The Inclusion Toolbox

D1591719

The Inclusion Toolbox

Strategies and Techniques for All Teachers

Jennifer A. Kurth

Megan Gross

CORWIN
A SAGE Company

A SAGE Company

FOR INFORMATION:

Corwin

A SAGE Company

2455 Teller Road

Thousand Oaks, California 91320

(800) 233-9936

www.corwin.com

SAGE Publications Ltd.

1 Oliver's Yard

55 City Road

London EC1Y 1SP

United Kingdom

SAGE Publications India Pvt. Ltd.

B 1/I 1 Mohan Cooperative Industrial Area

Mathura Road, New Delhi 110 044

India

SAGE Publications Asia-Pacific Pte. Ltd.

3 Church Street

#10-04 Samsung Hub

Singapore 049483

Copyright © 2015 by Corwin

All rights reserved. When forms and sample documents are included, their use is authorized only by educators, local school sites, and/or noncommercial or nonprofit entities that have purchased the book. Except for that usage, no part of this book may be reproduced or utilized in any form or by any means, electronic or mechanical, including photocopying, recording, or by any information storage and retrieval system, without permission in writing from the publisher.

All trade names and trademarks recited, referenced, or reflected herein are the property of their respective owners who retain all rights thereto.

Printed in the United States of America.

A catalog record of this book is available from the Library of Congress.

ISBN: 9781483344157

Acquisitions Editor: Jessica Allan

Associate Editor: Kimberly Greenberg

Editorial Assistant: Cesar Reyes

Project Editor: Veronica Stapleton Hooper

Copy Editor: Sarah J. Duffy

Typesetter: C&M Digitals (P) Ltd.

Proofreader: Wendy Jo Dymond

Indexer: Karen Wiley

Cover Designer: Michael Dubowe

Marketing Manager: Amanda Boudria

This book is printed on acid-free paper.

14 15 16 17 18 10 9 8 7 6 5 4 3 2 1

Contents

Part I of this book focuses on activities that would be completed in preparation for an inclusive program. Typically, these activities are completed in the days and weeks before the beginning of the school year. By completing these activities and using the strategies outlined in this part of the book, inclusion facilitators will have laid the essential groundwork for an inclusive school.

PART II: IMPLEMENTING INCLUSIVE EDUCATION   61

Part II of this book describes the ongoing activities that sustain and strengthen inclusive education for students with disabilities. These are activities and strategies that will be completed throughout the school year.

Chapter 5 Implementing Inclusive Instruction   63

Chapter 6 Engaging Students and Families   87

PART III: EXPANDING INCLUSIVE PRACTICES   181

Part III of this book focuses on the strategies and activities that may be completed to maintain, strengthen, and expand existing inclusive programs. Typically, these activities are used in the years following initial implementation of inclusion, when the inclusion facilitator is comfortable with and confident in his or her role and has established collaborative relationships at his or her school site.

Chapter 12 Co-Teaching   183

Chapter 13 Peer Supports   191

Tools Appendix Website

Chapter 1

Inclusive Education Self-Assessment
Barriers and Solutions to Inclusion Brainstorming Worksheet

Chapter 2

Developing a Vision for Inclusion

Chapter 3

Roles and Questions for Newly Hired Paraeducators
New Hire Orientation Checklist
Written Schedule Example (Elementary Level)
Written Schedule Example (Secondary Level)
Class- or Activity-Specific Instructions
Paraeducator Observation Tool

Chapter 4

IEP Master Calendar
IEP School Team Member Contacts and Schedules
Elementary Schedule Template
Secondary Schedule Template

Additional materials and resources related to *The Inclusion Toolbox: Strategies and Techniques for All Teachers* can be found at http://www.corwin.com/theinclusiontoolbox.

List of Pictures

Preface

As experienced inclusion facilitators and staunch advocates for inclusive education, we've often observed that others were interested in inclusive education, but
unsure of how to actually implement inclusive practices on a day-to-day basis.
Over time, we've chatted together about this observation and realized that we have quite
a few tried-and-true strategies that we've found useful and were eager to share them
with others. We believe that inclusive education is important for students with and without disabilities, and we hope to share with others the many practical strategies we have
identified. We also believe that many educators have learned strategies and tips in workshops and teacher preparation programs that are difficult to implement in everyday
practice. The strategies in this book are based on our own experiences as inclusion
facilitators searching for practical tools in books and on the Internet, re-creating resources
shared at workshops, and independently developing tools to further inclusive education
at our schools.

With this experience in mind, we set about writing this book as a practical tool for
educators (special and general education teachers), support staff (paraeducators and
administrators), and parents who are interested in promoting inclusive practices. We
have shared with our readers the many tools and strategies we have gathered on our
journey toward more inclusive schools and share them on a website so that our readers
can adapt the tools for their own use and particular circumstances. For these reasons, we
also call our book a toolbox: Like any good toolbox, we want to stock it full of a variety
of useful tools so that the inclusion facilitator can find, and use, the right tool for the job.

The book is organized into three main sections: Part I: Setting Up Inclusive Education,
Part II: Implementing Inclusive Education, and Part III: Expanding Inclusive Practices.
Part I focuses on activities that are most useful in newly developed inclusive programs or
at the beginning of a new school year. The tools in this section focus on laying the groundwork for effective and efficient inclusive education. Part II describes the variety of ongoing, day-to-day practices that are done to keep inclusive education working for students,
teachers, and parents. Finally, Part III focuses on those strategies that would be used in
established inclusive programs, with the aim of strengthening and expanding inclusive
services. The book contains many tools and case studies at elementary and secondary
levels demonstrating possible uses of the tools in real-life situations. In these ways, this
book is unlike others available. We do not focus on inclusive education as a value, but
instead provide practical, everyday tools to make inclusive education a reality. The tools
we provide are based on our experiences working as inclusion facilitators for many years,
our research in inclusive education, and the tips we have learned from others on our
journey. We think that the tools and strategies shared in this book are useful for all who
believe in inclusive education and seek to promote it, from the novice to the experienced
inclusion facilitator who is eager to add tools to his or her toolbox.

Acknowledgments

We wish to thank many dear friends and colleagues who have helped us learn to be better inclusion facilitators and have provided guidance and support in writing this book. We are in debt to Carly Reynolds, Jennifer Conlon, and Lisa Yamasaki, who read our first drafts and provided invaluable feedback.

We are grateful for the opportunities we've had to work as inclusion facilitators and for our students who showed us that inclusion really does make a difference. Several years ago, we had the good fortune to teach at the same school and share a classroom, and we will always be grateful to the incredible students, staff, and friends of J-55. We would especially like to thank Renay Marquez, who first planted the seed that we should write a book.

We are also thankful for the resources of our public university libraries. We started the heart of our first draft, typing and talking together, in a research room at Arizona State University Library. Without that first quiet room, and free Wi-Fi, this book might not exist! We've also benefited from a quiet space to type at San Jose State University and the incredible journal collections of Northern Arizona University and the University of Kansas.

Our families and friends have endured our writing process and we are grateful for their support. Megan is especially grateful to Stephen and Mason, who understood that "just one more minute" meant she'd be writing for 45 more minutes. She is also thankful for grandparents Dale, Noreen, Carl, and Linda, who provided hours of babysitting so she could write. Jennifer is thankful for the support and encouragement from Mark and Laurie, in all things, big and small.

Finally we wish to thank Corwin for its support of our project. We are grateful for the enthusiastic support of our editor, Jessica Allan, and her incredible staff that made this book a reality.

Publisher's Acknowledgments

Corwin gratefully acknowledges the contributions of the following reviewers:

Gretchen Gall, Instructor
Instructional Assistant/Paraeducator Program
Moraine Park Technical College
Fond du Lac, WI

Dr. Kathryn H. Ellis, Educational Program Specialist
East Georgia Learning Resource System
Augusta, GA

Lisa Parisi, Classroom Teacher
Denton Avenue Elementary School
New Hyde Park, NY

Sherry Markel, Associate Professor
Northern Arizona University, College of Education
Flagstaff, AZ

Barb Keating, Educational Consultant (Retired Elementary Principal)
Canada

J. David Smith, Professor
University of Richmond, University of North Carolina, and Virginia Commonwealth University

Pam Wall, Guidance Counselor/Former Special Education Teacher
Riverside Middle School
Greer, SC

Patti Palmer, Teacher/Resident Educator Coordinator
Wynford School District
Bucyrus, OH

Dr. Scott Mandel, Classroom Teacher
Los Angeles Unified School District
Los Angeles, CA

About the Authors

Jennifer A. Kurth, PhD, is an assistant professor of special education at the University of Kansas. Her academic interests include methods of implementing inclusive education, such as embedding critical instruction within the context and routines of general education while providing appropriate supports and services for individual learners. She also studies how teacher candidates develop their dispositions and skills in inclusive practices. Jennifer's research interests in inclusive education also include examining outcomes of inclusion in terms of skill development and quality-of-life indicators for students with disabilities. Prior to coming to the University of Kansas, Jennifer was an inclusion facilitator for students with mild to severe disabilities at both the elementary and secondary levels.

Megan Gross is a special education teacher in San Diego, California. She has taught and facilitated inclusion for students at both the elementary and secondary levels. Her professional interests include developing curricular modifications to increase student access to general education and facilitating professional development for paraprofessionals. Megan has presented at regional and national conferences and has published an article in *The Journal of the International Association of Special Education.*

PART I

Setting Up Inclusive Education

The first part of this book, Chapters 1 through 4, focuses on activities that would be completed in preparation for an inclusive program. Typically, these activities are completed in the days and weeks before the beginning of the school year. By completing these activities and using the strategies outlined in this part of the book, inclusion facilitators will have laid the essential groundwork for an inclusive school year.

We recommend that new and veteran teachers review Part I annually to plan for the upcoming year. We believe these are critical activities that must be completed annually to have an effective and efficient inclusive program.

1

Introduction to Inclusion

The definition that we use for inclusion has more to do with social equity and applies to all kids, not just kids with disabilities. For example . . . kids with second language issues, gifted kids, and kids who qualify for Title 1 programs because of circumstances of poverty. Our view of inclusion is about all kids.

—Wayne Sailor on "The Inclusive Class Podcast"

It seems today that most schools claim to be inclusive. And why wouldn't they? We know from over 30 years of research in special education that inclusive schooling results in tremendous gains for students with and without disabilities. And what's more, inclusive schooling reflects the inclusive lives that exist in our families and communities—in other words, inclusion *is* the real world!

But many schools that claim to be inclusive are, in fact, practicing mainstreaming rather than inclusion. Mainstreaming involves allowing students with disabilities to participate in some, but not all, general education activities. These mainstream activities generally involve the "specials" such as lunchtime, art, and music. Some schools practice *reverse inclusion* in which students without disabilities are brought into segregated special education courses for select activities, again, generally specials.

We, on the other hand, are advocating for true inclusion. To us, this means that a student, regardless of his or her disability label, is a full member of an age-appropriate general education classroom. The general education classroom is the *homeroom*, and the general education teacher is the *teacher of record*, with special education teachers and support staff assisting the general educators in providing all of the supports and services the student needs to be successful in that general education setting.

Furthermore, inclusive education is relatively easy to do poorly, and when it's done poorly it reinforces the idea that inclusion cannot work. Doing inclusion well requires thought, organization, and a commitment to making it work. It is not successful by accident!

BOX 1.1

Inclusion survives as an issue only so long as someone is excluded.

– Michael Giangreco (1997)

And this is the purpose of our book: to provide you, the inclusion facilitator who is a teacher (general or special education), support staff member (paraprofessional or related service provider), administrator (principal, director, inclusion specialist), or family member with practical tools to make inclusion work, and work with relative ease, at your school or district by giving you the tools to organize, strategize, and implement inclusion.

This book is unlike other books in that we do not develop inclusive strategies for a specific population of students (such as students with autism or students with learning disabilities). We believe that good teaching and good planning are good for all students, regardless of label. As inclusion facilitators for many years, we have developed or been taught a myriad of teaching and planning tools and strategies that we have found to be effective, and we pass them on to you in this book. We hope that you find them as practical as we have!

❖ Box 1.2   What Does the Research Say?

Outcomes of Inclusion

Desegregation has been important as a social movement for decades. In the 1950s, Gordon Allport's *The Nature of Prejudice* outlined the roots and nature of prejudice and promoted what he calls the *intergroup contact theory*. Allport's theory addressed race relations, but is applicable to special education. Namely, Allport argues that prejudice is reduced when majority and minority groups have common goals, a perception of common interests, and common humanity between the groups. Superficial contact, such as when students with disabilities are mainstreamed into select activities in the school day, can be detrimental to group relations. But when students work to achieve common goals, get to know one another as individuals, and work together on equal footing, prejudice and discrimination are reduced (Allport, 1954).

Beyond theoretical constructs, inclusion matters as well. Research over several decades documents that inclusive education is associated with improved cognitive and academic skills (Dore, Dion, Wagner, & Brunet, 2002; Fisher & Meyer, 2002; Hedeen & Ayres, 2002; McLeskey, Henry, & Hodges, 1998; Meyer, 2001), self-determination skills (Hughes, Agran, Cosgriff, & Washington, 2013), social skills, and peer acceptance (Causton-Theoharis & Malmgren, 2004; Cawley, Hayden, Cade, & Baker-Kroczynski, 2002; Dore et al., 2002; Mastropieri & Scruggs, 2001). In a review of the literature in 1998, McGregor and Vogelsberg documented a number of positive outcomes of inclusive education for students with and without disabilities, including skill acquisition, social development, and impact of inclusive education on students with and without disabilities, their parents, and teachers.

What is inclusive education?

Simply placing children with disabilities in the classroom and school they would attend if they did not have a disability is a first step toward inclusive education (Austin, 2001; Cook, 2001; Downing & Eichinger, 2008; Giangreco & Broer, 2005). Placement alone, though, is not an indicator of inclusive education. In fact, we think that just getting in the door is more like dumping a student off than inclusion. Instead, inclusion means that the student must have access to all of the supports and services he or she will need to participate fully in general education activities and curriculum (Burstein, Sears, Wilcoxen, Cabello, & Spagna, 2004; Downing & Eichinger, 2008; Mulvibill, Cotton, & Gyaben, 2004; Pivik, McComas, & LaFlamme, 2002). This indicator of inclusion suggests that services will come to the student, rather than the student going to the services. Inclusive education also embodies a philosophy of accepting, valuing, and respecting all students (Carrington & Elkins, 2002).

Inclusion facilitators accept that all students learn at different paces and in different ways, and value the contributions of this diversity to their classrooms. Inclusive schools are also accommodating to all learners (Thomson et al., 2003): The school facilities are accessible, as are curricula and activities. Inclusive education means that students with disabilities are full-time members of general education (Foreman, Arthur-Kelly, Pascoe, & King, 2004), not "visitors" who come to the class for certain activities and not others. Full membership extends beyond the classroom to the playground, lunchroom, and extracurricular activities (Kleinert, Miracle, & Sheppard-Jones, 2007). Inclusion facilitators collaborate to ensure the entire school experience, from the playground to the dance floor, is accessible and inviting to individuals with and without disabilities. Last, inclusive education means that each child, regardless of his or her learning style, pace, or preference, is given a high-quality education with meaningful curriculum and effective teaching (Ferguson, 1995). In other words, each student is provided with a challenging, meaningful learning experience that will enable every student to reach his or her maximum potential.

What is successful inclusion?

Knowing when a child is "successfully included" can be rather difficult to describe or rate. We have chosen to use the criteria for successful inclusion outlined by Cross, Traub, Hutter-Pishgahi, and Shelton (2004):

- The student made progress on his or her individualized goals.
- The student made gains in personal development, including acquiring knowledge and skills that are anticipated for all children.
- The student was welcomed by teachers, staff, and peers and accepted as a full member of the group.
- The student's parents were pleased with their child's growth.
- The student appears to be comfortable, happy, and part of the group setting.

Districts, schools, and individuals will be at different stages of implementing successful inclusive education, and frankly, the process of implementation is never really done. There will always be improvements to be made and challenges to overcome. A simple self-assessment, as shown in Figure 1.1, can be used as a guide to assess a school or district's commitment to and preparation for inclusive education.

Case Study: Mrs. Simpson Self-Assesses

To determine the state of inclusive education in her current school setting, Mrs. Simpson, a special education teacher at Harvard High School, completes a self-assessment to identify current practices, barriers, and facilitators of inclusive education in her school district. Her reflections are included in Figure 1.1.

| Figure 1.1 | Inclusion Education Self-Assessment |

	Yes, Describe	*No, Describe*
1. Do all students attend their "home school," or the school they would attend if they did not have a disability?		Students are bused to district programs (e.g., autism self-contained program at Holmes High School).
2. Do students with disabilities experience the same options for participating in curriculum, activities, and extracurricular activities as nondisabled peers?	Mainstreaming into art, PE, home ec classes	No participation in core academics, no participation in school sports teams or school activities like school plays, afterschool dances
3. Are a range of supports available and provided in general education settings, including assistive technology (AT), related service providers, adapted curriculum and materials, and social facilitation?	Paraeducator supports are available (can be shifted from self-contained setting to general education classes); AT equipment can be shifted; specialized equipment (e.g., CCTV) can be brought to a particular classroom.	Need to develop or locate adapted curriculum, teach related services providers to work in push-in model (rather than pull-out), and identify opportunities for social inclusion such as peer buddies
4. Is there an attitude of acceptance of diversity, or there is an "us" and "them" mentality at the school?	Teachers and administrators are friendly to students and special education staff. School has diversity goals in strategic plan.	I think the other teachers consider these "my" students (aka primary responsibility is mine).
5. Are the school facilities entirely accessible? Are curricular and extracurricular activities accessible to all learners and participants?	School buildings and restrooms are ADA-compliant.	The automatic door opener for wheelchair users in the library needs to be repaired. A range of options for curriculum (e.g., audiobooks) is needed.
6. Are students with disabilities full and equal members of classrooms and school activities?		At this time, students with disabilities receive most instruction in self-contained classrooms. Students with significant disabilities eat lunch together at a separate lunch table in the cafeteria.
7. Are the needs of students with disabilities considered in the planning of school activities, such as dances, parties, and playgrounds?	Rooms/buildings are physically accessible.	10% of desks should be adjustable height. Invite parents/students to plan activities to consider sensory and physical needs of students during extracurriculars.
8. Do general education teachers and administrators support the efforts to include children with disabilities?	Gaining allies—Mrs. Jones (English), Mr. Honbo (Home Ec) are supporters.	Principal is open—needs more information. Other staff is either unaware or doesn't have enough information yet.

	Yes, Describe	No, Describe
9. Are hiring (e.g., interview) practices in place that reflect an ongoing commitment to inclusive education?		Not now—need to get on hiring panels, talk to principal.
10. Are whole-school professional development opportunities available to support full membership of special educators and a commitment to inclusive education (e.g., curriculum committees)?	We had a diversity assembly last year, which included information about "Best Buddies" and students with disabilities.	I need to get on grade-level teams so that I contribute to curriculum adoption decisions. At this time our professional development is content specific (e.g., math teacher workshops). We need to be included on some of those professional development meetings to learn together.

Upon completion of this self-analysis, Mrs. Simpson is able to identify the resources that are already available to her as well as those factors that are not yet in place that will be necessary to make inclusion "work" in her school.

How do I start an inclusion program?

As you read this book, you may be in a situation in which your school is still segregated, whereby students do not attend their home school, do not attend general education classes, or do not participate in the full range of general education classes and activities. In this section, we discuss tips for beginning inclusive education for the first time or renewing a commitment to inclusion.

Build a team

Inclusion is not something that can be done alone. It is important to have a team in place. This can be done in many informal ways. For example, educators and administrators can simply eat lunch with other staff or complete extra duty together to get to know one another and share information and ideas. Educators and parents can provide plenty of support and encouragement to new allies. Educators and parents can also share their work with school and district leadership, sharing plans for inclusion and being open to their feedback. Finally, educators can use the tools throughout this book to create an inclusion plan to share with school and district leadership, including how students will be supported and their learning progress documented.

Inspire, don't dictate

It is easy to try to persuade others to implement inclusion by citing federal law (e.g., the Least Restrictive Environment provision of the Individuals with Disabilities Education Improvement Act), case law (e.g., *Oberti vs. Board of Education*, 1993), or the research support for inclusion. However, educators are a practical group. Educators tend to believe it when they see it and support those things that work. Thus, the surest way to a teacher's heart is through inspiration. Work closely with teachers to help assuage any fears. Demonstrate for them the support they will receive, professionally and for their students. Be prepared to "get your hands dirty" and problem-solve together.

BOX 1.3

The mediocre teacher tells. The good teacher explains. The superior teacher demonstrates. The great teacher inspires.

—William Arthur Ward

Meet people where they are

Have frank conversations with your colleagues or your child's teacher(s) about inclusion. Ask them about their biggest fears, and help them find solutions. Ask them about their greatest skills or gifts. Build on their strengths, beliefs, and desires. Nobody is going to be 100% prepared, ever. If we wait until 100% of people feel 100% prepared, we will deny generations of students the opportunity to learn and develop. Every day is a learning experience and a chance to grow. Make sure everyone knows that they will be respected and supported for doing their best and that perfection is not expected.

Be prepared to start small, but do it well

Many of us aim to have all of our students fully included and supported immediately. It may be necessary, however, to start inclusion on a limited basis (e.g., supporting inclusion for one student at a time) while you build allies and skills. The ultimate goal is that all students will be fully included. The pace of progress will vary based on the needs and skills of individual teams and schools. No matter the pace of implementing inclusion, make sure that those students who are included are well supported, as are their teachers.

Don't give in to failure or the naysayers

Expect imperfection. Expect setbacks. Implement your strategies to the best of your ability, all of the time. Gather data to know what is working and what is not. Make changes to address problems as they become known. Highlight what is going well, and be prepared to learn from those who disagree. When faced with "we don't do that here," take a step back and look at the individual child's needs. Identify the first step that you can take immediately even without financial resources; maybe mainstreaming during recess or lunch is possible at this time. Again, "all means all," and the end goal is that all students are always included. But building success one step at a time is reasonable. When you find yourself faced with a disagreement with school staff or colleagues, refrain from a quick retort. Instead, propose to talk later and take time to reflect on the other person's statements. Consider the person's perspective and what he or she might need or be feeling. Is the person unsure of what to do? Lacking resources?

Be prepared to be an "attitude ambassador"

Showing up with a positive attitude is contagious. Others will want to be near you. This is perhaps one of the easiest strategies for gaining allies and support. You might want to send your colleagues or child's teacher(s) specific notes, highlighting the positive things you've noticed they are doing for students and the school and their efforts toward inclusion.

Identify obstacles, barriers, and setbacks

Understand what has not worked or what acts as a barrier or obstacle to inclusion. This could be physical, such as having classrooms on a second floor with no elevator access; practical, such as course and supervision schedules; or attitudinal, such as a belief that only some students are capable of learning. Also identify your setbacks. Oftentimes, our first intervention or idea does not work. Once these obstacles, barriers, and setbacks are identified, they can be addressed. It will be critical to employ your allies in this task. A chart such as the one in Figure 1.2, showing concerns in one column and solutions or "let's try this" in the column next to it, can be used to facilitate a full discussion of inclusion. Also, consider gathering data on student performance, and be open to trying things in different ways.

Case Study: Mrs. Simpson Problem-Solves

In an effort to identify barriers to inclusion at her new school site, Mrs. Simpson meets with paraeducators, parents, general education teachers, and administrators to identify current barriers to inclusive education. As a group, they first brainstorm the list of barriers. Mrs. Simpson writes down each concern. After the concerns are listed, the team turns its attention to possible solutions, as seen in Figure 1.2.

| Figure 1.2 | Barriers and Solutions to Inclusion |

Barrier to Inclusion	Possible Solution
No staff training—how can we do something we aren't trained to do?	Use early release days for ongoing training. Invite faculty from local university. Devote professional development day.
Bullying	School assemblies; peer tutors; start a circle of friends/best buddies program. Educate! Contact other schools in district and set up sharing program.
Lack of materials (leveled readers, AT devices, etc.)	Lending library? Find materials online.
Not enough time	Designate common planning times for each grade level. Consider block scheduling?
Class size is too big already	Keep natural proportions (not all students with disabilities will be in same class).
Money (never enough)	Move resources from self-contained class to general education classes or a common pool (materials, funds).
Test scores, making Adequate Yearly Progress?	Make sure students take correct assessment, including alternate if appropriate. Use special education expertise to support all students in class, not just those with designated special needs (e.g., floating paraeducator, co-teaching).
Science lab is not safe, accessible for students with physical disabilities	Assign paraeducator and/or peer tutor to ensure safety as needed. Provide adapted desks and other equipment in science lab so that it will be accessible.

With this brainstormed list of concerns and ideas, Mrs. Simpson and the team can now divide responsibilities, as needed, to work on implementing the plan. For example, Mr. Jones, the science teacher, will obtain wheelchair-accessible desks in the science lab. Mrs. Simpson will contact the other schools in the district to see what adapted materials they have already created. The principal, Ms. Martinez, will investigate professional development opportunities for her staff. Thus, at the end of the meeting, voices of concern have been heard and validated, and a plan of action has been put in place!

Be prepared to provide information

Many of your colleagues or child's teachers may have limited experience with diversity and designing lessons to accommodate diverse learners. Discuss strategies for differentiation and ensure that providing inclusive education is not akin to lowering expectations. Rather, guarantee that through differentiation and universal design, expectations for all students will remain high; students will just demonstrate their knowledge of those high expectations using varying means. Provide information to your colleagues about individual students, including their strengths, needs, and preferred accommodations.

❖ Box 1.4   Differentiated Instruction and Universal Design for Learning

What Is Differentiated Instruction?

Differentiated instruction (DI) simply means teaching the way the child learns. It is a proactive approach in which the learning needs of students are identified and planned for ahead of time. For example, some students are visual learners; providing visual aids during lessons and teaching students to create graphic organizers while working are methods of differentiating instruction and supporting the needs of diverse students in a classroom.

What Is Universal Design?

Like differentiated instruction, universal design for learning (UDL) is a proactive framework that acknowledges that not all learners have the same learning needs. Instead, educators can provide multiple means of representation (how information is presented), multiple means of expression and engagement (how students demonstrate what they know), and multiple means of engagement (how to build student motivation and interest).

An Analogy

The goal for students in our current educational system is to meet state, or Common Core, educational standards. We can think of meeting these educational standards as the peak of a mountain (C. Lanterman, personal communication, November 9, 2012). Our goal, or high expectation, is for students to reach this peak by the end of the school year. How one meets that goal, however, can vary. For example, some people might hike up a peak via the most direct and steep route. Others may plan a path that is less direct and less strenuous, winding their way up the mountain. But there are even more ways to ascend a mountaintop! Some people may ride to the top on horseback. Others may ride a ski lift. Still others may take a helicopter to the top. In short, there are more ways than one to reach the peak of a mountain. Likewise, there are more ways than one for students to learn and demonstrate their knowledge and reach learning standards. Through knowing student learning styles and preferences, and matching instruction to student needs with UDL or DI techniques, educators can ensure the learning of all students.

Have a big bag of tricks

All teachers should have a big bag of tricks. No students learn the same thing in the same way at the same rate. We must be able to try many different teaching strategies to reach all of our students. It is critical to gather data and make reflective decisions about if or when changes in instruction are needed to help students learn.

How do I maintain an inclusion program?

Once inclusion has been established, there must be a committed effort to sustain and strengthen it. Research into failure of school reforms has identified a number of factors that contribute to failure; inclusive education has been shown to fail to maintain over time when there are changes in leadership, teacher turnover, and changes in state and district assessment policy (Sindelar, Shearer, Yendol-Hoppey, & Liebert, 2006). To help ensure that inclusion is maintained over time, we suggest a number of strategies.

Build on your successes

It will be important to recognize what is going well, and why, so that those successes can be strengthened and expanded. Frequent discussions with colleagues, sharing of information, and problem-solving will be essential. Similarly, identify any challenges or setbacks, and develop strategies to address them. And take some time to toot your own horn! Invite district administrators and school board members out to observe inclusion in action. Applaud the efforts that have been made, and take time to recognize what is working (and why it should be supported and valued), by writing letters to school board members or school administrators to celebrate and recognize what is going well.

Develop strong leadership for inclusion

One of the reasons inclusion failed in the study by Sindelar and colleagues (2006) is that the leadership for inclusion ceased to exist. Leadership would ideally come from administrators, but passionate, effective, and committed teachers and parents can also be instrumental leaders. Teachers who fill this leadership role may take on schoolwide responsibilities, such as being department chairs at their schools; participating in interview panels to make sure any new teachers, paraeducators, or administrators share a commitment to inclusion; and maintaining a focus on inclusion in the school and district, such as making sure the school website or mission statement demonstrates a commitment to inclusion (see Chapter 2 for more ideas). Parents who fill this leadership role may host parent information nights, meet with school board members, sponsor professional development for teachers, collaborate with their site administrators and teachers to identify supports and resources needed to make inclusion a reality, participate in the parent-teacher association to give voice to the needs of diverse learners, and do many other actions to support inclusive education.

BOX 1.5   *Administrator Insight*

Throughout this book, we'll provide insight boxes targeted for administrators. If you happen to be a school or district administrator, this box is for you! If, on the other hand, you are a teacher, paraprofessional, or parent, you might use the information in these boxes as a starting point to strike up conversations with school or district administrators.

The administrator insight in this chapter is advice for administrators who have adopted, or are planning to adopt, an inclusive school model (Janney, Snell, Beers, & Raynes, 1995).

Advice for District Administrators	*Advice for Principals*
• Give a "green light" to do what is best for all students. • Direct without dictating. Focus on participatory planning and decision making.	• Set a positive tone. • Start with teachers who volunteer to include students. • Involve everyone in planning and preparation. • Provide resources; offer to handle the logistics. • Start small and build on your successes. • Give teachers the freedom they need.

Source: Janney et al. (1995, pp. 72–80).

Commit to collaboration and shared decision making

The maintenance of inclusion cannot rest on one person; rather, a dedicated team must be created. This team can consist of any number of individuals, including parents, paraeducators, and general and special education teachers. It is important, however, that this team collaborates frequently and shares responsibility for making decisions and maintaining inclusive practices. The best collaboration doesn't necessarily happen during district-mandated collaboration time, but during day-to-day interactions.

Commit to ongoing training

Inclusion facilitators must commit to ongoing training to implement best practices and keep updated of any changes in knowledge, skills, or laws. Ongoing training will also help inclusion facilitators differentiate fact from fiction, thus guiding parents and other educators through the complicated maze of information that can be found online and in other popular media.

What are the tools in this book?

The purpose of this book is to give inclusion facilitators the organizational tools needed for implementing inclusive practices with all students. In our experiences we have noticed that educators and parents often attend conferences or read books about inclusive practices and feel, "This is great! I want to do this! But I don't have the time." We propose that having in place the organizational structures, such as scheduling supports, collaborating with others, developing "teacher as executive skills," and developing and implementing inclusive individualized education programs *will enable educators to have more time!*

In each chapter, you'll find tools we've designed or been taught, and used ourselves in schools, to support students, families, and teams. We include case studies to model the purpose and how to use the tools in our schools. In our daily practice we adapt each of our tools to meet an individual student or teacher's need and invite you to do the same by downloading files from our website and editing to suit your purposes.

Why is this book divided into three parts?

We've divided the book into three parts (Part I: Setting Up Inclusive Education, Part II: Implementing Inclusive Education, and Part III: Expanding Inclusive Practices) to meet the needs of our readers who are likely in different stages of developing or providing inclusive education services to students. While we certainly encourage reading the book from beginning to end, we know parents and educators have limited time to read and research in the middle of the school year and often need a go-to resource for addressing a specific need. We encourage you to begin with the chapters that address your current starting place and needs and then recommend furthering your reading when you're ready to move on to the next phase of inclusive education planning or improvement.

Please be sure to go to the website (http://www.corwin.com/theinclusiontoolbox) to download the forms and resources from this chapter!

2

Leadership for Inclusive Schools

Above all, we need leaders who remind us of the moral purpose of our profession. The very nature of our profession calls upon us to devote ourselves to making a difference in the lives of others. The success or failure of our efforts will affect the aspirations, opportunities, and quality of life for all our students.

—Rick DuFour

In our experience, the successful inclusion of one student, or all students with individualized education programs at a school site, or in a district, is built on the leadership skills of a small group of teachers who work together to implement best practices in inclusive education and successfully lobby their administrators and community for support. We believe teacher leadership and advocacy for inclusion are essential to developing inclusive classrooms and school communities in which students and staff thrive. In this chapter we describe the leadership role and skills of special educators, in particular, and offer practical strategies and tools for implementing a vision for inclusion.

What Inclusive Education Leadership Looks Like

A special educator's responsibilities in the areas of coordinating services and instruction for students with disabilities and supervising the work of paraprofessionals require skills in management—of both people and paper. We believe the teachers who are successful

❖ Box 2.1   What Does the Research Say?

The majority of teacher leadership research is focused on the characteristics of teacher leaders, models of leadership, general education instruction, assessment, and professional learning communities, with few references to special educators as teacher leaders (Billingsley, 2007; Lieberman & Miller, 2004). York-Barr and Duke (2004) define teacher leadership as "the process by which teachers, individually, or collectively, influence their colleagues, principals, and other members of the school community to improve teaching and learning practices with the aim of increased student learning and achievement" (p. 288).

Special Educators as Teacher Leaders

Billingsley (2007) examined the various special education teacher leadership roles in collaboration, university partnerships that include supervising student teachers, and providing professional development to colleagues. The role of a special educator who works as an inclusion facilitator has been compared to that of a business executive, since both need to effectively lead, communicate, and collaborate to be successful (French & Chopra, 2006). Special educators demonstrate leadership or professional competence in the areas of instruction, interpersonal communication, and management of paraeducators and special education caseloads (York-Barr, Sommerness, Duke, & Ghere, 2005).

Barriers to Special Education Teacher Leadership

Although the research is limited, possible barriers to special education teachers acting as leaders are the separate evolution of general education and special education teachers that leads teachers to continue to work in isolation or separate from each other, the fact that often principals may be less familiar with the work and needs of special education teachers, time-consuming paperwork and district focus on teachers meeting legal mandates, and high turnover in the special education workforce (Billingsley, 2007).

managers and leaders recognize and fulfill the responsibilities inherent in being a teacher and also contribute to their school community through

- advocating for their students and inclusion of all students;
- demonstrating excellence in their work, hence leading by example;
- developing a vision for their students and an inclusive school and using this vision to motivate themselves and others to continue to improve practices.

Advocating for Students and Inclusion

Inclusive education requires a shift in thinking for veteran educators and administrators, similar to the shift from an individual teacher isolated in a classroom to an individual teacher as a member of a professional school community (Lieberman & Miller, 2004). This shift in thinking from "my" students to "our" students requires the inclusion facilitator to reach out to administrators and like-minded educators and advocate for students' needs in the school community. Regardless of your perspective on high-stakes, standardized assessments, the federal mandate that all students with disabilities are also included in these assessments provides a starting place for a special education teacher to advocate for the needs of students with disabilities on campus. Many schools are identifying strategies and resources to address the needs of students who are at risk of not meeting high achievement standards, and inclusion facilitators have a unique set of skills and knowledge to aid administrators, teachers, and students in evaluating appropriate interventions and support strategies. Inclusion facilitators who reach out and offer assistance or consultation as needed to administrators and colleagues, or become a member of the school team to address the intervention needs of all students, help initiate the shift in thinking from "my" students to "our" students for themselves and colleagues.

Committees and Politics

Sharing ideas, knowledge, and resources with colleagues helps inclusion facilitators develop legitimacy among their colleagues, especially if they are new to teaching. Some inclusion facilitators choose to participate in department or schoolwide committees, such as the school leadership team, intervention team, school climate committee, parent-teacher association, and many others. At first glance, participating in one of these committees may not directly relate to special education caseload or advocating for inclusion. Some committees provide an opportunity to learn more about the school culture, organization, and ultimately the politics of the school and district. This will help inclusion facilitators in identifying potential resources for their students to access and develop relationships with other professionals who are supportive of inclusive schooling. Being an active member of a school committee can also demonstrate a teacher's commitment to the school community as a whole. When inclusion facilitators include themselves in the school community and share their perspectives, it paves the way for including students with disabilities (Gaylord, Vandercook, & York-Barr, 2003).

Participating in school- or district-level committees also provides inclusion facilitators with an understanding of how decisions are made, where resources are allocated, and how to acquire more resources and supports for students (York-Barr et al., 2005). In our experience, the teachers who are knowledgeable about their school or district budget, curriculum adoptions, or process for hiring paraeducators and participate in these processes (e.g., volunteer to be a member of interview panel for paraeducators) are more effective advocates for students, and inclusion, because they know how to acquire the appropriate resources.

Collaborative Relationships

Developing relationships with teachers, both general and special education, and administrators is essential to successful advocacy for inclusion. These relationships take time to develop and are often the result of daily interactions on campus, such as talking during recess duty, chaperoning events at the secondary level, or eating lunch with colleagues. Building trust and rapport with colleagues and successfully communicating and negotiating with different groups are a couple of the skills required to lead and advocate for inclusion (Fisher, Frey, & Thousand, 2003; Lieberman & Miller, 2004). When inclusion facilitators develop collaborative relationships across disciplines, traditional roles begin to blur, and special education teachers might begin to teach lessons in a general education class while general education teachers independently adapt or modify curriculum for all of their students; see Chapter 7 for more information (Fisher & Frey, 2001).

Collaborative relationships with families are also essential to developing a sustainable inclusive education program. While an inclusion facilitator can be a powerful advocate in a student's life, families are lifelong advocates and should be treated as an ally in their student's education and inclusion. Teachers who work successfully with families will find that families become partners in building awareness in the community about the benefits of inclusive education with other families. Families can also advocate for continuing to improve or enhance inclusive education opportunities with site and district office staff. See Chapter 6 for more information and resources for developing collaborative relationships with families.

Demonstrating Excellence

When a teacher demonstrates competency and is perceived by others to be a knowledgeable and skilled educator, her advocacy is more effective. Fisher et al. (2003) suggest inclusion facilitators demonstrate their leadership in the following ways:

- instruction (teaching, knowledgeable about strategies, using peer supports)
- coordination of special education services
- supervision of paraeducators

In our experience, when inclusion facilitators excel at these core skills they are able to provide meaningful inclusive education opportunities and quality instruction to students, while simultaneously earning the respect of families, colleagues, and administrators. The remainder of the book focuses on developing these skills and offers resources for organization and management.

Developing a Vision for Students and Inclusive Education

Effective inclusion facilitators manage the day-to-day details of their work while simultaneously keeping their eye on the big picture of the inclusion program as a whole (York-Barr et al., 2005). Developing a vision for an inclusive education program and articulating it to yourself and others provides a foundation on which to build a community (Dotger & Ashby, 2010). Building a community of individuals, including families, paraeducators, colleagues, and administrators, who support inclusive education at your school is essential for sustainable inclusive opportunities that aren't reliant on one teacher or one administrator. Table 2.1 provides guiding questions for developing, implementing, and improving an inclusion program. When you reflect on your vision for inclusion, consider the following:

- Talk with students, teachers and families. Understand their needs and preferences.
- Evaluate what is working well and what needs fine-tuning.
- Problem-solve as a team whenever possible.
- Be accountable for your actions.
- Implement changes based on team input.

Successful inclusion facilitators reflect on what inclusion actually looks like for their students on an almost daily basis. Then they proceed to fine-tune and make changes as necessary in order to provide students with the supports and materials they need to learn and to keep working toward a better inclusive education system for all involved.

Case Study: Mrs. Simpson Develops an Inclusive Education Vision Action Plan

At the start of the new year, Mrs. Simpson takes some time to reflect on the inclusive education opportunities during the first half of the school year and then decides to do some planning for the upcoming spring and fall. During her planning process, whenever she regularly meets with paraeducators, teachers, administrators, related service providers, and families, she remembers to ask questions about how to improve inclusion for her students, colleagues, families, and school. Mrs. Simpson records the ideas and feedback she receives on her vision-planning tool. To identify things that she and her colleagues could do at the district level, she asks her friends that work as inclusion facilitators in her district to share their ideas during a regularly scheduled weekly meeting. The other inclusion facilitators also share what is currently working at their school sites and offer to share resources. Once Mrs. Simpson has developed a draft plan, she seeks to follow through with actions required to implement plans by identifying general education colleagues to work with, training and delegating paraeducators to implement student specific supports in classrooms, and advocating for the needs of her students, the special education department, or the general education program at a weekly student intervention meeting or monthly school site council meetings.

Table 2.1 Developing a Vision for Inclusion

Level	Vision	Plan	Action	Reflection
Student	What do we want to see our students learning across the school day (academics, behavior, communication, social)?	Identify classes and extracurricular opportunities. Identify curriculum needed. Prepare adaptations and modifications if needed. Identify personnel or intervention supports needed, including peer tutors.	Instruct students. Use curriculum and any adaptations or modifications required. Continue to create and edit adaptations and modified materials. Communicate with instructional staff regularly. Communicate with families about coursework, goals, and homework. Provide training to staff and students on effective instructional strategies.	Inclusion in science is working well; gen ed lesson plans available 1 week in advance; need to increase use of peer supports for Kate. Need adapted novels for English courses.

(Continued)

Table 2.1 (Continued)

Level	Vision	Plan	Action	Reflection
Classroom	How should all of our students learn the academic, behavior, communication, and social skills they need?	Review curriculum. Collaborate with colleagues to develop new projects, strategies, and cross-curricular lessons. Develop lesson plans. Identify any training or resources needed to implement instructional strategies. Prepare classroom environment (desk arrangement, classroom organization, etc.).	Attend available trainings. Identify ways to acquire needed resources. Teach students curriculum and how to use specific instructional tools or strategies. Assess student learning. Communicate and problem-solve with colleagues on a regular basis.	Need to better implement use of augmentative and alternative communication (AAC) device and technology in classroom settings. Teachers and paraeducators really liked monthly team meeting; can we do again?
School	What do we want to see and feel when we walk into a classroom, the library, the cafeteria, the gymnasium, the office, or the playground?	Review school policies, especially surrounding behavior management and discipline. Collaborate with families and school staff to develop an inclusive community. Identify any facilities or routines that need to be adapted to increase accessibility (e.g., lockers, set up for assemblies, fire drill supports). Identify strategies to provide dedicated collaboration time for teachers and support staff. Provide training and resources to teachers and support staff.	Implement inclusive school policies. Implement schoolwide positive behavior support strategies. Ensure collaboration time is available and utilized by staff. Assess student, teacher, and family satisfaction. Modify any routines or facilities as needed.	Vice principal implementing schoolwide positive behavior supports (PBS)! What else could students do at lunch that was inclusive? Distributed disposable earplugs for staff to keep in emergency backpacks in case of unplanned fire alarm.

Level	Vision	Plan	Action	Reflection
District	What do we want our schools to provide for our students, families, and staff?	Collaborate with site-level teams (including families, teachers, support staff, and administrators). Identify resources needed for student achievement (e.g., curriculum adaptations, technology). Identify areas for districtwide training or parent education nights. Review state and federal legislation for special education.	Provide time to collaborate with site-level teams. Allocate resources. Provide districtwide training to staff. Provide parent education nights. Train staff on special education policies and law.	Ask special ed director for release time for transition observations prior to meeting. Ask special ed director to allocate $ for staff to attend TASH conference next year. Inclusion teachers presented at Beginning Teacher's Support Meeting about accommodations and modifications.

Informal Inclusion Support Team

In the midst of the daily work of including students in general education, you are likely to have found a few like-minded general education teachers, counselors, or support staff who also believe in educating *all* students. These individuals are your inclusion allies and can become an informal inclusion support team on your campus. Inclusion facilitators who develop positive relationships with two or three general education teachers and meet with this team to reflect on practices and ways to improve outcomes for students report feeling less isolated and overwhelmed (York-Barr et al., 2005). In our experience, developing relationships with colleagues who support inclusive education, through talk and action, yields opportunities to further inclusive education at your school in ways previously thought impossible. These colleagues may facilitate increasing opportunities for students to be included in school activities (e.g., assemblies, awards ceremonies, field trips), automatically develop necessary adaptations or modifications with lesson planning, or support your ideas or concerns in a staff meeting.

Sustaining a Vision for Inclusion

An observation of students successfully included in general education classes and campuses yields inspiration for teachers, administrators, and families. It is exciting to share observations with colleagues like these: *Did you see Sam and Alex reading together quietly? I loved watching Sam ask his tablemate how his weekend was. Did you see Tom ask Sam to join four square at recess? Mrs. Harper is great to work with, she incorporates all of Sam's*

BOX 2.2   Tech Byte

Some inclusion facilitators do not have the good fortune of working with many like-minded inclusive colleagues. So how does one find a system of support for inclusion? We have found social media to be a great resource for professional support!

- *Twitter:* Twitter is a fast, easy, and fun way to follow inclusion facilitators and organizations. Some of our favorites are the Inclusive Class, Kids Included Together, Paula Kluth, Leah Kelley, and Paraeducate.
- *Facebook:* Facebook is another fun way to keep up to date about inclusion and a way to find friends with similar interests. Some of our favorite Facebook pages are those of TASH, the Maryland Coalition for Inclusive Education, Think Inclusive, and the Thinking Person's Guide to Autism. However, many of our favorites are regional; you can find regional resources by doing a search on Facebook for "inclusive education."
- *Pinterest:* There are useful tools and resources all over Pinterest, and this is one more way to stay motivated and feel part of a community. You can search for pins related to inclusive education and find a large and supportive community here as well!

symbols into her lessons and encourages all students to use them. When students have an opportunity to progress toward achieving their goals in an inclusive environment and special education teachers have an opportunity to work with teachers and administrators who "get it" and support inclusion, the rewards are bountiful and motivating.

Staying Motivated on the Road to Inclusion

Unfortunately, including students with disabilities, especially if they have severe cognitive disabilities, health needs, or behavior challenges, is not the norm in every school or community. Navigating the path to inclusion for a student may, at times, require overcoming significant challenges related to breaking down barriers in a classroom, lack of support from teachers or administrators, or changing the cultural norms of a school community. When these challenges begin to feel insurmountable, and you find yourself questioning your leadership abilities, we feel it is helpful to reflect on what resources and supports you need to stay motivated so you can continue to persevere and pave the way for the next student to be included. The following are some of the ways we stay motivated in our careers as inclusion specialists:

- *Meet with supportive colleagues on a regular basis.* Take a moment to vent, and then move on to talk about what is working or ask for help identifying new support strategies.
- *Celebrate the little things that occur during the day.* Maybe your student remembered to bring her glasses to school or a teacher said hello to you in the hallway.
- *Reach out to former professors and ask for guidance.*
- *Read a book.* If an inclusion "textbook" doesn't seem like the right choice, find a memoir written by a person with a disability to offer you guidance.
- *Watch a movie.* Like books, there are many disability-related films and documentaries that are inspiring. Dan Habib is a documentary filmmaker who has many excellent films about inclusive education.
- *Attend local trainings or conferences on inclusive education.*
- *Utilize social media to learn from persons with disabilities, families, and teachers.*

- *Take a break.* Many teachers we know work countless hours after school and on the weekends, but we all need to take time for ourselves. Go to the movies, a museum, the beach, or do some retail therapy. Chances are, while you're out, you'll find some inspiration that you can take back with you when you return to work Monday.

Reallocating Resources to Build Inclusion

An inclusion facilitator can take a leadership role in devising strategies to reallocate existing resources to better support and promote inclusive practices. One place to start is examining the special education teachers at a school site. Teachers who work in inclusive settings are no longer tied to a classroom and are free to support students across the school. These teachers may be reassigned loads based on grade level or content area. For example, an elementary school with three special education teachers may divide case loads by grade level so that one teacher acts as the case manager and inclusion facilitator for students in kindergarten and Grade 1, another for students in Grades 2 and 3, and another for Grades 4 and 5. Or an inclusion team at a secondary school may decide that one teacher will be the primary support for language arts, another for science, and another for math. This type of "chunking" of teachers is particularly useful so that inclusion facilitators can be part of grade-level teams and facilitate co-teaching in core subjects.

BOX 2.3   *Administrator Insight*

School administrators play an important role in supporting teacher leadership. Help teacher leaders identify important committees to be on, such as committees for adopting new textbooks. School administrators can also support teacher leadership by allocating time or resources to support teacher leadership, such as permitting teacher leaders to attend leadership or management conferences and providing release time for teachers to engage in leadership activities. Last, and perhaps most important, school administrators can support teacher leadership by creating space for teacher leadership. This can be done by sharing insights and rationales and by providing emotional support to teachers who take on these important leadership roles.

Conclusion

Teacher leadership for inclusive education takes many forms. Some teachers are effective leaders through sharing their knowledge of curriculum and learning strategies with peers or mentoring student teachers or new teachers in special education, while others are effective leaders through department or school committee positions. Before you sign up for every committee, consider your strengths, interests, and available time and then pursue a leadership role in your school that is an ideal complement. If you choose a manageable leadership role, chances are you'll be a successful advocate and you'll be happy, too!

Please be sure to go to the website (http://www.corwin.com/theinclusiontoolbox) to download the forms and resources from this chapter!

3

Supporting Paraeducators to Facilitate Inclusive Education

Coming together is a beginning; keeping together is progress; working together is success.

—Henry Ford

A unique aspect of inclusive settings is the number of educators involved. A segregated special education program may have 10 students of multiple grades in a self-contained classroom and three paraeducators. When these 10 students are included in their grade-appropriate general education classes, students are generally in many different classrooms, and paraeducators are working out of the direct line of sight of the special education teacher for large portions of the school day. Thus, inclusive education can be more challenging for special education teachers in terms of providing supervision and feedback to paraeducators.

This chapter outlines a number of strategies for engaging in supervisory practices in inclusive settings. While it is geared more toward teachers and administrators, this chapter is also a resource for parents in understanding the roles of paraeducators in inclusive classrooms and as a tool in guiding parents to discuss how they would like to see paraeducators who are working with their child be prepared and supervised.

Hiring New Paraeducators

Many teachers have the good fortune of having a stable and consistent staff of paraeducators (also called paraprofessionals, teacher aides, instructional aides, or classroom assistants) to

---

❖ Box 3.1 What Does the Research Say?

Pre- and In-Service Preparation of Paraeducators

Unfortunately, many paraeducators (working in self-contained and inclusive settings) report that they received little to no preparation for their position (Drecktrah, 2000; Giangreco, Edelman, Broer, & Doyle, 2001). Notably, paraeducators have consistently been found to receive little to no preparation before the job, with few opportunities to receive preparation once employed (Downing, Ryndak, & Clark, 2000; French, 1999b; Hilton & Gerlach, 1997; Katsiyannis, Hodge, & Lanford, 2000). Downing and colleagues (2000) note that paraeducators reported their preparation as consisting of "teaching themselves . . . by reading, observing, and recalling their own experiences in school" (p. 177). Additionally, the research consistently finds that other paraeducators are typically teaching new paraeducators (Riggs & Mueller, 2001) with little direct supervision from credentialed teachers.

Additionally, there is a consistent lack of accurate job descriptions for paraeducators across the country (Downing et al., 2000; French & Chopra, 1999; Giangreco et al., 1997; Hilton & Gerlach, 1997; Marks, Schrader, & Levine, 1999; Wadsworth & Knight, 1996). As a result, paraeducators are often unsure of the parameters of their job, including what roles and responsibilities they are accountable for, what policies apply to them, and even basic information regarding who their supervisor is and how they are evaluated (Riggs & Mueller, 2001). Because there is often no role definition in special education, the paraeducator typically fills in as needed and is left completing a job of enormous scope and importance (Giangreco et al., 1997).

Teacher Supervisory Practices

Special education teachers typically report that they feel unprepared to supervise paraeducators (Marks et al., 1999) and do not frequently receive adequate preparation for their role as supervisors of paraeducators. This lack of preparation is well documented in the literature (French, 1999a; Giangreco, Edelman, Broer, & Doyle, 2001; Marks et al., 1999), and the absence of preparation typically exists at pre- and in-service levels. In fact, as of 2001, only two states had credentialing policies in place that require teachers to be prepared to supervise paraeducators (Wallace, Shin, Bartholomay, & Stahl, 2001). Despite the overall lack of formal supervisory preparation, 75% of special education teachers supervise one or more paraeducators, yet only 12% had preparation other than on-the-job experience to prepare them to supervise paraeducators (French, 2001). Most troubling, French (2001) notes that a number of disorganized supervisory strategies were employed by teachers, leading her to conclude that while teachers' implicit supervisory strategies were often sufficient, their lack of preparation often created legal, ethical, and liability concerns. Finally, despite lack of preparation, teachers are overall very happy with the performance and helpfulness of paraeducators under their supervision.

---

work with from year to year. Many other teachers, however, experience turnover of paraeducators for one reason or another and need to hire and prepare new colleagues. The hiring process varies across different districts, but it is a good idea to be involved in this process if possible, and certainly to be hands on in the preparation of paraeducators so they have the skills and confidence needed to succeed in their important work with students.

When hiring a new paraeducator, the process typically involves interviews, contacting references, and/or a proficiency exam. We advocate for teacher involvement in this entire process, including describing the nature of the position in the job ad, developing interview questions, contacting references, and developing the competency exam. While this may seem to be beyond the scope of teacher duties, it's important to have a good fit between teacher and paraeducator. After all, you will be spending a good deal of time together and collaborating regularly to meet the needs of students. This investment of time and energy will surely pay off.

During the process of hiring a new paraeducator, it is a good idea as an educator to reflect on your own teaching philosophy, communication styles, and teaching styles. Then listen and look for similar styles in the paraeducator applicant. Figure 3.1 provides some guiding questions for reflection.

Preparing a Newly Hired Paraeducator

Once you have decided which paraeducator to hire, or have been assigned a newly hired or transferred paraeducator, your role in preparing this person for his or her new role begins. Many effective strategies exist for helping the new paraeducator feel welcomed, supported, and equipped for this important role. First and foremost, simple orientation to the school, colleagues, and roles can go a long way toward making a person feel welcomed. Orientation can include showing the new paraeducator the locations of the staff restroom, break room, copy machine, mailboxes, and a safe place to leave personal belongings. Introduce the new paraeducator to the current staff, including other paraeducators, general and special education teachers, the office staff, and anyone else who will be important for the new paraeducator to know. Ideally you will also be able to take the newly hired paraeducator around to the classroom(s) she will be working in, and allow her to briefly meet the students, see the classrooms and materials, and even observe the class in action before jumping in to work. Last, it will be important to describe the roles of individuals the paraeducator will be working with. For example, whom should the paraeducator call if she will be out sick? Who will be responsible for making lesson plans? Who will lock up the classroom at the end of the day? Take a moment to reflect on these roles, and be sure to clarify them for your new colleague.

Figure 3.2 illustrates how Mrs. Simpson, a special education teacher and inclusion facilitator at Harvard High School, completed this task for a new paraeducator, Samantha.

Case Study: Roles and Responsibilities at Pine View Elementary School

Mr. DeMarco has created this handout on roles and responsibilities to orient Molly, a new paraeducator at Pine View Elementary.

Figure 3.1   Guiding Reflection Questions

Teaching Philosophy	Communication Style	Teaching Style
• Who is your teaching role model? What makes that person a great teacher? • What are your objectives as a teacher? • How do you believe students learn? • How does a good teacher interact with students?	• What mode of communication are you most comfortable with (e.g., face to face, email, notes) for general interactions? For more difficult interactions? • Do you seek or avoid confrontation?	• How do you believe a teacher should best meet the wide range of needs in a typical classroom? • How should a day and/or activity be presented and organized? • Describe your ideal lesson format. • How should challenging students best be addressed?

Figure 3.2	Roles and Questions for Newly Hired Paraeducators

	Issue or Question	*Who Is Responsible? Whom Should I Contact?*
Accessing general education	Who is responsible for making lesson plans?	Mrs. Simpson
	Who is responsible for making long-term adaptations to the curriculum?	Mrs. Simpson
	Who is responsible for making on-the-spot adaptations?	Samantha, with input from Mrs. Simpson
	Who will gather data? How often? Who will decide what data to gather and what forms to use?	Samantha; twice a week; Mrs. Simpson will provide forms and train on data collection
	Who is responsible for obtaining information about upcoming assignments, projects, or exams?	Samantha; speak with gen ed teachers weekly
	Who is responsible for communicating with general education teachers about student progress, needs, or successes?	Mrs. Simpson
Daily routines	Who will unlock and/or lock up the classroom each day?	Mrs. Simpson or Robert (paraeducator)
	Who will contact parents if there is a question or concern? Who will maintain daily or weekly communication with parents?	Mrs. Simpson only
	Who will need to be notified if a staff member is out? By when?	Mrs. Simpson, and call the sub-finder system
	Who will need to be notified if a student is out? By when?	Mrs. Simpson, and write this in the communication book
	Where is a safe and unobtrusive place to keep my belongings when I am at school?	Locked mail room in the school office
	Whom should I contact if I get injured on the job?	Mrs. Simpson and principal (Mrs. Presley)
	What are the emergency procedures (e.g., fire alarm)? What do I do and where do I go in these situations?	See postings on all doors; take emergency backpack with you
	Whom do I contact if I have a question or concern during a class? How do I find that person?	Mrs. Simpson; see staff schedules
	Whom should I ask if I have questions about pay, hours, my contract, or other personnel issues?	Human Resources representative Jody Franklin
Evaluations and duties	Who will evaluate me? When will this happen? On what will I be evaluated?	Mrs. Simpson and Mrs. Presley, once in January and once in May; you will be evaluated on the duties outlined in your job description (see your binder)
	What are my specific day-to-day duties and expectations? What are the day-to-day duties of my colleagues (general and special education teachers, related service providers, etc.)?	See your binder for specifics on duties; see role definition chart

Issue or Question	Who Is Responsible? Whom Should I Contact?
How can I get feedback on my daily performance?	Please ask Mrs. Simpson to observe you
Are there opportunities for training or professional development?	YES; see communication book, and additional trainings will be announced in weekly staff meetings
Are there rules I should be expected to know, such as dress codes, confidentiality provisions, use of cell phones, etc.?	Yes, see your staff binder

Paraeducators

Paraeducators who work with students with disabilities in inclusive settings have a variety of roles depending on the unique needs of the students with whom they work. These fall under several broad topics:

- Implement teacher-planned instruction:

  o Complete activities and curriculum directed by teacher
  o Support students during classroom activities (e.g., tutor, mentor) using modifications for lessons as needed
  o Record and chart data
  o Reinforce skills taught
  o Implement teacher-made modifications; you may also be responsible for creating your own modifications with approval from the teacher
  o Communicate with the teacher and other team members regarding student progress, programs, etc.

- Supervise students:

  o At lunch time
  o At playground and recess
  o As they arrive and depart on buses
  o Between classes
  o In various activities (e.g., assemblies, library, field trips)

- Clerical and general duties:

  o Operate media materials (e.g., video machines, LCD projectors)
  o Create bulletin board displays
  o Photocopy materials
  o Maintain daily logs
  o Maintain records
  o Set up and clean up after class activities

- Behavioral and social support:

  o Implement behavioral management plans developed by the teacher or team
  o Communicate with team members about a student's program and behaviors
  o Observe, record, and chart student behavior responses
  o Facilitate peer interactions

- Support individual student needs:
  - o Assist in implementing student individualized education plan (IEP) goals/integrating IEP goals and objectives
  - o Carry out instructional plans for students
  - o Assist in personal care, including feeding, toileting, and hygiene support
  - o Assist students with unique motor or mobility needs
  - o Assist students with unique sensory needs

Classroom Teacher

General education teachers instruct groups of children in one or more curricular areas. These groups include a wide range of students, including students with disabilities.

- Plan, implement, and evaluate instruction and assess students
- Adapt learning activities for students
- Take responsibility for the education of each member of the class
- Direct the classroom activities of paraeducators
- Communicate with parents regarding student progress
- Set the rules, guidelines, and expectations for the classroom

Special Education Teacher

Special education teachers provide specially designed instruction to children with disabilities in both special education and general education settings.

- Collaborate with the classroom teacher to assess, plan, implement, and evaluate instruction for students with disabilities in the general education classroom
- Design students' IEPs
- Adapt curriculum, materials, and equipment
- Incorporate individual education goals for students in classroom activities and interactions
- Oversee the implementation of IEPs
- Provide academic assessment and observations of student performance
- Consult and train members of students' educational teams
- Direct the class activities of paraeducators
- Communicate with parents regarding student progress

Related Service Providers

These specially trained professionals (e.g., speech therapists, occupational therapists) work with students in particular educational areas. They may work directly with students (direct service) in small groups or individually. They may provide this direct service in a pull-out setting (remove the child from class to work with him or her) or in the general education classroom. These service providers may also do consultative services to help skills generalize. When consulting, professionals may provide instructions to others to help students work on skills in a variety of settings as the opportunity occurs during the day. Frequent support providers at our school include the following:

- *Speech therapist*: This person works with children to improve communication skills. Communication can include intelligibility (e.g., articulation) and language (e.g., social skills, sentence structure).

- *Physical therapist (PT):* This person works to restore or improve a child's motor ability or skill level. This includes building muscle strength, improving endurance, coordination, and range of motion.
- *Occupational therapist (OT):* This person works with students to improve their ability to do everyday activities such as cutting, handwriting, and overall motor abilities related to education.
- *Adapted physical education teacher (APE):* This teacher focuses on motor skills related to physical education and exercise, and helps children participate in physical activities at school.
- *Transition coordinator:* This person works in secondary schools, primarily with children aged 14 and over, to develop job skills and may act as a job coach in high school.
- *Psychologist:* This person coordinates IEP meetings and evaluates students' cognitive and psychological abilities.

Additionally, Mr. DeMarco has provided Molly with the following brief outline of general rules or expectations of all support staff at Pine View Elementary School.

Confidentiality

As a paraeducator you will be working with different students and have contact with many adults both in and outside of your school site. It is very important to maintain confidentiality. This means not discussing the following: student records, student behavior, or anything concerning a student's family. You may discuss these things with the special education teacher or other professionals (speech therapist, OT, PT, APE) that work directly with the student.

Students' files, including IEPs, test scores, and all information about their diagnosis, are confidential and should never be discussed in public. Do not keep personal notes or files on students.

Professionalism

The paraeducator is an important part of the school site and must appear professional at all times. As an employee of the district, the paraeducator represents the school district as well as the teaching profession. What does it mean to "be professional"?

- Dress in a way that reflects that you are a professional. It is suggested that you wear clothing that is comfortable and appropriate for the age/needs of the students with whom you are working.
- Be aware that you are a role model for students.
- Be on time.
- Call the sub-finder for an absence and notify your teacher.
- Personal correspondence should be limited to break and lunch times.
- Do not speak about the students you work with or their families in front of others.

Sometimes a student's family or guardian will ask for information. It is appropriate and important to communicate what has happened during the student's day. This should be done in an objective way. For example, "Susan played with three students at recess, she ate all her lunch, she finished 4 of 10 math examples" is objective reporting. "Susan was in a really bad mood; I think she's not able to handle fifth-grade curriculum" is not objective reporting. If you are unsure of how to answer, then refer the family to the special education teacher.

When orienting a newly hired paraeducator, Mrs. Simpson made a brief checklist (Figure 3.3) to remind her of important topics to cover with a new paraeducator, in this case, Samantha.

Creating Staff Binders

One effective and efficient tool for providing information to paraeducators, and substitutes who may cover for an absent paraeducator, is staff binders. Staff binders

Figure 3.3 New Hire Orientation Checklist

Task	Completed?
School building orientation	
Office	
Staff lounge	
Staff restrooms	
Gym/cafeteria/etc.	
Bell schedule	
Mailboxes	
Obtain keys	
Classroom orientation	
Where materials are kept	
Overview of classroom rules	
Where personal belongings should be kept	
How to log on to computers	
How to use the telephone	
Student orientation	
Student goals	
Student learning styles	
Student accommodations or modifications	
Student communication style	
Student behavior supports	
Student health care plans/other concerns	

include all of the information the paraeducators will need for a school day, including their daily schedule, information about the student(s) they are supporting, and lesson and data collection plans to implement.

Staff binders can take many forms and contain important information. They should be individually created, reflecting the daily schedule and activities for each paraeducator at the school. The following is some useful content for each staff binder.

Written Schedules Showing the Location of Teachers, Paraeducators, and Students by Hour or Class Period (or Other as Pertinent)

It is helpful for the paraeducator to know where other staff members are at any given point in time as well as where students are. The daily written schedule also provides an hour-by-hour or class-by-class schedule for the paraeducator to follow, which will alleviate any anxiety about not being sure where to go or what to do. That being said, the schedule should include room numbers, teacher and student names, class/activity, and any other paraeducators or special education staff members who will be present. The schedule may also need to include transition guides so that the paraeducator knows where students should be going to and coming from. The schedule should further reflect any regular schedule changes (such as block-scheduling days).

Schedule of Activities to Be Performed by Teacher and Paraeducator at Each Point in Time

This can include lesson plans, adaptations/instructional plans, and data collection tools for paraeducators to refer to and complete. The lesson plans would include what each student should be working on in each class and how progress should be measured and what level of performance should be expected. Teachers should create these lesson plans. Adaptation plans, also called instructional plans (see Chapter 5), describe what adaptations to the curriculum, assessment, or activity must be made beforehand or on the spot to enable the student with disabilities to successfully participate in the general education curriculum, assessment, and activity that will occur. Often, paraeducators and teachers work together to create these plans. Last, data collection tools should be included for each class or activity so that the paraeducator can successfully gather meaningful data. This data should be shared regularly with the special education teacher so that instructional changes can be made, if needed.

Schedule Times for Breaks and Meetings

Each paraeducator should be allotted specific, duty-free times for breaks on a daily basis. Government (e.g., Department of Labor) and school district policies should be consulted when determining the length and frequency of these breaks. Regardless of policies, generally people are more effective and efficient with their job duties when they receive ample duty-free time (no supervision, no job-related tasks to complete) on a regular basis throughout the day. In addition to scheduling times for rest and lunch breaks, scheduling times for staff meetings is also essential.

Student-Specific Information, Including IEP Goals, Health Care Plans, Behavior Support Plans, and Data Collection Tools

Another essential component of the staff binder is information about the student(s) the paraeducator will be supporting each class period or activity. This should include the IEP goals each student is working on and what supports and services should be provided to assist the student in working on those IEP goals and accessing the general education curriculum. For example, student accommodations or modifications (e.g., extra time, added visuals, rephrasing instructions) should be included in the binder so that the paraeducator can implement the IEP with fidelity. The paraeducator should also have information about how the student learns best (e.g., kinesthetically, visually) and any health or behavior supports that should be in place.

Staff Binder Organization

The binder should be clearly organized so the paraeducator can quickly and easily find information. We suggest placing this content in a three-ring binder (one binder for each paraeducator) with tabs separating each class period or activity. A cover page with an overview of the entire workday should be provided. Then provide specific information (as outlined earlier) for each class or activity period.

BOX 3.2 Tech Byte

You might consider creating digital staff notebooks, rather than the three-ring binder notebooks we described. You can use "Notebook" view in Microsoft Word to create digital notebooks, complete with tabs to easily find pages. You can even store these notebooks online, such as on Google Drive or Dropbox. In doing so, it is easy to update the binders anytime and anywhere!

Permit, and Expect, Some Flexibility

We suggest creating these binders before the first day of the school year and providing them to the paraeducator to use as a guide on the first day (and days thereafter). While the inclusion facilitator will create this first version of the notebook for each paraeducator, the paraeducator can keep it up to date the rest of the year by collaborating with the inclusion facilitator and adding or subtracting pertinent information about the class and student (e.g., class schedule, student IEP goals), as details often change during the course of a school year. Thus, if the paraeducator is absent and substitutes are provided, the paraeducator will have an up-to-date substitute binder to facilitate a smooth transition for the student(s) and substitute.

Case Study: Mrs. Simpson Creates a Daily Schedule for a Paraeducator

The first thing Mrs. Simpson will do is create a daily schedule for each paraeducator (more details about this are covered in Chapter 4). As a first step, she simply transfers the full-day schedule for each paraeducator into the template in Figure 3.4, which shows each class period, room number, the names of students the paraeducator will be supporting, the class, and the teacher's name.

Figure 3.4 Paraeducator Daily Schedule

Period	Time	Room	Student(s)	Class	Teacher
1	8:20–9:12	49	Ayden	English 12	Mr. Carey
2	9:16–10:08	13	Wesley	US History	Mrs. Upton
3	10:13–11:13	57	Rachel, Josue	Geometry	Mrs. Olson
4	11:17–12:09	Gym	Allison, Jason, Jamie	Physical Education (9th and 10th grade classes)	Ms. Jones (9th grade) Mr. Hancock (10th grade)
Your lunch break 12:09–12:40					
5	12:44–1:35	53	Ayden, Casper	Earth Sciences	Ms. Roddy
6	1:39–2:35	34	Brandon, Ramona, Tomica	English 11	Mrs. Peeples
7	2:39–3:30	27	Brandon	Economics	Mr. B

After creating this overall schedule, Mrs. Simpson creates class-specific instructions (see Figure 3.5), so that paraeducators will know the overall class activity schedule, student goals to work on, student accommodations, and other relevant information about the student(s) they will be supporting during the class.

Figure 3.5 Class-Specific Instructions

- **Teacher:** Carey
- **Room:** 49
- **Student(s):** Ayden

Class Schedule

1. Students listen to a music selection (each student will sign up to bring songs). They will write while listening.

    a. Prompt Ayden to answer questions, such as "Do you like this song?" "What does this song make you think of?" "How does this song make you feel?" "Do you want to hear this song again?"

2. Students complete an editing question, presented on an overhead projector. Mr. Carey will randomly call on students to come to the overhead and share their corrections.

    a. Provide Ayden with two corrections to make—capitalization and punctuation. He will type his corrected sentence. If he is called on, he should bring the AlphaSmart to the overhead projector to show the class.

(Continued)

Figure 3.5   (Continued)

3. Students listen to a lecture or have a class discussion about a novel or writing activity.

   a. Summarize the lecture or question for Ayden.

   b. Prompt Ayden to draw a picture or select a picture representing the discussion topic (e.g., "Are we talking about Kino or Juana?").

4. Students read a novel together aloud or in small groups.

   a. Priming: Speak with Mr. Carey to be sure Ayden is prepared to read a specific section.

   b. Ayden can draw pictures of what is happening in the story.

5. Students write responses to a writing prompt.

   a. Provide a word bank for Ayden to use to write responses.

   b. Provide AlphaSmart to type his responses.

Student Information

- Ayden is a hard worker, but he needs frequent breaks after he has completed work. Encourage him to communicate—even write scripts if necessary. Ayden answers "yes" to almost anything, so refrain from asking open-ended questions; give him choices instead (e.g., *not* "Do you like yellow?" but "Do you like yellow or orange?")
- Ayden becomes anxious in unexpected routines. Provide him with a check-off schedule. Provide 2-minute transition warnings.

Goals for the Class

- Participate in activities.
- Write a sentence with noun, verb, and adjective.
- Type a four-word sentence with correct spelling, capitalization, and punctuation.
- Answer three literal comprehension questions (who, where, what, when).
- Read at second-grade level.

Health Care Plan

- Not applicable

Student Strengths, Interests, and Learning Style

- Ayden is a visual learner. Provide visuals to support the concept. Write down important topics for him. Ayden will repeat phrases you say (or he says) to be sure it was understood clearly. You can write down what you or he said to ensure comprehension.
- Ayden is interested in video games, Disney movies, and Disney characters.

Behavior Support Plan

- Provide 2-minute transition warnings.
- Provide *if–then* chart (if you finish this, then you get that).
- Provide a schedule for each class and the whole day.

Modifications/Accommodations

- Use of visuals (photographs or line drawings); assignments reduced by 50%; time and a half to complete tests; assignments and tests to focus on main ideas only; frequent sensory breaks

Communicating With Paraeducators

In an inclusive school setting, special education teachers and paraeducators are typically spread across a school campus throughout the day. Sharing important information (e.g., student illness, changes to schedules due to fire drills or assemblies) may be difficult. Simple tools such as communication books can help address this potential communication barrier. A confidential communication book can be placed in a private place (e.g., the school office, the staff room) where inclusion staff can write notes to one another. All staff members can then read or write in the book between class periods, during downtime, or during breaks and stay informed.

BOX 3.3   *Administrator Insight*

While many administrators receive some preparation for supervising and supporting adults, frequently teachers do not have this type of training. In fact, most teachers learn supervision skills on the job and will likely need your support in handling a variety of situations, particularly when there are problems or issues that need to be handled. Some administrators may believe that paraeducator supervision is a human resources task. However, teachers guide the day-to-day and lesson-to-lesson activities of paraeducators. Teachers must provide these adults with frequent feedback and instruction, yet are often uncomfortable or unsure of how to best do this. Administrators can support teachers in developing needed supervision strategies by providing mentoring, assisting teachers in developing supervision skills by referring them to resources or trainings, and having an open-door policy so that teachers know they can receive assistance from administrators without fear of feeling insecure about their abilities. Last, administrators can assist in checking on the fidelity of the implementation of inclusive practices. This can be done by leading the team in defining roles and responsibilities, and providing regular check-ins to see that each team member is supported in fulfilling her or his roles and responsibilities.

Regular Staff Meetings

In addition to communication books, regular staff meetings are essential to facilitating a successful inclusive program and are a means to stay informed of student needs and supports, staff needs, and ideas and techniques (Chopra, Sandoval-Lucero, & French, 2011).

Staff meetings should be held regularly, ideally weekly. They should be held at a regular time that is "duty-free" for all participants. Teachers should work with administrators at their site or district to help facilitate these important collaboration meetings. Often, meetings can be held during work, but non-student, hours. For example, many schools have an early-release or a late-start day once a week; a high school may typically have first period start at 8:30, but most Wednesdays the school starts at 9:15 to allow for teacher collaboration or preparation. As paraeducators are being paid (usually) starting at 8:30, these are ideal times for meetings. If a school has no regularly scheduled early-release or late-start days, other opportunities can be found, such as after or before school. It is not recommended that meetings be held outside of work hours unless they can be planned well in advance and include some compensation. For example, a weekly meeting for Monday after school for half an hour may be planned. Paraeducators may not be paid after school, but the teacher can compensate this by adjusting work hours. For example, a paraeducator may come in 5 minutes late each day, thus building a bank of 25 minutes that can be used for a 25-minute afterschool meeting on Mondays. Regardless of how the meetings and compensation are worked out, the meetings should be at a consistent time and place so that paraeducators can make necessary arrangements and be able to attend for the full meeting, each time.

The purpose and content of the meetings should be determined in advance. We suggest providing an agenda at the meeting so that all participants know what topics will be covered and can contribute to developing the agenda (see Figure 3.6). In doing so, all participants will feel a sense of buy-in for the meeting as their needs will also be addressed.

The meeting agenda also assists in making sure the discussions at the meeting are pertinent and efficient. That is, some small talk and catching up may be appropriate, but should not be the main purpose of the meeting. Rather, important information about students, curriculum, or schedules should be covered. The meeting should likewise be positive and oriented at problem solving. Some time for sharing successes may be included (e.g., birthdays, useful student supports or accommodations, behavior support break-throughs). Then the business of the meeting (as determined by the teacher and paraeducators) should take place.

Figure 3.6	Inclusion Team Staff Meeting Agenda

"Great teachers empathize with kids, respect them, and believe that each one has something special that can be built upon." —Ann Lieberman

1. Celebrations and inspiration ☺

    - Staff back from illness
    - Shared student successes

2. Student discipline issues

    - Discussed para's role in providing discipline in gen ed classrooms. Some paras feel like they are trying to follow teacher directions but aren't supported.

3. Behavior support plans and data tracking

    - Review inclusion students who have data tracking re BSP.
    - Discuss strategies for involving gen ed teacher in implementation of BSP. Teachers seem unsure of how to respond and strategies to use. Concern that some teachers are not reading BSPs or student IEP profiles.
    - Lacking collaboration time to discuss with gen ed teachers about student needs and support strategies. Gen ed teachers are responsive to specific directions and want to know what to do.
    - Also discuss over-reliance at times on paras (some teachers are hands-off for students with more severe needs), who is responsible for modifications, how to use peer supports more in gen ed classes.

4. Please collect student work samples (e.g., essays, tests, projects)

5. Announcement

6. Other items

    - Concern about lack of communication in our department. Strategies to improve: use staff communication book more, all staff write in binder about absences, lunchtime activities. Share in person about specific student issues or behavior needs.
    - Paras would like next year for all staff meetings to address:

        a. The paraeducator's role in gen ed classroom
        b. What is inclusion? Changing the conversation from *your* student to *our* student

7. Small groups: discuss students in J-55 and J-54

    - Tabled until March (or informally in the meantime)

Last, the meeting should take place in a setting where instructional materials are available and that is free from distractions or interruptions. That is, teachers should be able to use this time to model instructional techniques, implement and problem-solve lesson plans, review data and to discuss all of the preceding with paraeducators. It is important, then, that the meeting location is free from interruption and is private so that confidential matters such as student needs and progress can be openly discussed.

Evaluating Paraeducators

Often, teachers are part of the formal evaluation process for paraeducators. Teachers may be asked to complete evaluation forms alone or with an administrator to determine a paraeducator's performance. This formal (often annual) performance evaluation is an important tool for providing feedback to paraeducators. Performance ratings often have an important bearing on whether a paraeducator's contract is renewed or extended, pay raises are provided, or promotions are granted. Teachers should speak with an administrator at their school or district at the beginning of the year to learn who completes these evaluations and what the evaluations are based on. That being said, it is a good idea for the teacher to have a copy of a paraeducator's formal job description and a blank evaluation form so the teacher is aware of what duties the paraeducator will be evaluated on. The timeline for completing evaluations should also be known and an agreement reached as to who will complete the written evaluation, if meetings about the evaluation will be held, and who would be present at evaluation meetings. If teachers have concerns about a paraeducator's work performance prior to an evaluation period, they should provide this feedback immediately to an administrator so appropriate action can be taken to improve the paraeducator's work performance or pursue termination. While this may not be the reason we joined the education field, it is important to follow district policies for evaluating employees so that only the best paraeducators work in our schools.

While formal evaluations are typically a required component of most school districts' retention policies, informal evaluations and feedback are critical to paraeducator professional growth, confidence, and growth of the teacher as a supervisor. Many strategies exist for providing informal evaluations, but the feedback should be regular, constructive, and informative. We adapted a tool from Pickett and Gerlach (2003) that can be used during a paraeducator observation. We suggest completing this tool (see Figure 3.7) during the observation and then meeting with the paraeducator to discuss his or her impressions of what went well, what could be improved, and to explain any errors or successes.

This tool can be useful in guiding professional development for teachers and paraeducators. Consider having general education teachers also provide feedback about paraeducator performance; often, these team members also have valuable insight that will help the whole team!

Figure 3.7	Paraeducator Observation Tool

Paraeducator:_____   Date:_____   Lesson/Class:_____

Rating Key: E = excels; P = performs well; D = developing; N = needs improvement; X = not observed

(Continued)

Figure 3.7   (Continued)

Skill	Teacher Rating	Paraeducator Self-Rating
1. Prepared for the lesson (has age-appropriate materials ready; implements teacher-made or approved lesson; adaptations and student supports, such as communication devices, are ready)		
2. Establishes rapport with the student		
3. Gives clear instructions after gaining student attention		
4. Uses appropriate prompting techniques that foster student independence		
5. Incorporates natural supports (such as peers)		
6. Student is on task, engaged, and participating in the general education lesson in a nonstigmatizing and nonsegregating manner		
7. Gives appropriate corrective feedback to the student		
8. Uses reinforcement correctly (correct type and frequency)		
9. Records data on student performance clearly and correctly		
10. Incorporates student behavior support tools, health care plans, and addresses specified IEP goals		
11. Uses time, resources, and supports efficiently and correctly		
12. Paraeducator reflection: a. What went well in this lesson? b. What did not go well in this lesson? c. What changes would you want to make before doing this lesson again? d. What can the teacher do to support you in this lesson?		

Conclusion

This chapter has considered the distinct supervision needs that exist in inclusive settings. When inclusion staff work independently and throughout a school building, there is inherently less opportunity to speak together, provide supervision, and give feedback. Thus, there is a need to make sure that these opportunities are created and maximized. In this chapter, we discussed the use of staff binders, communication notebooks, staff meetings, and informal observations to help meet supervision and collaboration needs in inclusive settings.

Please be sure to go to the website (http://www.corwin.com/theinclusiontoolbox) to download the forms and resources from this chapter!

4

Scheduling for Successful Inclusion

Good fortune is what happens when opportunity meets with planning.

—Thomas Edison

A typical school day for any student, teacher, support staff member, or parent revolves around at least one schedule. In most schools there are several schedules established to keep everything running smoothly: the master class schedule, the bell schedule (which usually has at least a few variations to accommodate for assemblies, block schedules, or special event days), individual student schedules, the schedule of special events for the year, individual classroom schedules, and more. Special education adds yet another level of scheduling related to developing and implementing individual education plans (IEPs). With so many different needs to meet in a school day, creating effective and complementary schedules can truly be a work of art. We believe it is also the foundation for a successful inclusive school. This chapter discusses strategies for scheduling the many activities the inclusion facilitator coordinates, including scheduling IEP meetings, developing student daily schedules, developing staff daily schedules, developing schedules for substitutes, and scheduling for meaningful student participation in inclusive settings.

Strategies for Scheduling the IEP Meeting

The term *IEP* is often used interchangeably to refer to a meeting and a document. The IEP meeting (and document) may be held for (a) initial assessments, if a student is suspected of needing special education services; (b) interim review, if a student has an existing IEP and has moved to a new placement, school, or district; (c) annual review, for yearly

---

❖ **Box 4.1   What Does the Research Say?**

IEP Scheduling

Scheduling the IEP meeting at a time and place that are convenient to all team members is an important step in facilitating team member participation (Menlove, Hudson, & Suter, 2001). Furthermore, IEP meetings should be held in comfortable spaces where differences in cultural beliefs regarding disability are accepted (Dabkowski, 2004). Last, team member preparation and participation in IEP development is facilitated when the IEP is sent to team members ahead of time (Menlove et al., 2001).

Student Schedules

Student schedules should be created that benefit student learning and decrease student anxiety. For example, many students will benefit from a consistent, predictable schedule (Bullard, 2004). However, when developing student schedules and making class placement decisions, all student-needed supports must be considered and provided in that placement (Worrell, 2008). Schedulers should take care to avoid mismatches between student IEP needs and schedule by prescheduling students, utilizing transition planning information, and involving the school scheduler in placement decisions (e.g., counselor; Bugaj, 2000).

Staff Schedules

Finally, staff schedules must be considered. Paraeducators report a desire for scheduled time for specific activities (e.g., making adaptations, staff development; Liston, Nevin, & Malian, 2009). A clear set of expectations and role clarification, which can be accomplished through scheduling, has been requested by paraeducators to reduce emotional exhaustion at work (Shyman, 2010). Finally, schedules must ensure adequate time for educators to work with students and provide needed supports and services in their daily schedules (Mastropieri, 2001).

---

updates to the IEP goals and services; and (d) triennial reviews, for 3-year reevaluations to determine if the student continues to require special education services. For each IEP meeting, it is important to make sure that all required team members are present.

The law (Individuals with Disabilities Education Improvement Act, 2004) says that the following people must attend every IEP meeting: parents, general education teachers, special education teachers, a representative of the school or agency, and a person who can interpret evaluation results (see Figure 4.1).

While students are not required to attend their IEP meetings, the law clearly states students should attend whenever possible and the student must be invited to any meeting when postsecondary goals and transition services are discussed. Of course, other people may attend an IEP meeting. For example, a parent may wish to invite a friend or an advocate, and other individuals who have specific experience or expertise may also be invited. As a rule of thumb, it is a good idea to invite all individuals who provide a service to the student at home and at school.

The image in Figure 4.1 shows seven people at the IEP meeting table. But this is a minimal number; because IEP team meetings can get quite large, scheduling the IEP meeting at a time when everyone is available can be challenging. Some schools leave the scheduling of IEP team meetings for teachers to do, whereas other schools have designated staff members who complete scheduling. Check the policies at your school or district first. If you are responsible for scheduling the IEP meeting, here are a few tips:

Figure 4.1	IEP Team Diagram

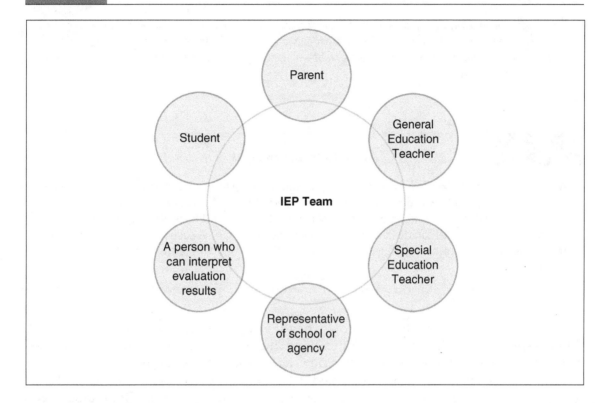

Scheduling Tips

- *Make a list of who needs to be invited.* You can refer to an existing IEP sign-in sheet or services sheet for the student for hints as to who came last time.
- *Obtain work schedule information from parents.* Many parents who are extremely interested in participating in IEP meetings fail to do so because the meetings are scheduled when they must be at work (Jones & Gansle, 2010). This puts parents in a difficult position of choosing to attend an IEP meeting and possibly losing pay or even their jobs. Simply ask parents when is the best time for them to be able to participate, and let them know how long the meeting is expected to last.
- *Obtain a copy of service provider schedules or dates of availability.* Many service providers work at multiple sites in a given week. If the speech-language pathologist works at the school site on Tuesdays and Thursdays, these would probably be the best days to hold IEP meetings at that site.
- *Schedule the meeting at a time and place where there will be few distractions.* Before or after school may be best. Also, check with your school site to determine if there is a designated time for IEP meetings. Be sure that your team members will be available for at least an hour, or the duration of the IEP meeting. Some schools hire roving substitute teachers to release teachers so that they can attend IEP meetings. If this is not possible, a teacher colleague who has a preparation period may be able to cover a class so that the teacher can attend the IEP meeting.
- *Provide detailed information when scheduling the IEP.* Tell the participants the type of IEP meeting (initial, interim, annual, or triennial) and provide details about what type of information they should give at the meeting (e.g., assessment results, progress updates, new goals, written reports).

BOX 4.2   Tech Byte

Online scheduling software can be a useful tool, especially when managing the often-conflicting schedules that many service providers may have. The IEP scheduler might use an online poll, such as the free and easy-to-use doodle poll (www.doodle.com) to survey when all meeting participants will be available (remember to survey parents as well!)

BOX 4.3   ***Administrator Insight***

Administrators play an important role in creating an appropriate schedule for all students, from deciding who teaches what and to whom to clarifying what is expected from school personnel and families during meetings and activities. Administrators can support the scheduling of IEP meetings by providing roving substitutes to release staff to attend meetings. Administrators can further support IEP meeting schedules by designating a non-teaching staff member to schedule IEP meetings, thus releasing teachers to focus on teaching duties.

The IEP scheduler should also know when IEPs are due for review for each student. Often a spreadsheet is a useful tool for tracking important dates. The spreadsheet is used to track IEP review dates, type of IEP review, and progress monitoring date. Remember, the law says that parents must be informed of their child's progress on IEP goals "at least as often as parents are informed of their nondisabled child's progress" (Individuals with Disabilities Education Improvement Act, 2004). Therefore, sending out IEP progress goal updates whenever report cards are released is a good rule of thumb to meet the minimal requirements of the law.

Case Study: Mrs. Simpson Creates an IEP Master Calendar

Mrs. Simpson has set aside an hour to create the IEP review date matrix for the 13 students she has on her caseload so far this year. She creates a master calendar (see Figure 4.2) that includes review due dates, the type of IEP, and a reminder of progress monitoring dates. At Harvard High School, report cards are sent out at the end of each quarter. Mrs. Simpson knows, then, that she must send out progress reports on IEP goals on this schedule as well.

Figure 4.2   IEP Master Schedule

Month	Student	IEP Review Date	Send Invitations by	Type of IEP Meeting	Request Permission to Assess by*
September	Allison	9/13	9/3	Annual	
	Wesley	9/27	9/17	Triennial	7/17
October (Progress reports due 10/20)	Jason	10/4	9/24	Annual	
	Jamie	10/15	10/5	Annual	

Month	Student	IEP Review Date	Send Invitations by	Type of IEP Meeting	Request Permission to Assess by*
November	Rachel	11/1	10/22	Annual	
	Josue	11/10	10/30	Triennial	7/30
	Brandon	11/18	11/8	Annual	
December	Ramona	12/5	11/25	Annual	
January (Progress reports due 1/28)	Michael	1/17	1/7	Annual	
February	Tomica	2/6	1/27	Annual	
	Ayden	2/15	2/5	Triennial	12/5
April	Casper	4/11	4/1	Annual	
	Alonso	4/26	4/16	Annual	
June (Progress reports due 6/15)	ALL				

*Permission requests only need to be completed when students will be assessed, such as for triennial reviews.

BOX 4.4   Tech Byte

In this tech-savvy world, apps exist to help schedule IEPs and keep important dates in mind. The app Schedule My IEP is available for free at the iOS app store for just this purpose!

Next, Mrs. Simpson creates a schedule for the IEP school team members with whom she frequently interacts (Figure 4.3). She can use this as an aid in scheduling meetings, but also to know when her team members plan to be on campus.

Figure 4.3   IEP School Team Member Contacts and Schedules

Name	Service/Role	Phone or Email	Days at Harvard
Ms. Thompson	SLP	555-5555	M, W, F
Ms. Franklin	OT	555-1234	M, Th afternoons
Ms. Rossi	PT	555-2345	W mornings
Coach Brown	Adapted PE	555-3456	M–F
Ms. Tate	Psychologist	555-4567	T–F
Mr. Johnson	Orientation and mobility	555-5678	W mornings

Developing Student Schedules

Prescheduling for Best Schedule

Before the school year can begin, all students must be assigned to classroom teachers. Sometimes a committee of teachers does this, sometimes school counselors develop schedules, and sometimes scheduling is completed by school administrators. It is always a good idea for the inclusion facilitator to be involved in scheduling students into general education classrooms. Often, students have learning needs that can best be met with a particular teaching strategy or philosophy, and so we can match students and teachers based on these characteristics. Sometimes the personalities of students and teachers are important to consider. Other times, simply knowing a teacher's organizational habits is important. Additional factors that an inclusion facilitator may want to consider when scheduling students into a specific teacher's class are listed in Figure 4.4.

Figure 4.4	Considerations for Scheduling

- **Teacher Characteristics/Teaching Style**

  - How organized is this teacher?
  - Does this teacher include visual and structural supports to provide organizational information to students?
  - Are there predictable routines and activities in this classroom?
  - Is this teacher amenable to collaboration? To co-teaching? To having adults in the classroom?
  - Are the assignments in this class manageable and adaptable?
  - Does this teacher provide for differentiated instruction or universally designed learning?
  - Does this teacher provide opportunities for social and character development (e.g., group work, table groups, clear rules and consequences related to bullying)
  - For secondary level: Is this class/teacher available at a time that matches student needs?

- **Student Characteristics/Learning Needs**

  - What are the student's needs for structure and routine?
  - What are the student's needs for organization and visual supports?
  - What level or types of adaptations to the curriculum will the student need to be successful?
  - What level or types of supports will be necessary for the student to succeed socially?

- **Overall Special Education Caseload**

  - Consider overall caseload size and seek natural proportions of students with and without disabilities in each class. For example, if 15% of students at a school have an IEP, then 15% of students in a given classroom would be expected to have an IEP. If 2% of students at a school have severe disabilities, then 2% of students in a general education classroom would be expected to have severe disabilities.

- **Supports Available**

  - How many paraeducators will be available to support each classroom?
  - What are areas of strength for each paraeducator? (Match strengths to class activities, class periods, or individual students.)
  - What are the training and certification backgrounds of paraeducators? Match certification areas to classes as much as possible.
  - Which students and/or teachers does each paraeducator work best with?

Often, prescheduling students who receive special education services can be helpful in making sure students have the best match of teachers to their distinct needs. Prescheduling, here, refers to assigning students with disabilities, and other students with distinct needs, to classes before general population students are assigned. Speaking with the scheduling committee, counselor, or administrator might be necessary to pre-schedule selected students for whom a good match is particularly important. Remember to obtain parent input in this process, particularly when considering the distinct learning needs and preferences of individual students.

Developing Comprehensive Student Schedules

Scheduling for Class Activities (Elementary)

Typically, students in elementary school are assigned a classroom teacher that they spend the entire day with. Sometimes, this is modified slightly so that a whole class will rotate together to a teacher for a special subject. For example, sometimes all of the third graders in Mr. Gray's class will go to Ms. Rodriguez for science lessons. To plan for class schedules and teacher assignments in elementary schools, then, it is important to have a good fit between the student and the primary (or only) teacher. It is also important to get information about class routines and schedules for individual teachers in elementary school.

Unlike secondary schools, where schedules are fixed by class periods, many teachers in elementary schools set their own daily schedules. For example, Mr. Gray may decide to teach reading, then art, then math in the morning, whereas Mrs. Leung teaches science, then math, then reading in the morning. Knowing teacher schedules and routines is critical in planning supports for students receiving special education services, especially paraeducator supports. To become familiar with the schedules for his students' teachers, Mr. DeMarco asks each teacher to complete a typical daily schedule, as shown in Figure 4.5. Mr. DeMarco has also accounted for the standard schedules at Pine View Elementary School, including recess breaks, lunch, and dismissal times for various grade levels. He has shaded cells when students are not in class in black (kindergarten is in the morning, and Grades 1 through 3 are released at 2:30, while Grades 4 and 5 are in school until 3:05). Mr. DeMarco will use this schedule later to plan for students, paraeducators, and related services.

Scheduling for Class Periods (Secondary)

Because students in secondary schools can enroll in a variety of courses, including electives, it is helpful to have a "big picture" in view to know student course needs and course requests. Creating a table listing the classes students want and need to take, gathered from the IEP team, along with any special needs or requests, can make the scheduling process a little bit easier. Consider Mrs. Simpson's scheduling needs, as shown in Figure 4.6. The typical school day at Harvard High School consists of seven class periods; all students have the option of taking only six periods instead of the standard seven. Harvard High School also has available various math courses based on assessed student need, a range of elective courses, and a Study Skills elective (previously a special education course) that is open for any student in need of

Figure 4.5 Typical Daily Schedules for Teacher's at Pine View Elementary School

Teacher → Grade → Student →	Mrs. Leung Kindergarten Kendra	Mrs. Davis 2nd Grade Sally	Ms. Cruz 2nd Grade Andy	Mr. Gray 3rd Grade James	Mrs. McAllen 4th Grade Michael	Mr. Brown 5th Grade Sarah	Ms. O'Neil 5th Grade Anthony
8:30–9	Circle Time	Morning Meeting	Morning Math Meeting	Morning Meeting	Bellwork	Science	Social Studies
9–9:30	Learning Centers	Math	Spelling	Math Workshop	Reading Workshop	Library	Math (Sullivan)
9:30–10	Snack	Snack Recess	Snack Recess	Snack Recess	Small Group Intervention	Math (Sullivan)	Music
10–10:30	Music	Language Arts	Reading	Writer's Workshop	Snack Recess	Snack Recess	Snack Recess
10:30–11	Play Outside	Writers Workshop	Music or PE	Music	Math	Language Arts (O'Neil)	Social Studies (Brown)
11–11:30	Read Aloud	Silent Reading	Lunch	Lunch	Writing Workshop	Technology	Library
11:30–12		Silent Reading	Language Arts	Science	Lunch	Lunch	Lunch
12–12:30		Science	Math	Reader's Workshop	Science or Social Studies	Music	Science
12:30–1		Art or Music	Social Studies	PE	Music	PE	PE
1–1:30		Recess	Recess	Recess	Small Group Intervention	Social Studies (Brown)	Language Arts (O'Neil)
1:30–2		Social Studies	Science	Social Studies	Recess	Recess	Recess
2–2:30		Clean Up	Clean Up	Art or Music	PE	Art	Art
2:30–3:05					Silent Reading	Class Meeting	Small Groups

| Figure 4.6 | Student Course Requests/Needs at Harvard High School |

Student	Grade	Math Class	Electives Desired/ Required	Core Classes	Special Requests or Needs?
Allison	9th	Alg 1	Computers	Eng 9, Biology, PE 9, US History	Six-period day
Wesley	9th	Alg 1	Computers	Eng 9, Biology, PE 9, US History	Study Skills
Jason	10th	Alg 1	Chorus	Reading, World His, PE 10, Physical Science	Study Skills
Jamie	10th	Alg 2/Trig	Arts and Crafts	Reading, World His, PE 10, Physical Science	Study Skills
Rachel	10th	Geometry	Spanish 2	English 10, World History, PE 10, Phys Sci	Study Skills
Josue	10th	Geometry	Chorus	English 10, World History, PE 10, Phys Sci	Study Skills
Brandon	11th	Alg 1	Library Asst. Foods, Weight Lifting	Eng 11, Economics, Chemistry	
Ramona	11th	Alg 2/Trig	Keyboarding	Eng 11, Economics, Chemistry	Six-period day, Study Skills
Michael	11th	Geom	Spanish 3, Arts and Crafts	Reading, Economics, Chemistry	Study Skills
Tomica	11th	Alg 2/Trig	Cross-Age Tutoring, Spanish 3	Eng 11, Economics, Life Sciences	Study Skills
Ayden	12th	Alg 2/Trig	Ceramics, Foods	English 12, American Studies, Earth Sciences	Study Skills
Casper	12th	Alg 1	Leadership, Band	English 12, American Studies, Earth Sciences	Study Skills
Alonso	12th	Geom	Spanish 4, Band; Foods	English 12, American Studies, Earth Sciences	Study Skills

extra time or assistance to study for classes, assistance with class work or homework, or assistance organizing materials.

At first glance, this "wish list" may seem daunting. By working with the scheduling team at her school (in this case, the counselors for Grades 9–12), Mrs. Simpson is able to assign students to classes so that their needs are met throughout the school day, as shown in Figure 4.7.

Developing Staff Schedules

Finally, student and staff schedules are combined to create a comprehensive special education program schedule. Chapter 3 has sample schedules for a single paraeducator;

Figure 4.7 Student Schedules, Fall Semester at Harvard High School

Student	Period 1	Period 2	Period 3	Period 4	Lunch	Period 5	Period 6	Period 7
9th Grade								
Allison	OFF	Alg 1	Biology	PE 9		Computers	English 9	US History
Wesley	PE 9	US History	Biology	English 9		Computers	Study Skills 9	Alg 1
10th Grade								
Jason	Reading	Alg 1	World His	PE 10		Chorus	Study Skills 10	Physical Sci
Jamie	Reading	Alg 2/Trig	World His	PE 10		Physical Sci	Arts and Crafts	Study Skills 10
Rachel	Spanish 2	PE 10	Geometry	Eng 10		Physical Sci	World His	Study Skills 10
Josue	Physical Sci	PE 10	Geometry	Eng 10		Chorus	World His	Study Skills 10
11th Grade								
Brandon	Weight Lifting	Alg 1	Library Asst	Foods		Chemistry	English 11	Economics
Ramona	OFF	Alg 2/Trig	Economics	Keyboarding		Chemistry	English 11	Study Skills 11
Michael	Reading	Geometry	Economics	Spanish 3		Chemistry	Arts and Crafts	Study Skills 11
Tomica	Life Sciences	Alg 2/Trig	Economics	Spanish 3		Cross-Age	English 11	Study Skills 11
12th Grade								
Ayden	Eng 12	Alg 2/Trig	Ceramics	Foods		Earth Sci	American Studies	Study Skills 12
Casper	American Studies	Alg 1	Eng 12	Leadership		Earth Sci	Band	Study Skills 12
Alonso	American Studies	Spanish 4	Eng 12	Foods		Geometry	Band	Study Skills 12

BOX 4.5   Tech Byte

We suggest creating schedules using software that is easy to manipulate, such as MS Excel or Word, simply because schedules are likely to change frequently, so writing them up and managing them by hand would be time-consuming. Some inclusion facilitators write up these schedules using dry-erase markers or sticky notes, and thus have the schedule in an easy-to-change format. The problem with this is that it is hard to share the schedule with others (such as the office staff, who may need to know how to find inclusion staff quickly in an emergency), if it resides in a physical location. Inclusion facilitators can easily share schedules with school staff that are created online by posting them in Dropbox (www.dropbox.com) or Google Drive (www.drive.google.com).

however, it is necessary to plan the entire workday for all staff so that student needs are fully addressed. A whole-staff schedule can also be shared with administration and the office so that school staff can be located if needed throughout the school day.

When assigning staff to work with specific students, it is a good idea to match staff and student personalities, characteristics, and strengths as much as possible. For example, a staff member who is particularly strong in math might be a good support person in math classes and activities.

BOX 4.6   *Administrator Insight*

Administrators can support the inclusion facilitator in developing schedules for paraeducators by providing the inclusion facilitator with final class lists and schedules prior to the start of school and, ideally, by providing a working day for the inclusion facilitator to develop schedules for paraeducators that match paraeducator strengths with class and student needs. The administrator can further assist with assigning paraeducators to classes by checking the certifications and qualifications of all staff members. Some paraeducators may be certified teachers, so matching these paraeducators to their content would be beneficial. Similarly, some paraeducators may be certified in first aid, so it makes sense to pair these paraeducators with specific students who have health care needs throughout the day. Because the transition to a new year or semester is much less anxiety-ridden and pleasant when everyone feels prepared, this workday will reap huge benefits to teachers and paraeducators.

It is also important to consider factors related to dependency when assigning paraeducators. Often, we have a temptation to assign a full-day, one-to-one adult to work with a student. Sometimes this seems logical because the student seems to be making good progress, because the paraeducator and student have a good relationship and enjoy working together, or because it is most convenient to do this. However, there are some real problems that can arise when a student has just one paraeducator. For example, crises can arise if that paraeducator is sick or moves and nobody else feels as comfortable or knowledgeable assisting the student. Long-term consequences for the student can also be problematic. One-to-one assignments can lead teachers (both general and special education) to disengage with the student and place responsibility on the paraeducator (Giangreco, Broer, & Edelman, 2001). The result of this disengagement is that student-paraeducator dyads become isolated from the rest of the class, further preventing teachers and peers from interacting with the student (Giangreco, Broer, et al., 2001).

Furthermore, one-to-one paraeducator assignments have a tendency to allow teachers to "disown" that student as their responsibility (Cook, 2004), instead relying on the paraeducator to make minute-by-minute instructional decisions. Students with disabilities themselves have reported that one-to-one paraeducators can act as a barrier between students with disabilities and their peers, making friendship development difficult (Broer, Doyle, & Giangreco, 2005). Certainly, paraeducators are valuable members of any educational team, but unhealthy relationships can develop when one-to-one assignments are the norm. So rather than having one adult work full day with a student with disabilities, we strongly advocate assigning at least two paraeducators to work with a student. We believe that switching up the support in this way enables students to learn to generalize skills better, helps them become less dependent on one person, and strengthens the skills of all educators in that they will see the student as approachable.

Box 4.7

Human Resources and the Inclusion Facilitator

The inclusion facilitator does not set a paraeducator's full-time equivalent (FTE); usually this is decided by human resources when the paraeducator is hired. However, the inclusion facilitator must play an important role in determining how that FTE is allocated on a day-to-day basis. In other words, human resources will likely not know when the paraeducator is scheduled to take a break, what classes he or she will work in, and so on. That is where the inclusion facilitator plays a critical role. The inclusion facilitator should work with human resources and administrators if there is any confusion or concern about how these day-to-day schedules are designed.

Perhaps the easiest way to assign paraeducators is by making a visual schedule. Earlier, Mr. DeMarco and Mrs. Simpson made student schedules for each student. Now the inclusion facilitators can determine the full-time-equivalent (FTE), or work hours, for each paraeducator and then assign paraeducators to students throughout the day. For example, an FTE of .75 means the paraeducator has been hired to work 30 hours per week. This is calculated by multiplying .75 by 40 hours in a full-time work week. Working with FTE is preferable, because the inclusion facilitator can then stagger work hours for all staff members so the whole school day is covered. For example, if each paraeducator has an FTE of .625 (25 hours/week, or 5 hours per school day) and there are 40 hours in a school week (8 hours per day), we want to make sure that all paraeducators don't go home at noon and leave the afternoons with no staff available. The inclusion facilitator may need to ask the school administrator or the human resources office for information about FTE for each paraeducator.

BOX 4.8	*Administrator Insight*

Administrators can support teachers in developing class schedules for students with IEPs by creating a working meeting for teachers to work with schedulers, before school begins, to have input into the course schedules for students on their caseload.

Mr. DeMarco and Mrs. Simpson first list each paraeducator and his or her FTE, then work hours so that there are paraeducators available all day (see Figure 4.8). Half an hour (unpaid) lunch breaks are also incorporated.

Figure 4.8   Paraeducator Staff at Pine View Elementary

Staff Name	FTE	Work Hours
Molly	.75	8:35–3:05
John	.625	9:05–2:35
Tammy	.5	8:30–12:30
Luke	.75	8:30–3
Anna	.75	8:35–3
Mr. DeMarco	1.0	8–4:30

Then Mr. DeMarco uses color-coding to assign each paraeducator (and himself) a color (see Figure 4.9). This book isn't printed in color, which is more visually appealing, so we use the term *color* but actually have different grayscale shading in each cell instead of an actual color.

Figure 4.9   Paraeducator Staff at Pine View Elementary

Staff Name	FTE	Work Hours
Molly	.75	8:35–3:05
John	.625	9:05–2:35
Tammy	.5	8:30–12:30
Luke	.75	8:30–3
Anna	.75	8:30–3

Next, the staff colors (or, in this case, patterns) are superimposed on the student schedule. This illustrates which staff member is supporting which student(s) at any given time of day. If there is no color at a certain time of day, that simply means no staff member is supporting the student at that time. And if a staff member is shown to be at two places at once (e.g., Anna at 8:30 is assigned to several classes), that means this staff member is "roving" or "floating," meaning that person is dropping in and checking on several students at this time.

Figure 4.10 Staff and Student Schedules at Pine View Elementary School

Teacher →	Mrs. Leung	Mrs. Davis	Ms. Cruz	Mr. Gray	Mrs. McAllen	Mr. Brown	Ms. O'Neil
Grade →	Kindergarten	2nd Grade	2nd Grade	3rd Grade	4th Grade	5th Grade	5th Grade
Student →	Kendra	Sally	Andy	James	Michael	Sarah	Anthony
8:30–9	Circle Time	Morning Meeting	Morning Math Meeting	Morning Meeting	Bellwork	Science	Social Studies
9–9:30	Learning Centers	Math	Spelling	Math Workshop	Reading Workshop	Library	Math (Sullivan)
9:30–10	Snack	Snack Recess	Snack Recess	Snack Recess	Small Group Intervention	Math (Sullivan)	Music
10–10:30	Music	Language Arts	Reading	Writer's Workshop	Snack Recess	Snack Recess	Snack Recess
10:30–11	Play Outside	Writers Workshop	Music or PE	Music	Math	Language Arts (O'Neil)	Social Studies (Brown)
11–11:30	Read Aloud	Lunch	Lunch	Lunch	Writing Workshop	Technology	Library
11:30–12		Silent Reading	Language Arts	Science	Lunch	Lunch	Lunch
12–12:30		Science	Math	Reader's Workshop	Science or Social Studies	Music	Science
12:30–1		Art or Music	Social Studies	PE	Music	PE	PE
1–1:30		Recess	Recess	Recess	Small Group Intervention	Social Studies (Brown)	Language Arts (O'Neil)
1:30–2		Social Studies	Science	Social Studies	Recess	Recess	Recess
2–2:30		Clean Up	Clean Up	Art or Music	PE	Art	Art
2:30–3:05					Silent Reading	Class Meeting	Small Groups

Mr. DeMarco might include himself in the color-coding schedule, or he might assign himself as a floater who assists in classrooms where paraeducators are also present to model and provide feedback. In our example, Mr. DeMarco decides to float and isn't assigned a color (see Figure 4.10).

Mrs. Simpson uses a similar process to assign paraeducators at Harvard High School. She begins by entering the names for each teacher each period. Then, she highlights each cell in the schedule to indicate the name of the paraeducator supporting the student(s) each class period. As in Mr. DeMarco's school, some paraeducators will be supporting more than one student each class period; other students are not in need of support and have no person assigned. However, Mrs. Simpson may float in to support students when no paraeducators are present. Likewise, she may provide modeling and feedback, while working individually with a student, even if a paraeducator is assigned to a class period. Finally, Mrs. Simpson co-teaches two classes each day. Mrs. Simpson has included herself on the master schedule (see Figure 4.11).

Figure 4.11   Staff Schedules at Harvard High School

Staff Name	FTE	Work Hours
Jessica	.75	8:30–3
Mary	.6875	8:30–2:30
Tom	.5	8:30–12:30
Greg	.75	9–3:30
Samantha	.75	8:30–3
Hilary	.5	11:30–3:30
Mrs. Simpson	.75	8:30–3

As did Mr. DeMarco, Mrs. Simpson then superimposes these colors onto the master schedule (see Figure 4.12), illustrating where all inclusion staff and students are throughout the day.

Substitute Schedules

All teachers need to be prepared for days they need to be absent. Substitute plans are a must. But as inclusion facilitators, your role can be different from what the typical substitute may expect. Writing up clear substitute plans and schedules is therefore essential. Providing the substitute with some basic information about your role, and the role of the paraeducators you work with, is essential. It is also a good idea to provide the substitute with a copy of your master staff schedule.

Mrs. Simpson has created a substitute plan that is on file at Harvard High School's office. A copy of this plan is shown in Figure 4.13.

Figure 4.12   Staff and Student Schedules at Harvard High School

Student	Period 1	Period 2	Period 3	Period 4	Lunch	Period 5	Period 6	Period 7
Allison	OFF	Algebra 1 Mr. Reynolds	Bio Ms. Smith	PE 9 Ms. Jones		Computers Mr. O'Keefe	English 9 Ms. Thomas	US His Ms. Lee
Wesley	PE 9 Ms. Jones	US His Mrs. Upton	Bio Ms. Smith	Eng 9 Ms. Reid		Computers Mr. O'Keefe	Study Skills 9 Mr. Clark	Alg 1 Mr. Reynolds
Jason	Reading Mrs. Simpson	Algebra 1 Mr. Reynolds	World His Mr. B	PE 10 Mr. Hancock		Chorus Ms. Salazar	Study Skills 10 Mr. Cruz	Phys Sci Mr. Diamond
Jamie	Reading Mrs. Simpson	Alg 2/Trig Mrs. Leonard	World His Mrs. Upton	PE 10 Mr. Hancock		Phys Sci Mr. Diamond	Arts and Crafts Mr. James	Study Skills 10 Ms. Shaw
Rachel	Spanish 2 Mr. Lopez	PE 10 Mr. Hancock	Geometry Mrs. Olson	Eng 10 Ms. Ballard		Phys Sci Mr. Diamond	World His Ms. Lee	Study Skills 10 Ms. Shaw
Josue	Phys Sci Mr. Diamond	PE 10 Mr. Hancock	Geometry Mrs. Olson	Eng 10 Ms. Ballard		Chorus Ms. Salazar	World His Ms. Lee	Study Skills 10 Ms. Shaw
Brandon	Weight Lifting Mr. Reed	Algebra 1 Mr. Reynolds	Library Asst Mrs. Keegan	Foods Ms. Yard		Chemistry Ms. Smith	English 11 Mrs. Peeples	Economics Mr. B
Ramona	OFF	Alg 2/Trig Mrs. Leonard	Economics Mr. Greene	Keyboarding Mr. O'Keefe		Chemistry Ms. Smith	Eng. 11 Mrs. Peeples	Study Skills 11 Mr. Ives
Michael	Reading Mrs. Simpson	Geometry Ms. Suarez	Economics Mrs. Upton	Spanish 3 Mr. Hancock		Chemistry Mr. Diamond	Arts and Crafts Mr. James	Study Skills 11 Mr. Ives
Tomica	Life Sciences Mr. Phillips	Alg 2/Trig Mrs. Leonard	Economics Mr. B	Spanish 3 Mr. Hancock		Cross Age Ms. Yard	English 11 Mrs. Peeples	Study Skills 11 Mr. Ives
Ayden	Eng 12 Mr. Carey	Alg 2/Trig Mrs. Leonard	Ceramics Mr. Houston	Foods Ms. Yard		Earth Sci Ms. Roddy	American Studies Ms. Kim	Study Skills 12 Mrs. Simpson
Casper	American Studies Ms. Kim	Algebra 1 Mr. Reynolds	Eng 12 Mr. Carey	Leadership Mr. Thomas		Earth Sci Ms. Roddy	Band Mr. Owens	Study Skills 12 Mrs. Simpson
Alonso	American Studies Ms. Kim	Spanish 4 Mr. Lopez	Eng 12 Mr. Carey	Foods Ms. Yard		Geometry Mr. Bryant	Band Mr. Owens	Study Skills 12 Mrs. Simpson
Mrs. Simpson	Reading	Alg 1 Mr. Reynolds (co-teach)	Floating Push-In/IEP Prep	Eng 10 Ms. Ballard (co-teach)	Lunch	Floating Push-In/IEP Prep	English 11/ American Studies	Study Skills

Box 4.9

Block Schedules and Other Considerations

Many secondary schools have different schedules, including block schedules, on different days of the week. For example, first period meets daily; on Monday periods 2, 3, and 4 meet; on Thursday periods 5, 6, and 7 meet; and on Tuesday, Wednesday, and Friday periods 1 through 7 meet. During these block schedule days, each class period meets for a longer time (e.g., 90 minutes rather than 50 minutes). This may appear to throw a wrench in the scheduling, but in fact it's not a big deal. The same paraeducators (and co-teachers) would meet in block schedules as in regular schedules, so in reality there is no change in the assignment of support staff.

| Figure 4.13 | Substitute Information |

Welcome to our classroom!
Mrs. Simpson
Inclusion Teacher
Harvard High School
Room 55

Thank you for subbing for me today. I teach students with moderate to severe disabilities. We are lucky to have several fabulous paraeducators who can support you today in each class. Feel free to ask them any questions or for help!

Mrs. Hart (another special education teacher) is next door in Room 54. Please let her know if you need any assistance with students. My student teacher Ms. Flores will be on campus today and is also a great resource.

My daily schedule:

Period	Class	Paraeducators
1st	Reading (Room 55)	This is a small-group instruction reading class with three students (Jason, Jamie, and Michael). Each student has a folder with their reading materials. Please have students work on their "Freak the Mighty" picture dictionaries (Carrie and the students know what this assignment is). A peer tutor (Carrie) will assist each student.
2nd	Algebra 1 (Room 36)	You will co-teach this class with Mr. Reynolds. Today, you will help students in need of extra assistance while Mr. Reynolds provides large-group instruction.
3rd	Floating/ Prep Period	You can use this time to check in on students in their general education classes (see attached master schedule); provide small-group or one-to-one direct instruction as needed.
4th	English 10 (co-teach) (Room 18)	You will co-teach this class with Ms. Ballard. Today, you will help students in need of extra assistance while Ms. Ballard provides large-group instruction.

(Continued)

Figure 4.13	(continued)

Period	Class	Paraeducators
Lunch		Your lunch break
5th	Floating/ Prep Period	You can use this time to check in on students in their general education classes (see attached master schedule); provide small-group or one-to-one direct instruction as needed.
6th	Eng 11/ American Studies	You will alternate between these two courses, providing individual supports (to any students) as needed during class.
7th	Study/ Transition Skills	Greg will assist you in working with all other students. Greg knows the classroom routine and will get students started on their planner check and homework. Students can work on homework today. I also have a peer tutor this period, Dustin. He will check in and then go to another classroom to tutor a student.

The following items are located in these places:

- **Lesson plans:** printed and attached to this sheet
- **Attendance sheet:** folder given to you by school secretary
- **Seating chart:** since it is the beginning of the school year, students are allowed to select their own seat (this is not a problem in any of my classes)
- **Emergency procedures:** posted on right side of entrance to classroom. *Please take GREEN/ RED "55" card with you in case of emergency or drill.*
- **Emergency backpack and binder:** located in first aid drawer (under stereo in back room, drawer is labeled with RED first aid sign). *This MUST be brought with you in case of an emergency/drill.*
- **First aid supplies:** Band-Aids and hand sanitizer, located in first aid drawer
- **School supplies:** paper, pencils, crayons, markers, colored pencils, and silent reading books are all located on back bookshelf. Students are allowed to use these supplies at any time. They may also take a pencil with them to use in their next class. Students should *not* access supply cupboards along back wall without a paraeducator supervising.

Our classroom procedures are as follows:

- **Out of seats:** If students are doing independent work they may leave their seat to get necessary supplies from bookshelf without raising hand.
- **Restroom:** Students may ask permission to use the restroom at any time other than lecture. They need to take the pass hung on the back wall.
- **Water fountain:** Students may use the water fountain at any time during independent work.
- **Discipline policy:** Students are expected to show respect to students and staff, and be prepared to work and participate in class activities. If students are having a hard time making good choices, please talk to them individually. You may also ask a paraeducator in class to intervene, as they have a rapport with the students. For *severe disruptions* please complete discipline referral and send to Mr. Dunn, vice principal.

Conclusion

Scheduling is an important factor in making an inclusion program run smoothly throughout the year. A variety of schedules must be considered, including IEP schedules, related-services schedules, and student and staff schedules. The tools introduced in this chapter will help create a plan for meeting the needs of students throughout the year. While ideally these schedules will be developed and implemented just once, it is important to keep in mind that change is an inevitable part of life, and each of these well-crafted schedules may need to be updated during the school year. Doing so will ease anxiety for all parties involved!

Please be sure to go to the website (http://www.corwin.com/theinclusiontoolbox) to download the forms and resources from this chapter!

PART II

Implementing Inclusive Education

Part II of this book describes the ongoing activities that sustain and strengthen inclusive education for students with disabilities. These are activities and strategies that will be completed throughout the school year.

The strategies and activities in Part II enhance the foundation that was laid in Part I; they will make the inclusive program function on a day-to-day basis.

5

Implementing Inclusive Instruction

If a child can't learn the way we teach, maybe we should teach the way they learn.

—Ignacio Estrada

When thinking about traditional special education instruction, the image of a small group of students sitting around a kidney-shaped table, working intently with a special educator, comes to mind. Or one may imagine a student and special educator sitting side by side, working on a skill, with the student receiving individual instruction. How do these common images of individualized instruction fit with inclusive education? Is it possible to provide special education effectively and efficiently in general education settings, and if so, how? Is there a trade-off between inclusion and individualization? Is simply providing curricular adaptations sufficient to help students with disabilities learn content in general education settings?

Collaboration Strategies to Implement the IEP

Soliciting Input From General Education Teachers in IEP Development

It is important to get input from all teachers and service providers during the IEP meeting. Sometimes general education teachers (and other service providers) are unsure of their role in an IEP meeting and how they might best contribute. Figure 5.1 shows a brief email Mrs. Simpson sends to general education teachers a week or two before Ramona's IEP meeting to remind them of the meeting and help them prepare for it.

❖ **Box 5.1   What Does the Research Say?**

A number of strategies have been identified for developing and implementing inclusive individualized education programs (IEPs). Soliciting general education teacher input is important (Menlove, Hudson, & Suter, 2001). Student profiles, or programs-at-a-glance, are another useful strategy. These tools provide valuable information that can be quickly and easily accessed by teachers and paraeducators throughout the school day (Janney & Snell, 2006).

Learning Opportunities

Research over the past several decades has demonstrated that students with disabilities can learn important academic skills, including mathematics (Browder, Spooner, Ahlgrim-Delzell, Harris, & Wakeman, 2008), sight-word reading (Browder, Wakeman, Spooner, Ahlgrim-Delzell, & Algozzine, 2006), and science (Courtade, Spooner, & Browder, 2007). We also know that this instruction can be delivered effectively in general education settings (Downing, 2010). Last, we know that students with disabilities need plenty of planned opportunities to learn and practice skills—we cannot simply leave learning opportunities to chance!

Embedded Instruction

Embedded instruction is based on naturalistic teaching and systematic instruction techniques. It uses systematic instruction procedures throughout the day to address specific skills. It consists of (1) defining the learning outcomes for the student in general education, (2) identifying natural instructional trials, (3) distributing instructional trials across typical routines, (4) scheduling the delivery of instructional trials across routines, (5) using systematic instruction, and (6) using data-based decision making (McDonnell, Johnson, & McQuivey, 2008). Embedded instruction is an effective manner of teaching skills to students with disabilities. It essentially uses systematic instruction to teach skills to students in natural, inclusive settings. Embedded instruction has been used to teach a range of skills *more effectively* than similar instruction in self-contained special education settings. For example, in one study a chain of behavioral skills (including phonemic awareness and word meaning) were taught with equal or greater effectiveness using embedded instruction compared to traditional special education (Jameson, Walker, Utley, & Maughan, 2012). Furthermore, paraeducators and special education teachers can effectively provide embedded instruction in general education settings (Jameson, McDonnell, Johnson, Riesen, & Polychronis, 2007). General education topics can be taught using embedded instruction (Johnson, McDonnell, Holzwarth, & Hunter, 2004).

Data Collection

Data collection has received increased attention as being essential to effective instruction (Etscheidt, 2006). When teachers collect data on student learning, they are better able to make timely instructional decisions, which in turn improves student performance (Powers & Mandal, 2011). While data collection is instrumental in day-to-day progress monitoring, assigning grades for students with disabilities who are included in general education classes is often problematic. Often, grades alone are low, are inaccurate, or lack meaning for students with disabilities (Silva, Munk, & Bursuck, 2005). However, personalized grading plans are effective tools in communicating student progress and determining how to grade students with disabilities in inclusive settings (Munk & Bursuck, 2001).

Figure 5.1   Email to Teachers to Prepare for IEP Meeting

Dear Teachers,

As a reminder, Ramona's IEP is scheduled for Dec. 3 at 2:30 p.m. in the office conference room. Your attendance is very important! I'm attaching a few guiding questions to help you be prepared to participate in Ramona's IEP. You may want to write out some responses or be prepared to verbally discuss this at the IEP meeting.

1. How is Ramona doing in your class(es)?

   a. Academically

      i. What is her grade?
      ii. How well is she completing assignments?
      iii. Is she up to date on all class work?
      iv. How is she doing on tests?
      v. Is her individual grading plan working?
      vi. Would you want to see any changes in this next IEP?

   b. Socially

      i. Does she complete group work?
      ii. Does she socialize too much or not enough?

   c. Behaviorally

      i. Does she arrive to class on time and prepared?
      ii. Does she follow the class rules?
      iii. Does she use the strategies outlined in her behavior support plan?

   d. Communicatively

      i. Is she communicating clearly and effectively?
      ii. Is her communication device programmed appropriately?

   e. Supports

      i. Does Ramona have the supports in your class that she needs to be successful (such as paraeducator support, peer support, adapted curriculum, adapted tests, etc.)?
      ii. Are there any changes you want to see in this next IEP?

2. How is Ramona using the adaptations (accommodations or modifications) provided in the current IEP?

3. Are these adaptations appropriate?

4. What changes would you want to see in this next IEP?

5. Do you have any specific positive feedback about Ramona?

6. Do you have any specific concerns to share about Ramona?

7. Are there IEP goals that you want to see expanded, added, or limited in your class?

Thanks again for all of your support and feedback! This will help us run a smooth IEP meeting! ☺ Mrs. Simpson

BOX 5.2 Tech Byte

Online forms can be used to collect information about students from teachers. For example, a document can be created on Google Drive (www.docs.google.com) so that the teacher can just go to the website and type in information. If the document is shared with all of the team members, this could be a useful way for teachers to see what their colleagues are thinking ahead of the IEP team meeting as well.

BOX 5.3   Tech Byte

Have an IEP team member who is not able to be present during the meeting? Consider using Skype (www .skype.com) so that the team member can be part of the meeting, even if he or she cannot be in the room. Remember to get parent permission ahead of time!

Student Profiles

It is also imperative that inclusion facilitators provide clear information about students to each of their teachers, including how each student learns, his or her IEP goals, the accommodations or modifications provided in the IEP, any specific health care information, information about behavior support plans, or any other relevant information. This information, or student profile, can be provided to each teacher in order to know students a little better (see Figures 5.2 and 5.3). Figure 5.2 is a student profile that Mr. DeMarco provides to Michael's general education teacher, Mrs. McAllen. Figure 5.3 is a student profile that Mrs. Simpson provides to each of Ramona's teachers.

Figure 5.2   Confidential Student Profile (Elementary)

Student: Michael Wilson
Case Manager: Mr. DeMarco

Time	Paraeducator	Notes
8:30–11:30	Anna	Anna will provide direct support for reading workshop, small-group work, morning recess, writing and math. Anna will primarily assist Michael, but she will assist all other students in the class as well.
11:30–12	Tammy	Tammy will float at lunch, providing assistance as needed to Michael and other fourth and fifth graders.
12–3:05	Luke	Luke will provide assistance to Michael during afternoon activities (science/social studies, music, small group, afternoon recess, PE, and silent reading). Luke will primarily assist Michael, but he will assist all other students in the class as well.
Daily	Mr. Demarco	Mr. DeMarco will drop in and provide floating assistance to Michael and any other student who needs assistance.

Student's Strengths

- Michael has a great sense of humor. He loves to tell jokes.
- Michael loves playing and watching sports. He aspires to be an ESPN announcer when he grows up.

Testing Results

Reading Level	Math Level	Writing Level
4.1	4.4	3.8
Grade equivalent	Grade equivalent	Grade equivalent

Helpful Strategies

- Michael was identified as needing special education support last year; he may need support and enthusiasm from teachers to encourage him to accept the additional support. Remember: *His special education classification is confidential.* Michael knows that he is going to receive support from Mr. DeMarco and paraeducators and understands he has learning difficulties but does *not* know he is labeled as SLD in special education.
- Provide work to Michael in small, manageable chunks (give him one page or half a page from a packet at a time).
- Reward on-task behavior with a ticket (on a schedule of one ticket every 5–10 minutes). The tickets are then entered into Ms. McAllen's (fifth-grade teacher) weekly lottery for prizes.
- Assign Michael to a group and seat in class. Do *not* let him choose his own group or seating arrangement, as he tends to sit with peers that distract him.
- Preferential seating (near front, middle, near quiet peers) is best.

Health Care Information

- Michael takes Adderall at home before school and at school during the lunch break. He will go to the nurse's office to take his medication (it is administered there).

Goals

- **Organization:** Use a daily planner to monitor homework completion and utilize resources (e.g., tutoring, HW club) to increase homework completion to 90% in all classes.
- **Academic:**
  - *Reading*: Michael will read a fifth-grade-level passage at a rate of 120 correct words per minute; he will decode fifth-grade-level passages with an accuracy of 90%; he will answer literal and inferential comprehension questions about a fifth-grade-level passage with 90% accuracy.
  - *Writing*: Michael will write a well-organized three-paragraph essay that consists of introductions, body (persuasion, expository), and conclusion and will edit his written work for grammar, spelling, and coherency.
  - *Math*: Michael will use a resource guide containing notes, equations, and word problem cues to solve fifth-grade-level word problems with 80% accuracy. He will check his calculations with a calculator.

- **Behavior:**
  - Michael will return to class on time after recess (that is, put away materials after first bell and be in line by second bell) 80% of the time.
  - He will raise his hand before speaking in class 90% of the time.
  - He will remain in his seat and remain on task, unless given permission, 90% of the time.

Classroom/Academic Accommodations/Modifications

- Extended time (time and a half for tests and an extra 3 days for long-term projects)
- Administer tests in library or alternate (distraction-free) location
- Provide work in small, manageable chunks
- Preferential seating: close to teacher, positive peer and/or board

Grading

- Personalized grading plan

I am available to discuss curriculum modifications, the role of the paraeducator, further details on student abilities, and any other concerns you may have. You can stop by the Resources room, leave me an email or a note in my box, or let the paraeducator know you'd like to speak with me any time.

Best of luck with the new semester,

Mr. DeMarco

Inclusion Facilitator

555-5000 ext. 253

| Figure 5.3 | Confidential Student Profile (Secondary) |

To: All Teachers

From: Mrs. Simpson

Student Name: Ramona Medrano

Case Manager: Mrs. Simpson

Primary disability: Ramona has been identified as having an intellectual disability. She has educational needs in all academic areas, and her intellectual abilities affect her behavior and ability to develop positive peer relationships.

Period	Paraeducator	Class	Teacher
1	N/A	OFF	
2	Jessica	Alg 2/Trig	Mrs. Leonard
3	Mary	Economics	Mr. B
4	N/A	Keyboarding	Mr. O'Keefe
5	Samantha	Chemistry	Ms. Smith
6	Tom	English 11	Mrs. Peeples
7	Samantha	Study Skills 11	Mr. Ives

Student's Strengths and Interests

- Ramona has a kind heart and thinks the best of people.
- She is interested in music, fashion, and dancing.
- She loves to do puzzles.

Core Academic Skills

Reading Level	Math Level	Writing Level
Grade equivalent 1.3	Grade equivalent 1.8	Grade equivalent 1.0
Ramona enjoys being read to. She has strengths in reading comprehension relative to decoding.	Struggles with setting up problems, is intimidated by word problems.	Ramona can write sentences using a word bank. She should type rather than write by hand.

Helpful Strategies

- Remember: *Her special education classification is confidential.*
- Ramona has a permanent break card to come to the nurse's office to take a 5-minute break. If you notice her behavior escalating, cue her to use her break card and visit the office for a few minutes.
- Provide work to Ramona in small, manageable chunks (give her one page or half a page from a packet at a time). Modify the work to focus on two to three key concepts and/or key vocabulary terms.
- Reward with positive praise and 1:1 quick chats. Ramona loves interactions and wants to develop relationships with people. She needs support developing positive relationships.
- Assign Ramona to a group and seat in class.
- Alert the vice principal, counselor, or Mrs. Simpson regarding any suspected bullying or harassment ASAP.

Goals

- Academic:

  o *Math:* Count with 1:1 correspondence up to 20.
  o *Math:* Use the dollar-up method to pay for items up to $20 with $1 bills (e.g., if the cost is $1.99, Ramona should give $2).
  o *Writing:* Write her name on all of her papers correctly.
  o *Writing:* Write a complete sentence using a word bank.
  o *Reading:* Read 20 high-priority sight words (e.g., Dolch words such as *the* and *are*).

- **Social Skills:** Following social skill instruction, identify at least two peers to interact with (initiate and sustain an interaction for at least 3 minutes).
- **Social/Communication:** Use positive communication strategies (eye contact, listening, using clarifying statements) and recognize social cues to monitor and repair conversations.
- **Behavior:** Request a break, using break card, in a calm manner without disrupting the class, and select an activity in nursing office (e.g., drawing, listening to music) to reduce frustration, anxiety and emotional distress.

Classroom/Academic Accommodations/Modifications

- Frequent breaks to reduce anxiety; use of permanent break card
- Copy of teacher/peer notes
- Extended time
- Take tests in Resources room or alternate location
- Provide work in small, manageable chunks
- Preferential seating: close to teacher, positive peer and/or board
- Homework: Parents will sign off after Ramona has completed 20 minutes of homework each night.

Grading

- Modified grading in each class. Ramona will be graded on the basis of progress on her IEP goals, participation, and effort in classes.

I am available to discuss curriculum modifications, the role of the paraeducator, further details on student abilities, and any other concerns you may have. You can stop by J-55, leave me an email or a note in my box, or let the paraeducator know you'd like to speak with me any time.

Best of luck with the new semester,

Mrs. Simpson

Inclusion Facilitator

555-5000 ext. 255

Grading Students in Inclusive Settings

Grading students who are completing different quantity, quality, or type of assignments and tests can be a challenge to successful inclusion, particularly in this age of accountability. In fact, this type of "nuts and bolts" issue can act as a barrier to inclusive education because teachers simply lack information on how to overcome this. Legally, schools may assign modified grades if all students (not just those with IEPs) may also receive modified grades (Salend & Duhaney, 2002). Personalized grading plans (PGPs) can help describe what is expected of a student with an IEP and how to assign grades to that student on assignments, tests, and report cards.

Many strategies exist for adapting grading procedures (Silva et al., 2005), including assigning grades based on the following:

- *Progress toward meeting IEP goals and objectives:* Teachers assign grades based on mastery of IEP goals and objectives, rather than progress on state standards.
- *Improvement over past performance:* Teachers assign grades based on how well they determine the student is improving over past performance.
- *Performance on prioritized, modified work:* Teachers assign grades based on accuracy of completing modified assignments and assessments.
- *Improvement in student learning process (rather than product):* Teachers assign grades based on student demonstration of learning to complete a task, rather than the quality or the quantity of the final product.
- *A system of modified weights and scales:* Teachers assign grades based on a modified system of assigning grades, so that, for example, only 50% accuracy is required to earn an A, whereas students without a personalized grading plan would require 90% accuracy to earn an A.

A PGP is considered a fair and effective way to describe how a student will be graded and consists of the following elements (Munk & Bursuck, 2001):

- A rationale as to why a grading adaptation was needed, including how the student's disability affects her or his school performance
- What grading adaptations would be needed
- The instructional or curricular adaptations already in place for the class or activity
- The roles and responsibilities of the student and all other team members
- A statement of agreement to adhere to the PGP, signed by all team members

Mr. DeMarco created a PGP (see Figure 5.4) for Michael in the areas of reading and writing.

Figure 5.4   Personalized Grading Plan

Student: Michael Wilson

Class/activity to have modified grading: Reading, writing (class and homework)

1. **Why is a PGP needed?** The student's current report card grade is lower than desired because Michael works at a slower pace on his reading and writing activities. Because of this, he earns lower grades on his tests and quizzes in class. He also spends too much time on homework, leading to frustration and a dislike of reading. The class requirement to read 20 pages a night, then, is not appropriate for Michael.

2. **What adaptations are already in place?**
   - ☐ Extended time (time and a half for tests and an extra 3 days for long-term projects)
   - ☐ Administer tests in library or alternate (distraction-free) location
   - ☐ Provide work in small, manageable chunks
   - ☐ Preferential seating: close to teacher, positive peer, and/or board

3. **What grading adaptations will be needed?**
   - ☐ Progress toward meeting IEP goals
   - ☐ Improvement over past performance

☐ Performance on prioritized work
☐ Improvement in learning process
☒ System of modified weights and scales

Explain:

☐ Self-paced assignments (including homework, projects, and class participation) need to be given more weight to the final grade.
☐ Participation points need to be given more weight (to also address the IEP goal of maintaining attention and participating).
☐ More points should be awarded for recording and completing assignments (use of agenda).

4. What changes will be made to the current grading system?

☐ An additional 3% of points will be given to self-paced assignments (see above).
☐ Participation points will count toward 10% of the total grade.
☐ An additional 2% of the grade will consist of recording and completing assignments (using his agenda).

5. Roles and Responsibilities

Team Member	Responsibility
General education teacher	Make changes to grade book, consult with Mr. DeMarco
Special education teacher	Review grade progress with Mrs. McAllen weekly
Paraeducator	Implement teacher-made modifications
Other	Parents will sign off on homework (30 minutes per night, total)

6. The grading adaptations outlined in this PGP will be attached to, and used in conjunction with, the student's IEP. My signature indicates my agreement to use this PGP when assigning report card grades for this student in this class/activity.

General Education Teacher: Mrs. McAllen   Date: 1/17
Special Education Teacher: Mr. DeMarco   Date: 1/17
Parent(s): Mrs. Wilson   Date: 1/17

BOX 5.4   Tech Byte

Consider working with the information technology staff at your school or district. It might be possible to have student profiles and personalized grading plans embedded on classroom attendance sheets or other online student information databases so that they are readily accessible to teachers (and maybe even provide visual prompts, through tags or highlighting student names, to call attention to them).

Embedded Instruction

Embedded instruction is a strategy that all inclusion facilitators should be familiar with. It is an evidence-based strategy for teaching academic skills in inclusive settings (Hudson, Browder, & Wood, 2013). Because a great, inexpensive, and brief book about how to implement embedded instruction already exists (McDonnell et al., 2008), we simply summarize it here. Instructional trials can be taught in massed trials (e.g., 30 trials of requesting an item in a single sitting) or be distributed across the day (e.g., find 30 times during the day to request an item). Distributed trials promote generalization across people, places, and materials (Collins, 2012). Embedded instruction refers to distributing instructional trials across natural, ongoing opportunities. Sometimes additional opportunities are created in natural, ongoing opportunities so students have enough instructional trials to learn a skill.

Embedded instruction can be used to teach very specific goals. For example, a student may have a goal to learn to read five sight words taken from the core vocabulary (e.g., two from U.S. History, two from chemistry, and one from home economics). Other times, embedded instruction can be used to teach a general goal. Most social and communication goals can be worked on at any time and are thus general goals. For example, a student can practice the goal of "responding to your name when called" in any activity. Likewise, a goal to "write your name correctly" can be worked on in any class. In fact, there are many natural opportunities to practice this skill when students receive handouts throughout the school day. McDonnell and colleagues (2008) describe natural teaching opportunities and embedded teaching opportunities. So what is the difference?

Natural Teaching Opportunities

Natural teaching opportunities are naturally occurring times when the skill is being worked on during a typical school day. For example, math time is a natural time to work on math goals; recess and lunch are natural times to work on social or communication goals. Remember, however, that while the time to work on a skill might be natural, the inclusion facilitator would use the same materials and activities to teach a skill for it to be truly natural and inclusive teaching. For example, during a third-grade math lesson, students are learning to graph. They are counting objects, voting, and using other opportunities to learn how to create graphs. Imagine a student with intellectual disabilities in this class who has a goal to count to 10 with one-to-one correspondence. This graphing lesson would be a natural time to embed instruction on counting (e.g., counting the colored candies to be graphed, counting how many votes an item received). It would not be inclusive (or embedded instruction) to pull the child with intellectual disabilities to a back table and work on counting separately. In other words, simply being in the same classroom does not make the activity embedded or inclusive. Embedded instruction asks inclusion facilitators to find opportunities to practice a student's important skills during a typical school day using the materials and activities that are present.

Embedded Teaching Opportunities

So, then, what do we mean by embedded teaching opportunities? This refers to instructional trials that are created by inclusion facilitators to teach a skill. This generally occurs if there are not enough natural opportunities in the school day to teach a skill, a child's learning rate dictates that more opportunities are needed, or it's simply a skill that is not used frequently enough in natural opportunities to have enough learning trials. Embedded teaching opportunities are then created. For example, imagine a high school student who has a goal to identify coins by name and value. The inclusion facilitator would first identify the natural times to practice this skill. Because most high school students have mastered money, it is not typically taught in high school. The natural times to practice money identification and counting, then, are in the school snack bar, which is open at lunch, and in the library, where students can purchase pencils. It is determined that these natural settings do not provide adequate opportunities to teach the skill, so opportunities for instruction must be created. The inclusion facilitator identifies noninstructional times during the day when the skill can be taught. For example, when students are standing in line at the cafeteria, the inclusion facilitator can present the student with coins to identify and label. Likewise, while the general education teacher is taking attendance, the inclusion facilitator can embed a few quick instructional trials on counting and naming coins. By finding such opportunities throughout the day to provide instructional trials, students in inclusive settings will have ample opportunities to practice and learn important skills.

Case Study: Mr. DeMarco Prepares for Embedded Instruction

Mr. DeMarco is considering using embedded instruction to teach sight word reading to Anthony, a fifth grader who has Down syndrome. Previously, Mr. DeMarco would pull Anthony and other students with disabilities from general education to provide direct instruction in reading in a pull-out classroom. During these pull-out sessions, Mr. DeMarco would provide intensive instruction in reading for 1 hour at a time, as is common in special education programming. Mr. DeMarco has learned about the benefits of embedded instruction and wants to try this approach with Anthony. He meets with Anthony's fifth-grade teacher, and the two determine the natural and embedded teaching opportunities that exist within a typical school day, noting these on the worksheet in Figure 5.5.

Figure 5.5   Identifying Opportunities for Instruction

Class or Activity	Natural Teaching Opportunities	Embedded Teaching Opportunities
Social Studies	• Textbook reading • Worksheets	• Transitions between activities • Organization time (e.g., attendance, returning papers, signing student calendars) • Natural breaks in activities
Math	• Textbook reading • Worksheets	• Transitions between activities • Organization time (e.g., returning papers, collecting homework) • Natural breaks in activities
Recess	• Materials checkout	
Library	• Leisure reading • Internet searches for book titles	• Transitions between activities • Organization time (e.g., attendance) • Natural breaks in activities
Lunch	• Reading menu items	• Natural breaks in activities
Science	• Textbook reading • Worksheets • Labs	• Transitions between activities • Organization time (e.g., returning papers, collecting homework, passing out lab materials) • Natural breaks in activities
PE	• Materials checkout • Team rosters/assignments	• Natural breaks in activities

(Continued)

| Figure 5.5 | (Continued) |

Class or Activity	Natural Teaching Opportunities	Embedded Teaching Opportunities
Language Arts	• Textbook reading • Worksheets • Leisure reading • Spelling • Writing passages	• Transitions between activities • Organization time (e.g., returning papers, collecting homework, passing out materials) • Natural breaks in activities
Recess	• Materials checkout	
Art	• Materials checkout • Material labels • Labs/project instructions	• Transitions between activities • Organization time (e.g., returning papers, collecting homework, passing out materials) • Natural breaks in activities
Small Groups	• Targeted instruction (massed trials)	

Inclusive Instructional Plans

In the introduction, we noted that students with disabilities are able to learn a range of important academic skills, but that this learning cannot be left to chance. Instead, it must be planned, programmed, and supported. In this section, we discuss some strategies for planning instruction that can be used in conjunction with embedded instruction. Developing inclusive instructional plans is one way to make sure that students are actively and meaningfully engaged in the curriculum (Aspy & Grossman, 2007). Inclusive instructional plans simply describe the typical routines and activities in a class, the necessary adaptations for a particular student, the supports required for the student, and instructional strategies (prompting, reinforcement, and error correction) that are needed for the student.

When developing an inclusive instructional plan, a series of components are addressed to prepare for the lesson:

- *Schedule of activities:* Here, the typical daily routine for a class period (secondary) or activity (elementary) are written in order. Observing the general education classroom, and/or collaborating with the general education teacher can generate this sequence of activities. More uncommon events, such as tests, may also be included so that there is a plan in place for any activity that may occur on a regular or semi-regular basis.
- *Skills to teach (beyond IEP goals):* A wonderful thing about inclusive education is that it provides plentiful opportunities to learn skills that are not included in an IEP. These skills might include turn taking, waiting, listening, oral comprehension, and so on. Of course, students without IEPs are working on these skills, too, even though they may not be state standards. In this column, list those extra skills that students are working on and may need support to learn. It's a good reminder for us all to find, and take full advantage of, teachable moments within typical routines. Completing this column can be a very useful activity in teaching peer tutors,

paraeducators, and sometimes general education teachers what the specific outcome or goal for each part of the activity is. It helps the entire team have a sense of the purpose of the student's participation. This can help avoid a focus on task completion and instead focus on key instruction.

- *Natural teaching opportunities (of IEP goals):* In this column, those IEP skills or concepts that the student will have natural opportunities to learn and/or work on during the activity are presented. For example, working on handwriting goals during a writing activity and working on reading goals while reading a science text book are natural learning opportunities.
- *Embedded teaching opportunities (of IEP goals):* In this column, the IEP goals that a student has a chance to work on, but are not a natural part of the lesson plan, can be listed. For example, during an art lesson a student might work on social communication goals. Or a student might work on a math goal while waiting turns to shoot free throws during PE. This column is just a reminder to find plenty of opportunities to practice IEP goals throughout a typical day.
- *Supports:* This section describes the materials, cues, and people that will be provided to help the student be successful. It includes many general adaptations (as described in Chapter 9). Examples of likely supports may include peer tutors, modified textbooks, word banks, paraeducator assistance, assistive technology, pictures of major concepts, assistive technology, and communication devices (programmed with needed words or phrases for the activity or lesson).
- *Adaptations:* For each activity, needed adaptations are described. The list of needed adaptations will include specific adaptations (see Chapter 9) and can come from the ecological assessment, the list of accommodations/modifications, and input from general education teachers. This section also lists the general adaptations needed by a student, for example, a wheelchair-accessible desk, access to sensory break items, weighted pencils, FM audio support systems, and so forth.
- *Reminders:* Finally, any reminders for educators should be listed. This may include information about behavior support plans, health care plans, and the like.

Inclusive instruction plans are excellent tools to organize and plan for student participation. By sharing them with the whole educational team (e.g., paraeducators, general education teachers), the student with a disability has a meaningful purpose for and manner of participating in general education. A sample inclusive instructional plan for two students is shown next.

BOX 5.5

Universal Design for Learning

Universal design for learning (UDL) is an important strategy to implement in every classroom. The inclusion facilitator can, and should, work with teaching colleagues to design activities, lessons, and assessments that reflect UDL principles throughout the school day. When this is accomplished, it will be that much easier to provide any needed adaptations for students and prevent students who do require adaptations from standing out from their peers.

Case Study: Mr. DeMarco Develops an Inclusive Instructional Plan for Sally

Mr. DeMarco plans for Sally, a second grader with attention deficit disorder and learning disabilities in the areas of reading and math. He focuses this instructional plan on math instruction. As you can see in Figure 5.6, the instructional plan combines information from the embedded instruction analysis to find times to specifically work on IEP goals (using natural teaching opportunities and embedded teaching opportunities if the student finishes early or there is downtime during that activity), while also providing instruction in skills that are important but are not IEP goals.

Case Study: Mrs. Simpson Develops an Inclusive Instruction Plan for Wesley

Mrs. Simpson is interested in making sure that Wesley, who has intellectual disabilities, has the support and instruction provided to him during ninth-grade biology to be able to meaningful participate in all science activities, while also learning the key skills that are included in his IEP. To help make this possible, Mrs. Simpson develops an inclusive instruction plan for Wesley (see Figure 5.7), which will be shared with his teachers, paraeducators, and peer tutors who are supporting him in this class.

Case Study: Mrs. Simpson Demonstrates Embedded Instruction in Biology

Mrs. Simpson uses Wesley's inclusive instruction plan as a tool to train the classroom paraeducator and peer tutor who will be supporting Wesley in class. When Wesley enters class and takes out his materials, she demonstrates to the peer tutor how to discreetly walk over to Wesley, welcome him to class, and complete a quick trial of sight-word flashcards. At the end of the trial, which takes approximately 30 seconds to complete while the class is transitioning, she prompts Wesley to complete his planner. While he is copying down the homework in his planner, Mrs. Simpson shows the peer tutor how to record data on the sight word trial. She has included a fluorescent index card in the stack of flashcards that has the list of words Wesley is learning. She teaches the peer tutor to record a + next to words Wesley reads correctly, and a – next to words that he is unable to read independently. Another opportunity to practice sight words will occur during the transition to lab activities. Once all of the students have recorded important information in their planners, the teacher introduces class to the warm-up activity. Wesley completes his adapted warm-up independently. While the rest of the class is completing their warm-up, Mrs. Simpson demonstrates to the class paraeducator how to support Wesley in practicing identifying the names and values of coins. Mrs. Simpson quietly walks over to Wesley and spends 1 minute with him practicing coins. She is able to complete two drills in this time. She also takes this time to check in on Wesley's answer to his warm-up questions and engages him and his classmate in a conversation about their upcoming lab. Later in the class, while students are working independently on a science writing project, the class paraeducator roves around the classroom. When she stops to check in on Wesley, she has him do a 1-minute coin identification break before she moves on to help other students. These quick, embedded trials maintain Wesley's attention and allow him to work on essential IEP goals throughout his day.

Figure 5.6 Inclusive Instructional Plan

Student: Sally R. **Class (or Activity):** 2nd Grade Math **General Education Teacher:** Mrs. Davis

Goal Summary
1. Read 150 high-frequency sight words
2. Read a first-grade passage at a fluency of 90 correct words per minute
3. Remain on task 80% of the time during group and individual activities for three out of five opportunities

Goal Summary, Continued
4. Count by 1s, 2s, 5s, and 10s to 100
5. Solve story problems involving addition and subtraction by setting up the problem and using the correct operation

Schedule of activities	Skills to teach (beyond IEP goals)	Natural teaching opportunities (of IEP goals)	Embedded teaching opportunities (of IEP goals)	Supports	Adaptations
Teacher introduces lesson Students listen to the teacher and follow along as she models how to solve problems.	1. Listen carefully to instructions/follow verbal instructions	<u>Goal #</u> 3		Roving paraeducator (assisting entire class) Fidgets (fine motor) to use at desk	Sit near teacher Frequent positive feedback Self-monitoring of on-task behavior
Individual practice Students work independently to solve math problems, such as worksheets.	Work quietly, without talking to peers inappropriately Attempt to solve a difficult problem before asking for help	<u>Goal #</u> 3, 4, 5	<u>Goal #</u> 1, 2	Word bank (to solve word problems) Manipulatives Roving paraeducator support (helping all students) Provide examples of completed problem	Highlight key words in word problems Color code worksheet (with text highlighted in corresponding color)
Group practice Students work in table groups or with partners to solve problems together.	Social communication skills On-task conversations	<u>Goal #</u> 3, 4, 5	<u>Goal #</u> 1, 2	Manipulatives Number chart Provide examples of completed problem	Self-monitoring of on-task behavior Highlight key words in word problems

(Continued)

Figure 5.6 (Continued)

Schedule of activities	Skills to teach (beyond IEP goals)	Natural teaching opportunities (of IEP goals)	Embedded teaching opportunities (of IEP goals)	Supports	Adaptations
Homework Students complete approximately 10 questions from a math workbook each night.	Turn in completed homework independently each day	Goal # 3, 4, 5	Goal # 1, 2	Sample problems Word bank Manipulatives Self-monitoring checklist (did I turn in my homework?)	Parents sign off after she works on homework for 10 minutes each night (works on math HW for no more than 10 minutes per day)
Quizzes/tests Assess knowledge of skills/concepts presented in class. Multiple-choice, fill-in, written responses required. Independent, quiet seat work.	Complete test independently with at least 80% accuracy	Goal # 1–5	Goal # NA	Word bank Manipulatives	Permit study guides on tests Extra time on tests (can take movement breaks)

Reminders

☐ Health care plan
☐ Behavior support plan
☐ Individualized grading plan (grading based on completion and percent accuracy of modified goals, as described above)
✓ Peer tutors
✓ Paraeducator support (roving support; paraeducator will assist all students in the class)

Figure 5.7 Inclusive Instructional Plan

Student: Wesley	**General Education Teacher:** Jackson		**Class (or Activity):** Biology		
Goal Summary: 1. Read 25 high-frequency sight words 2. Identify coins by name and value 3. Write full name legibly and correctly 4. Count with one-to-one correspondence to 25 5. Use calculator to compute addition and subtraction problems			**Goal Summary, Continued:** 6. Identify at least three peers by name 7. Respond to bids for interaction from peers within 5 seconds (respond to name, etc.) 8. Learn three vocabulary words (meaning) and decode three words (read independently) in each lesson unit from core subject courses		
Schedule of activities	*Skills to teach (beyond IEP goals)*	*Natural teaching opportunities (of IEP goals)*	*Embedded teaching opportunities (of IEP goals)*	*Supports*	*Adaptations*
Planner Independently fill in daily activities, homework in planner	Copy from the board Handwriting	Goal # 3	Goal # 1 (5 words, 1 trial)	Roving paraeducator (assisting entire class) Peer tutor Assignment written on board (to copy)	Adapted planner (larger lines and spacing) Homework folder
Warm-up question Copy question and write answer in notebook	Science concept (big idea) One key vocabulary word (meaning and decoding)	Goal # 8	Goal # 2	Word bank Simplified dictionary (with pictures of concepts)	Preprinted notebook (questions written, word bank provided) for each day
Mini lessons Listen to lecture. Material is introduced and reviewed. Students take notes.	Sit quietly Raise hand to speak Ask (at least) one on-topic question per day Copy at least five words written on the board	Goal # 3, 7, 8	Goal # N/A	Fidgets Red card/green card (red side = I need help, green side = I'm fine) Peer tutor to prompt to write and raise hand	Provide at least two questions student may ask Provide slot notes with word bank for any note taking
Lab Small-group or partner activities. Apply knowledge of current lesson. Students follow safety skills and use equipment appropriately. Maintain lab notebook.	Social communication skills Safety skills Write at least five words in notebook Identify main concept of lab	Goal # 1, 3, 6, 7, 8 (possibly 4 and 5 also)	Goal # 1	Pictures and names of lab partners Word bank	Adapted worksheets (highlighting one to three core concepts)

(Continued)

Figure 5.7 (Continued)

Schedule of activities	Skills to teach (beyond IEP goals)	Natural teaching opportunities (of IEP goals)	Embedded teaching opportunities (of IEP goals)	Supports	Adaptations
Workbook Independently and quietly complete one to two pages in class/for homework. Use text to find answers. Practice concepts presented in lecture.	Handwriting Vocabulary—identify three terms (both decoding and meaning) On-task behavior Look up three key pieces of information in text	<u>Goal #</u> 1, 3, 8 (possibly 2, 4, 5 also)	<u>Goal #</u> 2	Word bank Peer tutor Roving paraeducator support (helping all students) Provide examples of completed problem	Highlight key words in text, using removable highlighter tape Color code worksheet (with text highlighted in corresponding color)
Homework Students read ~10 pages in text per week. Answer comprehension questions in text. Turn in written assignments on time.	Read one page in modified book Answer two questions from modified book Turn in completed work independently	<u>Goal #</u> 1, 3, 8 (possibly 2, 4, 5 also)	<u>Goal #</u> N/A	Homework folder (work to complete on side A, work to turn in on side B) Self-monitoring checklist (did I turn in my homework?)	Modified science book (add pictures, simplify text) Modified worksheet (with two questions from modified book) Audiobook of regular science book
Quizzes/tests Assess knowledge of skills/concepts presented in class. Multiple-choice, fill-in, written responses required. Independent, quiet seat work.	Complete test independently with at least 80% accuracy	<u>Goal #</u> 1, 3, 8 (possibly 2, 4, 5 also)	<u>Goal #</u> 2	Word bank Pictures of key concepts Peer tutor for on-task reminders and reinforcement of effort	Modified test (focusing on two to three key concepts from the unit) Rewrite open-ended questions to be multiple choice

Reminders

☐ Health care plan
☐ Behavior support plan
✓ Individualized grading plan (grading based on completion and percent accuracy of modified goals, as described above)
✓ Peer tutors
✓ Paraeducator support (roving support; paraeducator will assist all students in the class)

Data Collection and Progress Monitoring

Mr. DeMarco and Mrs. Simpson have laid the groundwork for students to be successful in their general education classrooms and their IEPs. However, the role of the inclusion facilitator does not end once the IEP is written, the PGP developed, and inclusive instructional plans designed. The task of progress monitoring and data collection is just beginning! Despite the best efforts of the IEP team, it is possible that the instructional materials, curriculum, or supports provided will not be successful in helping the student make progress. Often, educators need to make adjustments in these areas to keep students on track to meet their goals. It is not possible to truly know, however, if a student is making adequate progress without gathering data.

Maintaining Data and Progress Monitoring Logs

Mr. DeMarco has created a "data binder" for each student. There is a binder for Michael, and all of his goals are in that binder. It is kept in the resource room, and Mr. DeMarco and his paraeducators will check out the binder once a week to gather data on how Michael is performing each of his goals. To facilitate this, Mr. DeMarco announces in the staff communication binder "Data Days" once a week. On Data Days, all staff are to check out binders for the students they are supporting and collect data that day. Mr. DeMarco tries to alternate data days so that they fall on different days of the week, in case student performance varies by day. Following data collection, the data is graphed for each goal. Then at progress report time or IEP review, Mr. DeMarco can simply review the contents of the binder and update Michael's parents and IEP team. The data sheet and graph shown in Figure 5.8 depict this strategy.

Other teachers may choose to use a data collection sheet in which all of a student's goals and data forms are on one piece of paper. Mrs. Simpson uses this strategy in her high school setting. Similar to Mr. DeMarco's data binders, Mrs. Simpson provides a data sheet for each student the paraeducator works with. These data sheets are kept in the paraeducator's binder (as described in Chapter 3). Each day, the paraeducator working with the student collects data on IEP goal progress. The form that Mrs. Simpson uses to monitor Ramona's progress is shown in Figure 5.9. As can be seen, this form is a

---

BOX 5.6   *Administrator Insight*

Implementing inclusive instruction can be a big shift for many teachers, who may be used to working fairly independently. With inclusive instruction, teachers must plan for grading students with disabilities, collaborate to decide how and when to implement instruction on skills that may be substantially different from instruction that is already happening in class, and work together to monitor student progress on learning outcomes. Administrators can support this shifting role by providing common collaboration time for teachers, assigning inclusion facilitators to various content- or grade-level teams, and providing mentoring and support to teachers as they navigate these new responsibilities. Administrators can encourage innovation in these new roles by further providing support to attend workshops and collaborate with other schools that are implementing inclusive practices, in person or via online meetings (e.g., www.gotomeeting.com) to assist in this process of instructional transformation. More than anything, however, administrators can support teachers by understanding that changing practices is challenging and may be frustrating; therefore, administrators should be open to suggestions and requests for assistance from teacher colleagues.

Figure 5.8	Data Sheet: Michael Reading Fluency

Date	No. of Words Read	No. of Errors	Correct Words Per Minute
9/10/14	101	3	98
9/17/14	102	2	100
10/3/14	107	4	103
10/8/14	112	3	109
10/16/14	105	3	102
10/27/14	120	5	115
11/4/14	119	2	117
11/10/14	125	4	121
11/17/14	119	3	116

"one-pager," with all of Ramona's goals on one page. It contains a column for each day of the week for an entire month. In each column, Mrs. Simpson or a paraeducator writes down how Ramona performed that day. At the end of the month (or the week, as shown in this example), the column labeled "x̄%" is calculated to demonstrate either an average x̄ (e.g., the average number of items Ramona counted) or a percent accuracy (e.g., the percentage of words Ramona read correctly).

For monitoring data on the frequency of behaviors, often a frequency chart is most useful. For example, a teacher may wish to track how frequently a student raises his hand or uses inappropriate language. Mrs. Simpson uses the chart in Figure 5.10 to document the frequency with which Ramona initiates interactions with her peers.

To use this graph, Mrs. Simpson simply places an X on the observed frequency (she can also use it as a tally, placing an X on the number each time she observers a target behavior). Then she draws a line connecting the observed frequency and can quickly see if the behavior is increasing, decreasing, or staying the same. In this example, we see that although her interactions initially decreased, during the most recent observations Ramona's interactions with peers are increasing.

Collecting Data on the Provision of Services and Supports

Finally, sometimes parents or administrators request that teachers track the type or level of support a student is receiving in an inclusive setting. For example, Michael's parents were very concerned about him receiving interventions in his general education classroom that were described in the IEP meeting. Therefore, Mr. DeMarco created a tracking form to communicate with Michael's parents the frequency and the duration of his supports and services (Chapter 6 provides more examples of methods to communicate and collaborate with parents). This tool can be used to both communicate and to track data. That is, Mr. DeMarco may use it to decide if Michael needs different supports or more intensive supports when he views this in combination with other data collection tools.

Figure 5.9 One-Pager Data Sheet

Student: Ramona
Month: October

Domain	IEP Goal	M	T	W	Th	F	M	T	W	Th	F	M	T	W	Th	F	$\bar{x}$	%
Math	Count to 20 with 1:1 correspondence (record highest number Ramona counts to)	12	11	12	12	11												$\bar{x}$ 12
	Use dollar-up strategy to pay for items up to $20	3/5	2/4	3/4	1/3	2/3												57%
	Read 3 words from core vocabulary lessons with 100% accuracy	2/3	1/3	2/3	1/3	2/3												53%
Reading	Read 20 sight words with 100% accuracy	3/5	2/5	4/5	3/5	4/5												64%
	Ask/answer comprehension questions with 80% accuracy	1/2	2/3	3/3	2/3	1/2												69%
	Write name correctly 100% of the time	3/7	4/7	2/7	5/7	4/7												51%
Writing	Write one correct sentence with a word bank	+	+	−	−	+												60%
Social	Initiate and respond to three social interactions from peers	Init	3	1	1	2	4											$\bar{x}$ 2.2
		Res	2	2	1	2	1											$\bar{x}$ 1.6
Access	Participate in academic unit/learn three facts of terms per unit	0/3	1/3	1/3	2/3	2/3												40%
Other																		

Figure 5.10   Behavior Frequency Data Sheet

Student: Ramona

Month: October

Observation Period: Lunch

Behavior Description: Interact with peers

Behavior Frequency	M	T	W	Th	F	M	T	W	Th	F	M	T	W	Th	F	M	T	W	Th	F	M	T	W	Th	F
15	15	15	15	15	15	15	15	15	15	15	15	15	15	15	15	15	15	15	15	15	15	15	15	15	15
14	14	14	14	14	14	14	14	14	14	14	14	14	14	14	14	14	14	14	14	14	14	14	14	14	14
13	13	13	13	13	13	13	13	13	13	13	13	13	13	13	13	13	13	13	13	13	13	13	13	13	13
12	12	12	12	12	12	12	12	12	12	12	12	12	12	12	12	12	12	12	12	12	12	12	12	12	12
11	11	11	11	11	11	11	11	11	11	11	11	11	11	11	11	11	11	11	11	11	11	11	11	11	11
10	10	10	10	10	10	10	10	10	10	10	10	10	10	10	10	10	10	10	10	10	10	10	10	10	10
9	9	9	9	9	9	9	9	9	9	9	9	9	9	9	9	9	9	9	9	9	9	9	9	9	9
8	8	8	8	8	8	8	8	8	8	8	8	8	8	8	8	8	8	8	8	8	8	8	8	8	8
7	7	7	7	7	7	7	7	7	7	7	7	7	7	7	7	7	7	7	7	7	7	7	7	7	7
6	6	6	6	6	6	6	6	6	6	6	6	6	6	6	6	6	6	6	6	6	6	6	6	6	6
5	5	5	5	5	x	5	5	5	5	5	5	5	5	5	5	5	5	5	5	5	5	5	5	5	5
4	x	4	4	x	4	4	4	4	4	4	4	4	4	4	4	4	4	4	4	4	4	4	4	4	4
3	3	x	3	3	3	3	3	3	3	3	3	3	3	3	3	3	3	3	3	3	3	3	3	3	3
2	2	2	x	2	2	2	2	2	2	2	2	2	2	2	2	2	2	2	2	2	2	2	2	2	2
1	1	1	1	1	1	1	1	1	1	1	1	1	1	1	1	1	1	1	1	1	1	1	1	1	1
0	0	0	0	0	0	0	0	0	0	0	0	0	0	0	0	0	0	0	0	0	0	0	0	0	0
Date	M	T	W	Th	F	M	T	W	Th	F	M	T	W	Th	F	M	T	W	Th	F	M	T	W	Th	F

Figure 5.11 Frequency and Type of Support Data Collection Sheet

Date	Type of Support			Support Provider				Time		Activity			Comments
	1:1	Small Group	Large Group	Spec Ed Teacher	Gen Ed Teacher	Para	Peer	Start	End	Reading	Writing	Math	
10/10		✓		✓				8:45	9:15		✓		
10/11	✓					✓		12:15	12:30	✓			Silent reading: reading fluency check
10/12	✓					✓	✓	8:45	9:15	✓			Reading "Where the Red Fern Grows" in class
10/13		✓		✓				10:15	11			✓	
10/14													Michael absent today
10/15	✓			✓		✓	✓	8:45 10:15	9:15 11	✓		✓	

> **BOX 5.7   Tech Byte**
>
> A number of free apps exist for iOS and Android phones and tablets for educational data collection. Be sure to search your app store, and check out customer reviews! Some of our favorites are TeachMe Skills, Tally Counter, D.A.T.A., AutismTrack, Super Duper Data Tracker, Intervals, and Behavior Tracker Pro.

Conclusion

In this chapter, we discussed methods of bringing evidence-based, systematic instruction for students with disabilities into general education settings. With these tools, it is possible to provide not only high-quality instruction in inclusive settings but effective instruction. As a final reminder, the inclusion facilitator is urged to take full advantage of the multitude of learning opportunities that exist in general education. There are so many chances to learn valuable and important concepts and skills in these settings that it is simply impossible to match these opportunities in special education settings. With a little creativity, and a cautious awareness of avoiding stigmatization, there will be no limit to how much, and how well, students with disabilities can learn in general education settings and activities!

> Please be sure to go to the website (http://www.corwin.com/theinclusiontoolbox) to download the forms and resources from this chapter!

6

Engaging Students and Families

Inclusion works to the advantage of everyone. We all have things to learn and we all have something to teach.

—Helen Henderson

As educators, our instruction benefits enormously from knowing our students and their families. By knowing the unique interests, learning styles, likes, and dislikes of students, we are better able to tailor our instruction to match their needs and preferences. Similarly, knowing families and helping them be more engaged in their child's learning, while also building on their strengths and preferences, will help students learn more and feel more supported at school. Finally, when peers at the school understand differences, including differences in how people look, move, speak, and learn, our schools are more accepting and welcoming of all.

Person-Centered Planning

Every IEP contains a Present Levels of Academic Achievement and Functional Performance statement that outlines the student's current skills academically, socially, communicatively, and so on. Reading an IEP and attending IEP meetings are methods of getting to know a student his or her family, but often this is not enough. IEP meetings tend to focus on student instructional planning for the upcoming year and tend to be rather clinical. It is important to have real conversations with families and students, and know them as individuals. One way to do this is with person-centered planning, such as using a Making Action Plans (MAPS) or Planning Alternative Tomorrows With Hope (PATH) planning meeting. These meetings bring together families and schools and use a collaborative process to learn about the student, discover a vision and plan

---

❖ Box 6.1   What Does the Research Say?

Student Involvement

Students' involvement in their own education, including individualized education program (IEP) meetings and development, is important for student self-determination. Self-determination skills are associated with improved access to the general education curriculum (Palmer, Wehmeyer, Gipson, & Agran, 2004). Student involvement is also key to person-centered planning, which is also associated with positive outcomes for individuals with disabilities (Claes, Van Hove, Vandevelde, van Loon, & Schalock, 2010). Person-centered planning has even improved parent and student involvement in the IEP process (Miner & Bates, 1997). Finally, student involvement in the form of disability awareness is found to be a best practice for supporting inclusion of children with disabilities (Mulvibill, Cotton, & Gyaben, 2004).

Family Engagement

Parent engagement in school has been associated with improved achievement for students with disabilities (Zhang, Hsu, Kwok, Benz, & Bowman-Perrott, 2011). One way to facilitate parent engagement is through the use of person-centered planning. Person-centered planning has been associated with increases in parent participation in IEP meetings (Miner & Bates, 1997), and it has a positive impact on student and family outcomes, including engagement and community participation. However, person-centered planning is not widely used in schools (Claes et al., 2010).

---

for the student, and then build supports to enable that plan to be realized (O'Brien & Lovett, 2000). Person-centered planning meetings can be useful in learning about the entire life of the student and his or her family, including the student's strengths, needs, interests, preferences, and priorities.

Usually, parents contribute a significant amount of information to a person-centered planning meeting (as well as to an IEP meeting). However, siblings, peers, and family friends can also provide valuable information and should therefore be invited to the person-centered planning meeting. Usually, information gathered is presented graphically using markers and whiteboards or large pieces of paper (see Figure 6.1).

The first step in person-centered planning is to develop a history or personal life story of the student.

Questions about the student's background include the following:

1. What is the student's background?
2. What were critical events in this student's life?
3. What, if any, medical issues have impacted this student's life?
4. What major developments, such as learning to walk or learning to read, has this student encountered?
5. Who are the important people in this student's life?

Next, a discussion of quality of life is shared. Questions often include the following:

1. How does this student participate in the community (e.g., shopping, religion, leisure activities)? Does the family and/or student desire more or different participation?

Figure 6.1 Person-Centered Planning Diagram

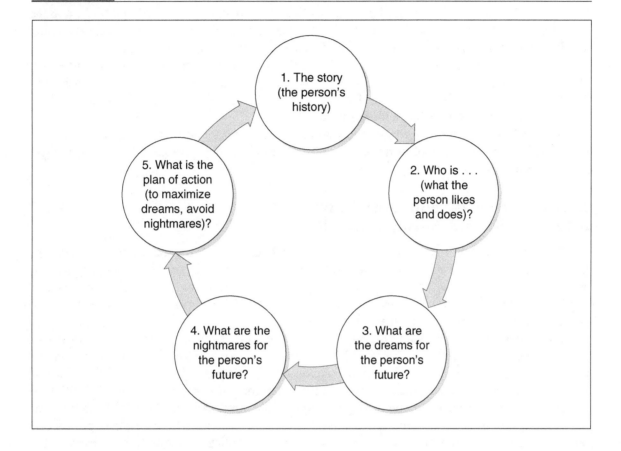

2. Does the student have age-appropriate choice-making skills and opportunities? Are the student's rights respected and protected?

Last, the personal preferences of the student are discussed. Questions include the following:

1. What does the student enjoy doing?

2. What does the student dislike doing?

3. What are the hopes and nightmares for this student's present and future?

During and following the person-centered planning meeting, participants are challenged to brainstorm ways to increase opportunities and diminish challenges for the student. Obstacles and opportunities are identified, and action steps are outlined to guide implementation of the dream.

It's important to remember that the person-centered planning meeting is not a replacement for an IEP meeting. Generally, a person-centered planning meeting happens a few weeks or months before the IEP, as a way for the team to find out about the real priorities of the student and his or her family. In this way, information from the person-centered planning meeting can be useful in identifying services and goals as well as setting up a climate of support and mutual interest between the school and family.

Family Involvement

Family involvement and collaboration are essential to inclusive education (Pivik, McComas, & LaFlamme, 2002). Families know the child best; they have lifelong experience with the child and know the child in different contexts than just school. Family involvement and participation in supporting what happens at school, and assisting in designing routines and activities, are also tremendously effective (Cross, Traub, Hutter-Pishgahi, & Shelton, 2004). Their insight is invaluable, and it is highly recommended that teachers invest efforts to establish and maintain a positive working relationship with families.

A less formal method of getting to know families is a parent and teacher gathering. Next we describe a back-to-school potluck Mrs. Simpson holds each year to set the tone for the upcoming school year.

Case Study: Mrs. Simpson Plans a Back-to-School Family Potluck

It is a few days before the school year is about to begin. Mrs. Simpson, a special education teacher and inclusion facilitator, is preparing for the new school year. She is buying school supplies, including spiral notebooks, pens, papers, and "fidget" items like squishy toys and paper clips. Mrs. Simpson is also learning to use the assistive technology (AT) tools her new students use, including Kurzweil and Proloquo.

While learning new tools and buying shiny new materials are standard practice for many teachers at the start of a new school year, Mrs. Simpson is also preparing herself and her school program to be as organized and functional as possible. She is preparing binders with information about students, IEP goals, and supports for each of the paraeducators she works with (see Chapter 3). She is spending some time with the school counselor, Ms. Leopald, to make sure her students are included in the proper general education courses where ample supports can be provided (see Chapter 4). And Mrs. Simpson is already collaborating with her general education partners to learn about the curriculum and activities they are planning for the upcoming semester and school year (see Chapter 7).

Finally, the day before school is to begin, Mrs. Simpson's efforts begin to pay off. Her efforts to lay the groundwork for a successful start, and duration, of the school year cap off with a back-to-school potluck. Participants include Mrs. Simpson, paraeducators, students, and families of students. This simple 1-hour potluck is a chance for apprehensive families and students to meet the staff they will be working with for the school year, to do a last-minute tour of the school and classrooms, and, most important, to set a climate of support and approachability. There is no set agenda to the potluck: Families and school staff simply chat over cookies and juice, getting to know one another.

Following the potluck, paraeducators feel more confident in their ability to know and work with students. Students feel less concern about who they will be interacting with and where. Parents feel supported by a special education staff that is committed to supporting them and their children. And Mrs. Simpson feels satisfied with her efforts to support her entire team and students, and she knows that the groundwork has been laid for a successful first day.

Home–School Communication

Often, parents ask their child, "What did you do at school today?" and inevitably children reply, "Nothing" or "I don't remember." While this is typical of many children, students with special needs may have memory difficulties that make it even more difficult to discuss their day, or they may lack the communication skills to effectively describe what happened. Inclusion facilitators can help families be engaged with their child's schooling through the use of home–school communication binders. These binders can be completely open-ended (i.e., a blank notebook that parents and educators can write in to share pertinent information). Or they can be more structured to help save time and make sure the information that is shared is relevant.

Figures 6.2 and 6.3 demonstrate these communication notebooks for elementary and secondary students. As you see, the content and structure differ slightly for different grade levels.

BOX 6.2   Tech Byte

Schools and families can use a traditional paper-and-pencil manner of communicating. However, some teams might prefer to use online resources. Many blogging platforms, such as WordPress (www.wordpress.com), have controls so that the blog can be shared privately. Writing blogs between home and school can be a useful way of sharing important information.

Figure 6.2   Elementary Home–School Communication Sheet

In Math, I . . .

Today we worked on telling time. We are estimating how long it takes to complete different activities.

In Language Arts, I . . .

We read our books and answered literal comprehension questions.

At morning recess, I did/played with . . .

I played with Heather, Josh, and Amanda on the monkey bars. We ate snack together, too.

In Writer's Workshop, I . . .

Finished my story about elephants. Next, I will work with you to edit my story. Then I'll type it.

In Science, I . . .

Watched a video about the oceans and animals that live in the ocean.

In Art or Music, I . . .

Today we did chorus with our fifth-grade buddies.

In Social Studies, I . . .

Made a map of my classroom and labeled North, South, East, and West.

At Lunch, I . . .

Ate inside because it was raining. We played board games. I played mostly with Heather.

Afternoon Recess, I . . .

We went to the gym for inside recess because of the rain. We played capture the flag.

Today I also did

☐ Art   x Music   ☐ APE

x Speech   ☐ OT   ☐ PT

☐ Social group

☐ Other:

_____

Notes from school

Great day today! Sally will need to bring a coat since it's getting colder. Also, remember the field trip to the aquarium tomorrow. Sally needs to bring a bag lunch. Homework is in her homework folder.

Notes from home

_____

_____

_____

_____

_____

_____

Figure 6.3   Secondary Home–School Communication Log

1st Period: Math

Took test today. Worked hard on it—used study guide independently!

Homework:

None

Upcoming Tests/Long-Term Assignments:

None

2nd Period: Art

Continued working on clay sculpture. Worked with Emily and Hannah.

Homework:

Donation letter to parents

Upcoming Tests/Long-Term Assignments:

Field trip to Community Art Center in 2 weeks

3rd Period: US History

Watched movie about start of Civil War, read diaries from soldiers.

Homework:

Read Chapter 7.1–7.3 in book

Upcoming Tests/Long-Term Assignments:

None

4th Period: English

Continued reading "The Giver" and class discussion. Began drafting five-paragraph essay. Worked on draft with Tyrell.

Homework:

Finish reading Chapter 3

Upcoming Tests/Long-Term Assignments:

Vocab test on Friday

Lunch

Ate lunch with Paul and Kyle. Played basketball outside with Paul and Kyle.

6th Period: Home Ec

Cooking demonstration

Homework:

None

Upcoming Tests/Long-Term Assignments:

Tomorrow the class will be baking squash.

7th Period: PE

Ran the mile—about 13 minutes! Ran with Casey and that made it more fun. ☺

Homework:

None

Upcoming Tests/Long-Term Assignments:

Home basketball game Thursday—extra credit if attend

8th Period: Science

Learning about elements of periodic table (gases)

Homework:

Finish worksheet that was started in class today

Upcoming Tests/Long-Term Assignments:

None

Today I also did:

□ Speech   □ OT   □ PT

□ Social Group   □ APE

□ Other: <u>None today!</u>

Notes From School

Good day—had a lot of fun playing basketball at lunch.

Notes From Home

Engaging Families in Preparing for the IEP

Parent engagement can be improved by recognizing the invaluable role parents play in the IEP process. Often, teachers send out notifications to attend an IEP, provide a copy of parents' due process rights, and ask if parents have any questions or concerns during the meeting. While this is all legally necessary, simple efforts can help parents be more prepared for the IEP meeting and better able to contribute to its development. Giving parents information about the IEP, and a copy of a draft of the IEP, a few days ahead of the meeting can make a huge difference in a family's ability to participate.

Case Study: Mrs. Simpson Prepares Rachel's Family for Her Upcoming IEP Meeting

Dear Parents of <u>Rachel Smith</u>,

You have been invited to participate in a meeting concerning your child's educational program. Since you know your child best and can offer helpful insights from a unique perspective, your participation is greatly valued as a member of the team. This *Parent Report Questionnaire* is one way for you to offer your input. Though filling out all or any part of this form is completely optional, your ideas and opinions will help the team better understand your child and guide us in developing an appropriate educational program. Please review the attached draft of your child's individualized education program (IEP), and return this form as soon as possible or at the educational meeting scheduled for (date) <u>November 1</u> at (time) <u>3:30 p.m.</u> at (location) <u>front office</u>.

Ability Awareness

Another important part of including students is providing information to peers about differences. Some children may have limited experience with people who move, speak, learn, and appear differently from themselves. As inclusion facilitators, we want to make sure that these differences are understood as something to be embraced, not something to fear. Often, simulations are used to teach children about differences. For example, a visual impairment is

---

Figure 6.4	Parent Input Questionnaire

1. What are your child's strong points and positive qualities?

2. What concerns or worries you about your child?

3. What are your goals for your child in the next year?

4. What are your future hopes and goals for your child (i.e., where do you see your child at age 25?)

5. Do you see any errors in the draft IEP?

6. Are there any additions or changes you would like to make to this draft IEP?

Copyright © 2014 by Corwin. All rights reserved. Reprinted from *The Inclusion Toolbox: Strategies and Techniques for All Teachers* by Jennifer A. Kurth and Megan Gross. Thousand Oaks, CA: Corwin, www.corwin.com

---

BOX 6.3   *Administrator Insight*

Family involvement is key to education, and the administrator can readily assist the inclusion facilitator in promoting family involvement. The administrator can provide paid staff days to engage with families before the start of the school year, as with Mrs. Simpson's potluck. If money is not available to pay staff, consider allowing flex time so that staff can bank and store time throughout the year (i.e., bank the time spent engaging with families early in the school year, and spend it to leave early or come late a few days to make up the difference, or to "buy out" extra duty, such as passing period or playground supervision). The administrator can also support student and family engagement by encouraging assemblies and schoolwide activities that promote disability awareness, adopting curriculum materials that include important characters with disabilities, and so on.

---

simulated by having students wear a blindfold, or a hearing impairment is simulated by having students put cotton balls in their ears. While these are pretty easy to do, they are problematic for many reasons. In fact, most people who have disabilities discourage simulations because (1) simulations oversimplify the disability (a simulation for a few minutes is nothing like experiencing a disability daily) and (2) simulations tend to evoke pity rather than respect and understanding.

So how can the inclusion facilitator evoke understanding and respect of diversity without using simulations? Luckily, there are many excellent and fun ways to teach children about disabilities without relying on simulations. Students might read books in which the protagonist has a disability; they might watch films that feature people with disabilities; or you might develop formal lesson plans that discuss disability as a form of diversity, the rights of people with disabilities, and ways to support people with disabilities in a nonstigmatizing manner.

There are websites and books listed at the end of this book that contain sample lesson plans related to teaching children about disability. Here, we discuss two strategies for an Awareness Day; we emphasize, however, that the lessons from this day are too important and too numerous to be adequately addressed in a single day. Instead, we urge inclusion facilitators to embed awareness activities throughout the year (by reading books with important characters who have disabilities and so on).

Strategy 1: Escorts and Allies

This strategy is highlighted in the book *Disability Awareness—Do It Right!* (M. Johnson, 2006). The idea is to have escorts, people with disabilities, assist in creating the Awareness Day activities. These escorts can be community members who are advocates or activists related to disability. You can identify these individuals by asking your local newspaper editor, the director of special education, university faculty, parent groups, or searching for local disability support groups online. Of course, you'll want to vet these potential escorts first to make sure they present a non-ableist and nonstigmatizing discussion. These escorts can provide first-hand accounts about their successes and struggles. The allies, your target audience, will learn through activities and discussion about disability and their role (however unintentional) in oppressing people who have disabilities. *Oppression* may seem like a harsh word, but it encompasses the daily acts, often done without thinking, that stigmatize and ostracize others. For example, at the start of an assembly, the principal asks all students to stand up and cheer, not accounting for the fact that a student who uses a wheelchair will be singled out and excluded from this activity. Likewise, a teacher who asks students to respond "Here!" when taking attendance, not accounting for a student who does not hear or speak verbally, prevents the student from participating in this daily activity. These are daily acts that we do unconsciously but that have a negative impact on people who have disabilities and have these experiences of being unaccounted for and unaccommodated day after day. The activity and the discussion, then, turn from feeling like disability is something that is pitiable to empowering allies to advocate for social change and awareness in their schools and communities.

Strategy 2: Student-Specific Meetings

The advocacy lessons from "escorts and allies" can be targeted toward a specific student, if appropriate. In some cases, a single student may have been bullied or misunderstood. Perhaps this student is teased because he wears odd clothing (but that, due to autism, it is the only comfortable clothing he can wear). Or perhaps this student is simply ignored because she has a hearing impairment and her peers do not know enough sign language to communicate with her. Other times, a student is seen as being a "bad" kid, because peers do not know that he has an emotional-behavioral disorder that makes it difficult to control his feelings when he is frustrated. In cases such as these, it might be useful to have a discussion with classmates about a specific student.

Certainly, parent permission must be obtained before doing this. Sometimes parents even want to lead this discussion with classmates. Other times, parents will provide information to share but will choose to have school staff lead the discussion. Sometimes, the child who has a disability will be present for the discussion. Other times, the child may choose to come for part or none of the discussion. In any event, a class meeting can be held and relevant information about the child's needs and behaviors explained. Classmates are given a chance to ask questions. The focus then shifts to problem solving: "Now that we as a class understand the problem, what as a community of learners can we do to support our friend and help him or her with the issues we've discussed?" Simply asking this question is usually very informative and inspirational. It's just amazing to hear the great ideas that classmates have and their willingness to be allies!

Case Study: Mrs. Simpson Organizes a Class Meeting

Josue is a 10th-grade student on Mrs. Simpson's caseload. He has an intellectual disability, uses a wheelchair for mobility, and has limited vision. He communicates by smiling, laughing, crying, and grunting. He is learning to use a voice-output device. Josue's teachers have noticed that he rarely interacts with his classmates, and some of the students even appear to be afraid of him due to his unexpected arm movements and vocalizations.

Mrs. Simpson first speaks with Josue's parents and informs them that she is concerned that he is becoming isolated at school and that she would like to speak to Josue's classmates to brainstorm ways to help Josue become more involved at school. The parents agree that this would be fine, and they tell Mrs. Simpson about Josue's birth story. He was born very premature and was not expected to survive. His parents and doctors fought for him, and because Josue is such a strong and brave person, he not only survived but has been living a happy and loving life, far exceeding anyone's expectations. They describe that Josue has a loving older brother and younger sister. He enjoys listening to them talk and play video games; he also enjoys going on car rides and playing with the family dog. His parents would rather not be present during the class meeting, and they feel it would also be better if Josue was not present. His parents suggest that perhaps Josue's brother, who is a senior at Harvard High, could attend the class meeting and share his perspective. Mrs. Simpson assures them that these are fine decisions and proceeds to meet with Josue's teachers.

All 10th graders at Harvard High School must take English 10, so Mrs. Simpson decides that addressing Josue's peers during English would be ideal. She tells the English teacher that she would like to have a 15-minute class meeting, and the teacher agrees that this would be useful. They decide to have the meeting during fourth period.

Mrs. Simpson begins the class meeting by introducing Javier, Josue's brother (who agreed to participate), and telling the class about Josue's life history: when he was born, who his family is, where he has lived, and other interesting information, including his likes and dislikes. Javier and Mrs. Simpson highlight Josue's interests and the things he has in common with other 10th graders (including video games and siblings). Next, Javier and Mrs. Simpson describe Josue's disability, including his movement, vision, and communication styles. The two then discuss that Josue is often lonely at school because it is difficult for him to interact with his peers. Javier describes the accommodations he makes when playing with Josue, such as describing what is happening in a video game, taking him on "bumpy" wheelchair rides (over rough terrain, which Josue enjoys), and other ideas. The class then has a shared discussion of what they can do, as allies, to support Josue at school so that he feels welcomed and part of the school. Mrs. Simpson writes down their ideas and asks for volunteers to start implementing some of the ideas (e.g., a lunch buddy, a person who will read the textbook and worksheets aloud to Josue). The meeting ends on a positive note, with the classmates feeling empowered and understanding.

BOX 6.4   Tech Byte

Sometimes sharing short videos about inclusion and disability can be a useful way to help students understand diversity and their role as advocates. Many useful videos can be found by doing a search on YouTube (www.youtube.com). We like the A Credo for Support video about diversity and advocacy: www.youtube .com/watch?v=wunHDfZFxXw. Some students might even feel inspired to create their own advocacy videos, as did the group of students who made an "Inclusion" Public Service Announcement for their school: www.youtube.com/watch?v=UJxUmDNPrps.

Conclusion

This chapter discussed simple tools and strategies to empower and involve families, students with disabilities, and their peers. We also discussed the advocacy roles that each of these groups plays in inclusive education. At the conclusion of this chapter, we would like to remind the inclusion facilitator that you are not alone: These groups (parents, students, peers) can provide such amazing insight and ideas; make sure to seek their advice and input—you will not be disappointed when you do!

Please be sure to go to the website (http://www.corwin.com/theinclusiontoolbox) to download the forms and resources from this chapter!

7

Collaborating With General Educators and Related Service Providers

There is only one way to look at things until someone shows us how to look at them with different eyes.

—Pablo Picasso

Positive, working relationships among paraprofessionals, teachers, administrators, related service providers, and families are at the heart of every successful inclusion program. These relationships are built through ongoing communication, follow-through, and organization. In this chapter, we focus on strategies for communicating essential individualized education program (IEP) information and working collaboratively with general education teachers and related service providers.

Identify Communication Styles and Preferences

Navigating colleagues' communication styles and preferences can be one of the more challenging job requirements for inclusion facilitators, especially if you are new to a school site or district. When introducing yourself to colleagues, let them know the best way to get in touch with you (e.g., stopping by a classroom, email, phone) and ask what their preferences are as well. If you know a colleague is inundated with emails, then finding time to talk with him or her in person is important. Be respectful of colleagues' time and ask if they have a minute to talk before jumping in to your list of questions, concerns, or needs.

❖ **Box 7.1   What Does the Research Say?**

Collaboration Is Essential to Inclusive Programs

Collaboration among school staff is an essential component to a successful inclusion program (Fisher & Frey, 2001; York-Barr, Sommerness, Duke, & Ghere, 2005). This includes teachers working together to improve student achievement (Lingo, Barton-Arwood, & Jolivette, 2011), communicating information about student IEPs and individualized needs (Fisher, Frey, & Thousand, 2003), and planning for instruction and creating curricular adaptations (Mastropieri & Scruggs, 2001). Conversely, lack of collaboration, particularly in coordinating instructional support and adaptations (York-Barr et al., 2005), and lack of a schoolwide collaborative system (Downing, Spencer, & Cavallaro, 2004) are noted as barriers to inclusive education.

Necessary Skills

Effective interpersonal and communication skills are the foundation for developing working, collaborative relationships. In York-Barr et al. (2005), teachers identified specific communication skills that inclusion facilitators need for working with many people: listening, reading the intentions and desires of other people, providing specific information in ways others can comprehend and apply, offering feedback that is not reacted to defensively, and affirming the contributions of others in supporting student learning (p. 207). In addition, Fisher et al. (2003) find special education teachers in inclusive programs are more successful if they are "masters of collaboration and skillful negotiators" (p. 46).

Outcomes for Students

Inclusive schools identify collaboration time as a critical component to student success (Villa, Thousand, Nevin, & Liston, 2005). Instructional teams that work together to plan for instruction and create curricular adaptations enable access to the core curriculum for all students, including those with significant disabilities (Fisher & Frey, 2001).

If you support students in multiple classrooms during the school day, it is helpful to check in with teachers and related service professionals frequently to see if there are any concerns, updates related to curriculum, service schedule changes, and so on. Frequent check-ins help all IEP team members stay on the same page, ensure appropriate supports and services for the students, and feel a part of a team. If there are concerns or needs presented during check-ins, it is important for the inclusion facilitator to problem-solve with team members and follow through in addressing the concerns or providing the appropriate resources or tools to meet the team members' needs. Communicating a timeframe for when you can address the concern is also essential and helps team members know they can depend on you.

Communicating IEP Information

Collaboration happens continuously during the school year. However, there is essential information that needs to be shared at the beginning of the school year, or at the start of a new semester, to help school staff organize their instruction and time.

School Site Staff

Teachers and paraprofessionals need to be aware of the nuts and bolts of a student's IEP: accommodations/modifications to the curriculum, goals, special education services, any related services (e.g., speech therapy, physical therapy, occupational therapy), and any specialized plans for health care or behavior. Providing a student's teacher and any para-professionals with a copy of the Student Profile (see Chapter 5) and reviewing this with school staff at the beginning of the year is an efficient way to provide this information.

Related Service Providers

At the beginning of the year, it is important to review IEP calendars and support schedules with therapists to ensure all team members have the same information to avoid scheduling conflicting services or meetings. In addition, it is important to discuss how services will be provided to a student. In some districts there is a high rate of turnover for speech-language therapists and occupational therapists, and new therapists may need support and resources for providing push-in services to a student, especially if they are new to inclusion. If providers are providing pull-out services, it is important for service times to be scheduled in consultation with the classroom teacher's classroom activities and routines so students do not miss core instruction. See Chapter 15 to learn more about strategies for providing inclusive related services.

Determining Team Member Roles

Identifying roles and responsibilities for school staff, related service providers, and families is an essential component to effective collaboration (Giangreco, Suter, & Graf, 2011). We think it is important to address this in a variety of collaborative forums, such as schoolwide staff meetings, grade-level or department meetings, and special education parent advisory meetings, so all team members or potential future team members have an opportunity to review and discuss. Schools and/or IEP teams should identify the roles and responsibilities of staff and families in order to clearly articulate how staff and families will work together to provide inclusive special education services. Figure 7.1 provides an example of how a school might delineate roles and responsibilities for team members. This tool could be developed at a collaboration meeting, with each group brainstorming responsibilities for their specific school site. Schools can also use a tool such as the Roles of Team Members in Inclusive Schools Needs Assessment to guide team members in identifying areas of strength and areas where more support is needed.

Case Study: Mr. Finn's Staff Meeting on IEP Team Member Roles

Mr. Finn is the principal at Pine View Elementary School. He asks Mr. DeMarco to assist him in leading a discussion on roles and responsibilities for IEP team members at the first staff meeting of the year. Mr. Finn gives each staff member a copy of a handout on expected roles and reviews the responsibilities all team members have (see Figure 7.1). Mr. DeMarco then reviews how roles differ among staff members. In addition to information about team member roles, Mr. Finn wants staff to have an opportunity to discuss the roles, identify strengths, and determine areas and supports that are needed in order to improve. Mr. Finn divides staff according to their role in an IEP team and asks them to complete the needs assessment on chart paper (see Figure 7.2). Following this activity, team members share their assessed strengths and needs with the whole group and brainstorm ways to improve.

Figure 7.1	Team Member Roles in Inclusive Schools

All members of the team are responsible for
- Actively participating in IEP team meetings
- Contributing to the development of students' IEPs
- Maintaining high expectations for all students
- Supporting inclusive opportunities on campus for students, staff, and families
- Facilitating peer relationships
- Being positive, active members of the school community

General Education Teachers	Special Education Teachers	Paraeducators
• Implement district curriculum • Provide team with lesson calendar, syllabus • Create universal design for learning lessons in consultation with special education team members • Ensure all students can access and demonstrate knowledge of curriculum • Be knowledgeable about students' IEPs • Train paraeducators • Grade student work • Provide input on progress monitoring	• IEP case management • Communicate with team members on a regular basis • Train paraeducators • Develop instructional plans for paraeducators • Set up IEP progress monitoring systems • Collaborate with team members to develop accommodations and modifications • Provide specialized health care, behavior supports, and so on as required • Develop knowledge of general education curriculum, standards, and class routines • Provide support to students and staff in general education classes • Identify or develop social opportunities for students	• Provide support to all students in class • Implement teacher-provided lessons and modifications • Develop modifications per teacher directions • Collect progress monitoring data • Provide specialized health care, behavior supports, and so on as required • Facilitate communication and interactions among classmates • Support students in participating in schoolwide activities (e.g., assembly, lunch) • Provide clerical support to faculty
Related Service Providers	Parents and Students	Administrators
• Provide services to students and staff in general education environment • Collaborate with team members to identify needed tools, supports, or strategies to increase student progress toward goals • Manage any specialized equipment or assistive technology devices • Provide families with resources to implement school-based strategies at home • Problem-solve with team members	• Communicate with team members on a regular basis • Provide opportunities for generalizing students' skills at home and in the community • Participate in school and community activities • Complete homework on a consistent basis • Utilize augmentative and alternative communication or specialized devices at home and in the community	• Provide resources for common planning time for team members • Consider team member needs in master scheduling • Support team members in problem solving in challenging situations • Advocate at the district level for student and school needs • Provide resources for professional development • Connect families to resources and organizations (e.g., PTA) in the school community

Copyright © 2014 by Corwin. All rights reserved. Reprinted from *The Inclusion Toolbox: Strategies and Techniques for All Teachers* by Jennifer A. Kurth and Megan Gross. Thousand Oaks, CA: Corwin, www.corwin.com

| Figure 7.2 | Team Members' Roles in Inclusive Schools Needs Assessment |

Group: Gen Ed Teachers

Current strengths:

- Role model for students
- Participate in IEP meetings, are knowledgeable about student IEPs
- Classroom environment
- Instructional planning for all students

Role	What We Currently Do to Address Role	Additional Supports Needed to Fulfill Role	Questions or Issues to Address
Differentiation; adapting and modifying curriculum	Meet with Mr. DeMarco. Review unit: identify essential vocabulary, main ideas, stories, activities, and assessments. Mr. DeMarco creates all modifications.	Address needs of students during grade-level planning meetings. Additional trainings on implementing universal design with mandated district curriculum and pacing guide.	Invite Mr. DeMarco to grade-level planning meeting or alternate time for all to meet and plan in advance. Release time for training or collaboration?
Co-directing paraprofessionals	Provide information about today's lesson, bring attention to potentially difficult portions of lesson, ask to make photocopies.	Take time to talk with paras outside of lesson time. There is not enough time during class to direct paras and teach; need a plan before lesson starts.	Think about how to avoid multiple/ conflicting directions given by admin, special ed, gen ed.

Identifying Roles in the Classroom

When reviewing a student's IEP information, it is also important for inclusion facilitators, teachers, and related service providers to discuss what special education services will look like in a classroom, how responsibilities for any specialized supports (e.g., assistive technology, AAC system, health care needs, positive behavior support plan) are going to be divided and who is going to support the student during different times of the day. Many teams can address a student's needs and identify team member roles and responsibilities by using an inclusive instructional plan (see Chapter 5). However, for some students with multiple disabilities and IEP teams with several related service providers, it is helpful to develop a reference tool identifying specific responsibilities for each team member in order to help keep everyone on the same page.

Case Study: Mrs. Simpson's Staffing Meeting for Tomica

Tomica is an 11th-grade student who is included in grade-level academic and elective courses. She uses a variety of assistive technology (AT) devices, including an iPad, laptop, and screen-reading software, to access the general education curriculum. In addition to receiving daily support from paraprofessionals and an inclusion facilitator, she receives weekly direct services from a physical therapist, occupational therapist, and speech therapist. Tomica also receives enlarged textbooks and mathematics manipulatives from the vision specialist. Mrs. Simpson and Tomica invite her team members to a meeting at lunch in the beginning of the year so everyone knows when Tomica will use specific AT devices and which team member is responsible for providing appropriate accommodations and adapted materials during each class period. Mrs. Simpson creates a chart of responsibilities (Figure 7.3), based on the team's conversation, and provides each team member with a copy at the end of the meeting.

Figure 7.3   Tomica's Team Member Responsibilities

Period 1 Life Science	• Science teacher will provide enlarged note-taking form at start of lecture. • SPED teacher will create adapted work packet and put it on a flash drive. • Para will help Tomica load digital textbook onto iPad and laptop, type daily homework into e-planner, provide reader and scribe services.
Period 2 Alg 2/Trig	• Math teacher will provide enlarged notes with space for para to scribe for Tomica and that follow lesson on overhead; will enlarge tests (120%). • Para will scribe class notes, type homework into e-planner, enlarge daily homework. • Vision specialist will consult with teacher to provide appropriate visual models; will provide enlarged talking calculator. • Tomica will use her iPad for facts practice games and use enlarged calculator. • OT will find Tomica an iPad stand and assist with organizing iPad and increasing proficiency.
Period 3 Economics	• Economics teacher will provide projects and tests to SPED teacher in advance so they can be enlarged or scanned. • Para will set up Tomica's laptop at start of class and type lecture notes (in enlarged font so Tomica can read), scribe written responses, type homework in e-planner, read aloud book. • Tomica will request videos from Netflix to provide background knowledge.
Period 4 Spanish 3	• Spanish teacher will provide projects and tests to SPED teacher in advance so they can be enlarged or scanned. • Para will set up Tomica's laptop at start of class and type lecture notes (in enlarged font so Tomica can read), scribe written responses, type homework in e-planner, read aloud book.
Period 5 Computers	• Computer teacher will collaborate with Tomica, para, and SPED teacher to adapt unit projects to meet Tomica's needs and IEP tech goals. • Tomica will use her iPad for research, increasing proficiency with apps (e.g., science review, flashcards) and email. • Paras will help Tomica scribe emails to teachers/parents and explain new apps. • PT will incorporate various sitting positions during elective time to provide opportunity for Tomica to get out of her chair.
Period 6 English	• English teacher will provide book list, materials, and tests in advance to SPED teacher. • SPED teacher will download to Tomica's laptop digital versions of novels from Bookshare. • Vision specialist will provide digital novels that are unavailable on Bookshare; will ensure enlarged text of story anthology. • Speech therapist will support Tomica in speech writing, comprehension practice, and improving oral responses. • Para will set up Tomica's laptop at start of class and type lecture notes (in enlarged font so Tomica can read), scribe written responses, type homework in e-planner, set up iPad on independent reading days with headphones.
Period 7 Study Skills	• Tomica will ask para or SPED teacher to load her e-planner and homework onto her USB drive to take home. • Tomica will dictate responses for homework to scribe or listen to audio texts on laptop/iPad. • Tomica will use iPad to quiz classmates (using flashcard game) or play a fun game during last few minutes of class on Friday. • Para will check that e-planner is complete, assist Tomica with packing appropriate supplies for homework.

Communicating About Curriculum

Inclusion facilitators need to be knowledgeable about classroom routines, activities, and content to provide the best support to students and teachers. General education teachers and special education teachers need to communicate on a regular basis about the curriculum and instruction in a classroom. Some teachers are extreme planners and organizers and can hand inclusion facilitators a folder stuffed with unit lesson plans, activities, and supplemental materials, while other teachers always seem to plan their lessons at the last minute. It is helpful if inclusion facilitators use their own organizational tools to plan for students' instructional needs and allow themselves an opportunity to prepare materials in advance, instead of always having to adapt quickly at the start of a new lesson.

BOX 7.2   *Administrator Insight*

Administrators can support lesson-planning articulation by asking all teachers to provide curricular maps at the beginning of each school year. The maps should include information about primary and supplementary texts and reading materials, activities for each unit, field trips or activities, and content covered in unit exams. These curriculum maps will be invaluable in supporting collaboration for inclusion.

Obtaining Lesson Plans and Course Information

The teacher talk sheet (see Figure 7.4) is a useful tool for identifying essential components of classroom instruction. Inclusion facilitators may use this tool during regularly scheduled collaboration meetings with teachers, or for a few minutes at the beginning of the week if collaboration time is not allotted. Inclusion facilitators may be able to increase their efficiency by checking a teacher's webpage (if updated regularly), classroom calendar, or homework agenda for the week. Then when meeting with the classroom teacher, an inclusion facilitator can confirm activities with the teacher and use meeting time to identify instructional strategies or adaptations instead of using precious time to write down all of the assignments for the week.

Related Service Providers

Inclusion facilitators can assist related service providers in connecting therapy sessions with classroom curriculum by providing them with information from the teacher talk sheet and a calendar of activities or lesson topics. This is especially important if services are provided in a pull-out setting. In our experience, therapists are more than happy to use and reinforce curriculum taught in a general education class. We have had occupational therapists support students in improving handwriting and introducing letters in the same sequence as they are presented in an elementary classroom and speech therapists review concepts from an English novel to help students prepare for an in-class oral presentation.

Case Study: Mr. DeMarco's Staff Create a Teacher Talk Sheet

John is a paraprofessional who works with Mr. DeMarco and helps facilitate inclusion for students included in Mrs. Davis's class. While he supports students in class, he pays attention to Mrs. Davis's announcements and checks her classroom agenda and posted calendar in order to prepare for the following week. Every Thursday, John checks in with Mrs. Davis at the end of class and reviews the list of assignments, tests, and important announcements she shared with the class. He then asks if there are any materials or projects that may need to be adapted for students to use the following week.

Following his conversation with Mrs. Davis, John checks in with Mr. DeMarco and provides him with an overview of the class for the following week. Mr. DeMarco and John then discuss any scheduling changes that may need to be made to provide

Figure 7.4	Teacher Talk Sheet

Teacher: Mrs. Davis
Week of: October 2
Class: 1st grade
Student(s): Erica

Subject/skills you will be covering next week (include chapters, topic, and any worksheets you will be using)

- **Calendar:** recording important dates in month of October
- **Reading:** phonics: /h/, /m/, /t/, and short /a/ sounds and spellings (including handwriting practice); sight words: *the, is, on, are*; Open Court decodables and workbook
- **Writing:** pumpkin poems
- **Math:** using part-part-whole model for addition, using blocks for creating subtraction sentences; read *How Many Seeds in a Pumpkin* and introduce predictions.
- **Fun Friday:** pumpkin patch field trip and afternoon seed counting to evaluate predications made earlier in week.

Tests you will be having next week:
Day: Thursday
Chapter or skills: sight words test
Study guide/worksheets:

Long-term reports/projects:
Due Date:
None

Schedule changes next week (field trips, assemblies, etc.)
Friday: Pumpkin patch field trip; parent drivers; students can bring spending money for train or purchase pumpkin. Leave at 9 am.

Concerns? Comments?
Missing permission slip for Valerie—double check with mom

additional support, such as when the class is taking a test or goes on field trips. In addition, if any adaptations need to be made, John and Mr. DeMarco set aside time to make them. John's completed teacher talk sheet is shown in Figure 7.4.

BOX 7.3   Tech Byte

Technology can be useful in facilitating collaboration. Here are a few tips:

- Use Google Drive (drive.google.com). You can use this website to create files (including documents and spreadsheets).
- When you share the file and allow anyone to write on it, an easy-to-access system occurs whereby anyone with Internet access can quickly add notes and information that can be shared with the whole team.
- Teacher talk sheets can easily be uploaded onto a Google Doc; teachers just need to type what's happening and it is automatically shared with the other team members.

Communicating About a Student's Day

Finally, general education teachers, related service providers, and inclusion facilitators need to find a method to communicate with each other about a student's daily performance. For some teams, this might be during a face-to-face daily check-in. Other teams may find sharing a daily student progress report to be more helpful. A daily progress report can be designed to record data on a significant goal related to academics, behavior, communication, or organization (see Figure 7.5). For example, in elementary school, a general education teacher may complete a daily progress report for one student related to using appropriate behavior in class, while another student may have a daily progress report related to completing and submitting classwork. In addition to being a tool to provide a quick snapshot of a student's day, it should be completed with the student. This will help the student develop an awareness of her or his goals, understand that all of her or his teachers are on the same page, and can help promote self-determination.

Case Study: Mrs. Simpson Reviews a Daily Progress Report

Mrs. Simpson meets with her students at the end of the day to give them support with homework and study skills. Brandon is a student who is currently struggling with organization, recording in his daily planner, and completing his assignments. Mrs. Simpson and Brandon's teachers decide to use a daily progress sheet, as seen in Figure 7.5, to help provide support to Brandon in developing his organization and accountability for materials and homework. Since Mrs. Simpson does not support Brandon in all of his general education classes, she is able to review his daily progress sheet and his daily planner and be confident that he has the information he needs to begin his homework. By reviewing this sheet daily, Mrs. Simpson is able to evaluate whether Brandon is improving in his organization and classroom assignments or needs different supports to understand his classroom assignments and responsibilities.

Figure 7.5	Daily Student Progress Report

Student Name: Brandon   **Date:** December 3

Period 1: PE   **Teacher Signature:** Ms. Jones

Overall performance	Yes	No	Factors contributing to this report
_X_ Excellent	X		All homework is up to date
____ Very Good	X		Submits complete assignments
____ Improving	X		Submits good-quality assignments
____ Unsatisfactory	X		Brings materials to class
____ Failing	X		Good behavior in class
_NA_			Homework for tonight is written thoroughly in planner, including unfinished classwork (if applicable)

Period 2: Math   **Teacher Signature:** Mr. Reynolds

Overall performance	Yes	No	Factors contributing to this report
____ Excellent		X	All homework is up to date
____ Very Good		X	Submits complete assignments
_X_ Improving	X		Submits good-quality assignments
____ Unsatisfactory	X		Brings materials to class
____ Failing	X		Good behavior in class
_X_			Homework for tonight is written thoroughly in planner, including unfinished classwork (if applicable)

Comments, as needed: Brandon is missing homework from Monday and Tuesday. Improving behavior and focus in class.

Period 3: Library Asst.   **Teacher Signature:** Mrs. Keegan

Overall performance	Yes	No	Factors contributing to this report
____ Excellent	X		All homework is up to date
_X_ Very Good	X		Submits complete assignments
____ Improving	X		Submits good-quality assignments
____ Unsatisfactory	X		Brings materials to class
____ Failing	X		Good behavior in class
_NA_			Homework for tonight is written thoroughly in planner, including unfinished classwork (if applicable)

Comments, as needed: Brandon assisted students in finding materials in the library. Great help today!

Period 4: Foods   **Teacher Signature:** Mrs. Yard

Overall performance	Yes	No	Factors contributing to this report
____ Excellent	X		All homework is up to date
____ Very Good	X		Submits complete assignments
____ Improving	X		Submits good-quality assignments
_X_ Unsatisfactory	X		Brings materials to class
____ Failing		X	Good behavior in class
_X___			Homework for tonight is written thoroughly in planner, including unfinished classwork (if applicable)

Comments, as needed: Group project today was challenging. We need to work on this. Independent work has been amazing.

Period 5: Science   **Teacher Signature:** Mrs. Smith

Overall performance	Yes	No	Factors contributing to this report
____ Excellent	X		All homework is up to date
____ Very Good	X		Submits complete assignments
_X_ Improving	X		Submits good-quality assignments
____ Unsatisfactory	X		Brings materials to class
____ Failing	X		Good behavior in class
_X___			Homework for tonight is written thoroughly in planner, including unfinished classwork (if applicable)

Comments, as needed: Great week! Turned in all late work today. ☺

Period 6: English   **Teacher Signature:** Mrs. Simpson

Overall performance	Yes	No	Factors contributing to this report
_X_ Excellent		X	All homework is up to date
____ Very Good	X		Submits complete assignments
____ Improving	X		Submits good-quality assignments
____ Unsatisfactory	X		Brings materials to class
____ Failing	X		Good behavior in class
_X___			Homework for tonight is written thoroughly in planner, including unfinished classwork (if applicable)

Comments, as needed: Brandon is missing his vocab four square from Monday night. Tonight: practice speech! ☺

BOX 7.4   Tech Byte

A useful tool for sharing information and collaborating about student progress is ThinkBinder (www.think binder.com). It is an online binder that lets users collaborate for free on a whiteboard, share files, update a calendar, and post status updates among group members.

Troubleshooting Collaboration

Inclusion facilitators communicate with a number of professionals on a daily basis, and even the most organized, competent facilitators encounter an occasional miscommunication or collaboration breakdown with a colleague. While these breakdowns can stir up an emotional reaction for the individuals involved, it's important to take time to reflect and identify ways to improve communication or repair the collaborative relationship, instead of immediately responding. Here are some tips to maintaining working relationships with colleagues:

- *Use "I" messages:* When an inclusion facilitator realizes a miscommunication has occurred, it is helpful to begin a response with a statement such as "I think I misunderstood . . ." or "I am unclear on . . . ." Using an "I" statement allows your communication partner to respond to you without feeling defensive.
- *Stop emailing and ask to meet in person:* Although we live in a tech-savvy world, sometimes the best thing an inclusion facilitator can do is ask to meet with a staff member in person. Meeting in person, even if just for a few minutes, often resolves a miscommunication because both people are able to talk and ask clarifying questions as needed. This is also a helpful strategy for inclusion facilitators to use when a staff member isn't responding to any emails. Catching someone in the hallway and asking, "Can we set up a time to meet? I have some questions regarding . . ." may help remind a staff member that he or she hasn't responded to several emails or provides the staff member with an opportunity to ask some clarifying questions he or she needed answers to prior to responding to the inclusion facilitator's email. We are all busy professionals, and sometimes emails get overlooked or misinterpreted; if we talk in person, the issues relevant to student needs can get sorted out.
- *Observe students and the class:* Whenever there are concerns about a student, it is helpful to take time to directly observe the student in the classroom or around campus. This observation time allows the inclusion facilitator to have the big picture in mind when identifying learning strategies, appropriate accommodations or adapted curriculum needs, and skill development needed in the area of communication and positive behaviors. Set up a time to meet with the classroom teacher and/or the paraprofessional after an observation time to discuss what you saw and heard and brainstorm strategies together to better support the student and staff.
- *Ask a trusted colleague for communication strategies:* If you know another inclusion facilitator or colleague on your campus has experience successfully communicating with another colleague, ask if that person would share with you the strategies he or she uses so you can improve your communication with the colleague as well. Your trusted colleague might be able to shed light on pet peeves or other missteps you might be unknowingly making.

In the event of a serious collaboration breakdown and after using the preceding strategies:

- *Meet with an administrator:* An administrator may be able to share additional strategies to improve communication with a specific colleague. In addition, if the collaborative relationship is really strained, the administrator may be able to facilitate a meeting with an inclusion facilitator and another staff member to help resolve the conflict and reestablish a working relationship.

BOX 7.5 — *Administrator Insight*

Administrators can assist collaboration by providing common time and space for team members to collaborate. This may include designating a standing space in the office for collaborators to meet, setting up a Dropbox account (www.dropbox.com) for collaborators to share documents, and providing common planning meetings, on a weekly or monthly basis, for team members. All of these actions not only support team members but also convey your support for collaboration in a meaningful, concrete manner.

Conclusion

This chapter considered the various types of collaboration that are needed to help make inclusion successful for the student and the student's team members. Inclusion facilitators foster collaborative relationships through good communication skills; the ability to share knowledge about students' support needs, curriculum, and services; and resourcefulness to obtain resources or supports for students or colleagues. This chapter is also a reminder that it's not feasible or sustainable for the inclusion facilitator to "go it alone." Find your allies, develop collaborations across campus, and use tools to help make collaboration fit into the busy schedules of all the professionals who are dedicated to supporting students!

Please be sure to go to the website (http://www.corwin.com/theinclusiontoolbox) to download the forms and resources from this chapter!

8

Social Facilitation Strategies for Inclusive Settings

The only way to have a friend is to be one.

—Ralph Waldo Emerson

What is your favorite memory from high school? Chances are, you answered this question with a memory of the fun things you did outside of the classroom— rather than the math or history content you learned. Participating in extracurricular and social activities, including sports, clubs, school dances, theater, choir, and being with friends, are memorable and enjoyable aspects of school life and growing up. This speaks to the important social aspects of school; children do not attend school for only academic reasons, nor is academic learning the primary outcome of schools. Instead, social learning and participation are critical to the school experience and quality of life. Think about this quote from Salman Rushdie: "Our lives teach us who we are." How do our social experiences influence our lives, teach us about ourselves, and teach us about the world we live in?

Peer Involvement and Age-Appropriateness

Inclusive education is not focused simply on student academic needs, but also on social and quality-of-life needs. Peer supports can help facilitate all aspects of inclusive schooling. And the benefits of peer supports extend beyond students with disabilities, helping

---

❖ Box 8.1   What Does the Research Say?

Why Is Social Inclusion Important?

Social skills and successful interactions are important for many reasons. Specifically, social success is associated with academic skill development, increased social competence, increased social support, the development of friendships, and improved quality of life (Carter, Hughes, Guth, & Copeland, 2005; Fisher & Meyer, 2002). Inclusive schooling supports social learning for students with and without disabilities. Students without disabilities in inclusive settings at both the elementary and secondary levels are more likely to be friends with peers with disabilities, and to demonstrate lower levels of teasing and bullying, than are students educated in schools with self-contained programs (Bunch & Valeo, 2004). Students who are included in general education also have higher social skills development when compared to similar students in self-contained settings (Fisher & Meyer, 2002). Last, students who are included in general education have better social relationships, are less lonely, and have fewer problem behaviors than children in self-contained settings (Weiner & Tardif, 2004).

Strategies for Teaching Social Inclusion

A number of strategies exist that can improve social inclusion. Peer buddies, or peers without disabilities who receive instruction in how to interact with peers who have disabilities, are effective in increasing social interactions (Carter et al., 2005). Teaching paraeducators how to promote social interactions has also been associated with increased social interaction (Causton-Theoharis & Malmgren, 2004). General education teachers, special education teachers, and paraeducators have rated special education teacher support, paraeducator support, and peer buddies as effective (Carter & Pesko, 2008). Peer supports are another effective ingredient to inclusive schools (Hughes et al., 1999).

Extracurricular Inclusion

Participation in extracurricular activities is important for students with and without disabilities. Extracurricular participation has been found to be associated with improvements in quality of life, developing friendships, and community integration (Modell & Valdez, 2002). Yet students with disabilities are at risk for having many fewer chances to participate in extracurricular activities when compared to their peers without disabilities (Wagner, Cadwallader, Garza, & Cameto, 2004). Teachers play an important role in challenging this trend by helping students engage in extracurricular activities, which has a profound impact on improving the quality of life of students with disabilities (Kleinert, Miracle, & Sheppard-Jones, 2007).

What Does the Law Say?

Extracurricular involvement is so important that the Individuals with Disabilities Education Improvement Act goes so far as to mandate that students with disabilities have support from schools to participate in extracurricular activities: "Each public agency must ensure that each child with a disability participates with nondisabled children in those extracurricular services and activities to the maximum extent appropriate to the need of that child. The public agency must ensure that each child with a disability has the supplementary aids and services determined by the child's individualized education program (IEP) Team to be appropriate and necessary for the child to participate in nonacademic settings" (34 C.F.R. §300.117).

---

teach educators about age-appropriate skills and interests. For example, a teenager with disabilities who has an interest in *Sesame Street* characters can learn about animation and puppetry through theater and anime clubs at school, bridging an age-inappropriate interest into something more socially acceptable and appropriate.

Social Inclusion Strategies (Elementary)

The following strategies are suggested for students in elementary schools to help facilitate social interactions during lunch, recess, and other social times. With a little thought, these could be adapted for secondary-age students as well.

Lunch Bunch

Lunch bunch is a lunchtime social event in which students with and without disabilities come together and have social interactions. Generally, there is a facilitator of the lunch bunch; this could be a special education teacher, a general education teacher, a paraeducator, a school counselor, or any other interested adult. The facilitator monitors and facilitates social interactions, providing any scaffolding as needed; arranges the time and place for the lunch bunch to meet; invites students to participate; and develops activities or conversation topics for the lunch bunch.

To organize a lunch bunch, the facilitator helps the student with disabilities identify three or four friends to participate. The most basic way is to invite existing friends to the group. However, some students might not have a friendship group for a variety of reasons, and other strategies can be used. For example, a class rotation can be set up (so that all students are eventually invited); one can also draw names from a hat or select peers who have similar interests and/or ongoing friendships with the student who has disabilities. It might be a good idea for parents to consent (via a permission slip) to allow their child to participate in lunch bunch.

The facilitator can take an active or more of a monitoring role in the lunch bunch. The facilitator might choose conversation topics for the students to discuss or organize games that can be played during lunch. If the student with disabilities requires more support, the facilitator might provide a bank of questions for the student to ask his or her peers and perhaps sentence starters for the student to use when answering questions or making comments. For students in need of less support, the facilitator might simply monitor the conversation and activity, and provide clarification or prompting as needed. The goal is always for the students to get to know one another and become friends; the goal of the inclusion facilitator should be to fade out his or her active participation as much as possible over time.

BOX 8.2   *Administrator Insight*

Where do students eat lunch on your campus? Do all students eat in a common area? Are some students with disabilities segregated in a classroom with adults? Check in with staff to ensure all students can access and eat lunch in a common area. For students who need assistance eating or require specialized health procedures, brainstorm with special education case managers ways to provide these supports at an earlier time so all students have the opportunity to participate in recess or lunchtime activities.

Case Study: Mr. DeMarco
Organizes a Lunch Bunch for Sarah

Recognizing that all of us have social needs, and that our lives are improved by having friendships and relationships, Mr. DeMarco seeks to facilitate the social lives of the students he supports. One method he uses at his school is a lunch bunch. Once a week (or more), Mr. DeMarco hosts a lunch bunch in a classroom during the lunch break for one of the students with disabilities that he supports. This time, the lunch bunch is hosted for Sarah, a student with Down syndrome. The lunch bunch meetings are somewhat special, with games available and music playing. Sometimes Mr. DeMarco brings in a special treat such as pizza or popcorn.

Prior to inviting any general education students to participate, Mr. DeMarco describes the lunch bunch to the entire fifth-grade class. He tells the students that this will be a fun time to get together and socialize, have lunch together in a special location (e.g., a classroom, the office), and that there are special treats for the students who participate (e.g., pizza parties, listening to music). Mr. DeMarco then passes out permission slips for each student to have his or her parents complete (see Figure 8.1). This way, Mr. DeMarco will know if there are any students who should not participate or who have special dietary or other restrictions.

Next, Mr. DeMarco works with Sarah to select peers to invite to the lunch bunch. Sarah chooses to invite four peers. She passes a note/invitation to Erica, Jocelyn, Amber, and Camille telling them when and where lunch bunch will be (see Figure 8.2).

Circle of Friends

Circle of Friends is another strategy for developing social relationships and social skills for students with disabilities. Different groups of peers without disabilities (six to eight students per group) support the student with disabilities in activities throughout

Figure 8.1   Lunch Bunch Permission Slip

I think Lunch Bunch is a terrific idea for my child _____ (first, last) to participate in!

Please indicate any dietary restrictions, allergies, or other concerns I should be aware of:

_____ Not Applicable

_____ Yes (describe):_____

I would prefer that my child _____ (first, last) not participate in Lunch Bunch at this time.

Please return to Mr. DeMarco (Room 45)

Figure 8.2   Lunch Bunch Invitations

Dear Jocelyn,	Dear Amber,	Dear Camille,
I'm having a lunch bunch	I'm having a lunch bunch	I'm having a lunch bunch
Thursday	Thursday	Thursday
in room 22	in room 22	in room 22
See you there!	See you there!	See you there!
From, Sarah	From, Sarah	From, Sarah

the day. A Circle of Friends group meets regularly with a facilitator (as with a lunch bunch, the facilitator can be any educator who knows the students), who provides ongoing support in how to model communication and social skills and problem-solve.

To begin, the Circle of Friends brainstorms with the facilitator the needs of the student with disabilities. These could include behavior regulation (e.g., how to calm down when upset), how to join social activities (e.g., how to enter a game, knowing the rules of a game), and how to sustain an interaction (e.g., taking turns in a game or conversation, sharing). Once the list of needs is generated, peers in the Circle of Friends generate strategies and assign tasks for themselves. For example, peers may decide to tell the student "just forget about it" when the student is upset. They may take turns inviting the student to play with them at recess. They might invite the student to go to a movie over the weekend. Clearly, the list of options is endless, but it is geared toward meeting the unique needs and interests of the student and peers in the Circle of Friends. Through this type of interaction and group problem solving, the Circle of Friends usually becomes a true group of friends who help and support one another.

Social Communication Books

Some students with disabilities have a difficult time communicating with their peers through sharing stories, making comments, and asking questions. This type of interaction is critical for establishing common interests (the basis of all friendships). Students who have limited verbal communication skills, who use augmentative or alternative communication systems, or who are very shy could benefit from social communication books. These books are created in picture albums or notebooks. They consist of pictures and/or sentences containing information and questions that can be used in conversations. Each page of the book contains a statement about the student with disabilities and a related question for peers. Based on the communication level of the student with disabilities, he or she may read the statement and question or hand the conversation book to a peer to read and answer.

BOX 8.3 Tech Byte

Talking photo albums are widely available today at most drugstores and online. They are quite inexpensive and can be used for social communication books. A same-gendered peer can record himself or herself reading the questions and comments about the student with disabilities. Then the talking photo album has a voice! Apps such as Kid in Story provide an opportunity to make digital talking books. Classmates would likely have fun making a digital story together!

Case Study: Social Communication Books

To help Erica engage in social communication with her peers, Mr. DeMarco creates a social communication book for her. He first speaks with Erica's family and receives photographs and information from them about her, including her family, past vacations, pets, and other topics for Erica to talk about. Mr. DeMarco puts those photos in a small photo album with topic questions, as in the example in Figure 8.3.

Figure 8.3	Social Communication Books

I like going hiking in the mountains. I think it's fun to swim in mountain lakes. Do you like to go hiking?	This is my cat Simba. Do you have any pets?

Social Inclusion Strategies (Secondary)

Best Buddies

Best Buddies is an international organization that matches students with disabilities with peers who do not have disabilities for the purpose of friendship. Best Buddies chapters can be established in middle and high schools. Best Buddies members organize activities for large groups or buddy pairs, such as attending dances, going to a movie, and so on. At middle and high schools, there is generally a teacher who helps with facilitation of the chapter. However, the idea is for students to take the lead in developing and organizing activities, as true friends would.

School Clubs

Many secondary schools have various clubs that meet during or after school. These clubs are typically organized around interests and activities. For example, schools may have theater clubs, gay/straight alliance clubs, robotics clubs, literature clubs, and so on. Middle and high school teachers can work with students to develop a club around the interests of students with disabilities. For example, a student who loves history might develop a history club, or a student who excels at video games may start a Wii club. These school clubs are excellent ways for students who often struggle in school academically or socially to have an avenue to "shine" and develop natural friendships with peers who have similar interests. Sometimes a teacher must host a club, which may involve providing a classroom space for the club to meet and facilitating the activities of the club.

Extracurricular "Homework"

Extracurricular activities, such as sporting events and school dances, are times for students to get together and have fun. New friendships are often forged in these activities, which makes them a ripe opportunity for social inclusion. Sometimes, however, students with disabilities have very limited experience attending these extracurricular activities. As part of a social curriculum, students can be given assignments to attend a certain number of extracurricular events each semester. The school can help facilitate this by having peer buddies (or Best Buddies) sign up to attend the activity with the student or by providing school staff support as necessary.

BOX 8.4   Tech Byte

Some students benefit from seeing video models of how to act and what to do during various social and extracurricular activities. Video modeling is a fast, fun, and effective way to provide these models. Video models are typically more effective than live models because students can pause the action to pay attention to relevant cues and also watch the scene multiple times for extra practice. Here are a few video modeling resources:

- *National Professional Development Center on Autism Spectrum Disorders.* This website (http://autismpdc.fpg.unc.edu/content/video-modeling) contains information on how to set up and complete video self-modeling. This is not just for children with autism but also is useful for all students.
- *TeacherTube:* This website (www.teachertube.com) is another great resource to see sample video modeling.

Case Study: Mrs. Simpson Assigns Homework

Mrs. Simpson has assigned the following homework to Jamie, a student who has autism, for the academic year: Jamie must attend at least one school dance, one sporting event, and one school club meeting. This homework was devised because Jamie has not participated in any extracurricular events. Mrs. Simpson has made it clear to Jamie (and her parents) that if she enjoys the activity, she will be supported to continue to participate in similar activities. If, however, Jamie does not enjoy the activity, she does not need to repeat it. This Friday, Harvard High School is having its first dance of the school year. Jamie will be attending.

Mrs. Simpson plans on devising layers of support for Jamie so that she will have the greatest chance of having fun at the dance. First, Mrs. Simpson plans adult supports. She has asked which paraeducators, if any, are interested in attending. Because the school does not pay for paraeducators to attend these events, Mrs. Simpson asks for volunteers. She will bank the hours that the paraeducators spend attending the dance; paraeducators can use those banked hours to leave early some school days, come in late, or go to appointments in the future. Mrs. Simpson will also attend the dance as part of her extra-duty assignments. In the future, she hopes to reduce the adult supports and build up natural (peer) supports as a replacement. For the first dance, however, Mrs. Simpson wants to make sure adults are available to problem-solve as needed.

Next, Mrs. Simpson plans natural supports. She invites Jamie's peers to a lunch meeting on Tuesday. Mrs. Simpson shares that Jamie will be attending the dance, but that she will need some support. Jamie and Mrs. Simpson describe to her peers that Jamie may need help paying to enter the dance, to be reminded to use her earplugs if the noise volume is too high, and to have somebody to hang out with during the dance. Jamie and her peers brainstorm any other supports she will need and decide which peer will be responsible for making sure Jamie's needs are met.

On the night of the dance, Jamie's friend Beth meets her in front of school. Beth and Jamie enter the gym together. Beth makes sure that Jamie is able to pay the entrance fee. Next, Beth and Jamie find the other girls and spend the night dancing, playing games, talking, and enjoying refreshments.

BOX 8.5

Administrator Insight

Some students may need additional support to participate meaningfully in extracurricular activities. Brainstorm with inclusion facilitators ways to allocate resources for this support. Here are some ideas to consider:

- Provide compensation for staff who work additional hours. Ideally these would be paid, time-carded hours. Some staff may also appreciate the flexibility of official comp time for performing extra duties.
- Recruit and train a set of volunteers from the school's parent organization who are interested in supporting all students at school functions.
- Problem-solve issues related to transportation. Students who receive district-provided transportation may need support with advocating for different drop-off or pick-up times.
- Recognize staff who put in extra time engaging and supporting students in extracurricular activities.

What to Do If the School Doesn't Offer an Activity That Is Accessible or Interesting to a Student

Sometimes schools already have a wide range of activities available, and it is easy to find several options for students to choose from. Other times, however, the school just doesn't seem to have an activity that meets the particular interests of some students. In this case, the inclusion facilitator might take a leading role in developing a new club or activity with the student of concern. For example, Alonso loves video games, but there is no outlet at school to enjoy this activity with others. Mrs. Simpson goes to the school administration to learn how to create new clubs and helps Alonso develop a "gamers" club. In this club, students who love video games can talk about games, research games and gaming strategies together, and play video games on donated equipment. Other times, finding an age-appropriate interest is the challenge. For example, a 14-year-old who enjoys spinning the wheels on matchbox cars is likely going to be isolated in this interest. With support, this interest can be shaped into a Monster Truck activity, so students can watch Monster Truck rallies, design trucks, and design tracks for the truck to travel on as an activity or club at school.

BOX 8.6

Common Core Connections

K–12 standards for speaking and listening in the Common Core focus on two strand areas: (1) comprehension and collaboration and (2) presentation of knowledge and ideas. Students with IEPs that include goals related to communication and social skills will greatly benefit from inclusion in social and extracurricular activities, as it will enable them to make progress toward their goals, participate in the general education curriculum, and make friends!

The process for starting new clubs or assisting students with disabilities to join extra-curricular activities will necessarily vary by student age, interests, and the nature of the activity. However, there will be a few common steps.

Obtain school support. This is usually done by going through existing channels at school, such as the school principal or counselor, who approve new extracurricular activities. Sometimes, no formal processes exist. Other times, it is necessary to draft letters of interest and obtain formal support. The Sparkle Effect website (explained in the Resources Appendix) has a draft letter to administrators that can be a useful template, so be sure to check out that resource.

Find students who share a common interest. This can be done through parent–teacher organizations, school flyers, talking to students and adults at school, and even student surveys (as Mr. DeMarco did). Be sure to check out the Sparkle Effect website for other sample flyers and recruitment strategies!

Case Study: Finding Members for the Gamers Club

Mrs. Simpson and Alonso meet to discuss recruiting other members for the gamers club. Together, they create an informational flyer to recruit members who have similar interests in gaming, as seen in Figure 8.4.

Find an adult who will sponsor the group, if needed. Sometimes extracurricular activities need adult support in terms of providing space (e.g., a classroom to meet in), supervising the activity, coordinating schedules and activities (e.g., transportation to events), and assisting in writing grants to fund the activity (if needed). Sometimes, the best adult is one who knows the student already. Other times, it's an adult who has an interest in the activity. For example, an art teacher may be a great sponsor for an anime club.

Decide how you will get any needed materials for the activity. Some activities are quite easy to implement, but others require a bit more creativity. Be creative in your fund-raising. You may ask for donations from the school, the parent-teacher association, and even local businesses. You may do fund-raising activities. You may even find grants. Many businesses, such as Target, Lowe's, and Walmart, regularly fund grants for schools. You can find these grants by visiting the websites of local businesses, conducting Internet

Figure 8.4   Recruitment Flyer

Do you love video games?

Harvard High School has a new

Gamers Club!

Members of this club must love video games!

We will share strategies, play games, and socialize about our favorites!

For more information, call Mrs. Simpson at 555–5555 or come to our first planning meeting.

Room 57

Wednesday at Lunch

searches for school grants, speaking with school administrators about opportunities, or even using social media. Sometimes schools have money set aside for these purposes, so be sure to ask your principal. The parent–teacher association might also be able to provide funding. And local charitable organizations (e.g., churches, Rotary Clubs) may be able to provide some funding, so be sure to ask them as well!

Strategies for Accommodating Student Involvement

Participation in extracurricular activities should be fun and meaningful. It should also be based on a student's interests and preferences. Therefore, sometimes a student might choose to be involved in an activity for which support and accommodations are necessary. As outlined in this chapter, many opportunities for school clubs already exist or can be created for students in K–12 settings. Accessibility may be an issue that the inclusion facilitator needs to address. Accessibility can refer to physical access (removing physical barriers), sensory accessibility (hearing and vision), attentional access (being able to pay attention for appropriate duration and to the most important features), social accessibility (having the communication and social tools to participate), and sometimes the types of roles students will be able to play in the activity (competitor, assistant, organizer, etc.). The inclusion facilitator needs to think flexibly and creatively at times to help make this happen. Figure 8.5 lists simple strategies to help students participate in some common extracurricular activities.

Figure 8.5   Sample Accommodations for Extracurricular Activities

Physical Accessibility		
Is this space free from clutter (i.e., has a clear path) for wheelchair users? Are materials used accessible to a range of students?	☐ Yes ☐ No	☐ Move extra chairs/tables out of the way to create a clear path. ☐ Hold club meetings in spaces where there are ramps and/or elevators, as needed. ☐ Provide balls, nets, goals, and other materials that have different sizes, if appropriate. ☐ Provide physical supports, such as t-ball stands, musical instrument grips, musical note stands that can be attached to wheelchair, and so on.
Are there multiple ways for people with physical disabilities to participate?	☐ Yes ☐ No	☐ Allow flexible means of participating (time, space, materials). ☐ Use peer buddies (to provide assistance and information).
Is the seating space accessible and conducive to full participation?	☐ Yes ☐ No	☐ Provide adjustable-height desks. ☐ Provide equitable seating options for all participants (no separate spaces for those with and without disabilities).
Does participation in the activity require movement between	☐ Yes ☐ No	☐ Identify the possible locations for the club (classrooms, hallways, gardens, playgrounds). Provide ramps, elevators, and sturdy walking surfaces.

two or more settings (e.g., indoor and outdoor)? Are both/all settings accessible for people who move with walkers, wheelchairs, or other supports?		☐ Provide a peer buddy to assist the student in navigating between activities. ☐ Provide accessible bathrooms and drinking fountains. ☐ Choose locations and activities that are navigable for people who move in different ways.
Does participation in the activity require fine motor skills (e.g., drawing, writing, moving game pieces)?	☐ Yes ☐ No	☐ Include weighted pencils or markers. ☐ Provide adapted equipment specific to the game, sport, musical instrument, or activity. ☐ Make available dictation software or partners. ☐ Add grips to game pieces to make them easier to hold/manipulate. ☐ Use peer buddies (to help move game pieces, write down ideas, etc.).
Sensory Accessibility		
Will participation and full access be limited if a child has a visual impairment or blindness?	☐ Yes ☐ No	☐ Add Braille. ☐ Add audio description to any videos. ☐ Provide auditory information (read scores aloud, state what number was rolled, etc.). ☐ Use peer buddies to help move game pieces or keep track of scores or information and to provide context about what is happening. ☐ Use balls, goals, stage directions with auditory cues. ☐ Provide auditory information (read scores aloud, whistle when the play or scene is about to begin).
Will participation and full access be limited if a child has a hearing impairment or deafness?	☐ Yes ☐ No	☐ Add closed captioning to any videos. ☐ Provide visual information (write down important information such as scores, give a hand signal when a play or scene will begin). ☐ Use peer buddies to provide context information about what is happening in the event.
Attentional Accessibility		
Is sustained, focused attention required to participate in the activity (e.g., watch an entire movie carefully so that it can be discussed)?	☐ Yes ☐ No	☐ Provide scaffolding so that the student knows what to look out for (e.g., cloze notes). ☐ Provide reminders of what occurred. ☐ Prime the student to look out for or pay particular attention to certain things. ☐ Encourage self-monitoring for on-task behaviors.
Is it necessary to pay attention to some, but not all, parts of the activity to be successful (e.g., a memory game, a drawing activity)?	☐ Yes ☐ No	☐ Bring attention to the most important features by highlighting them, writing them on a notecard, or verbally reminding students what is most important to pay attention to. ☐ Prime student to look out for, or pay particular attention to, something in the activity.

(Continued)

Figure 8.5   (Continued)

Social Accessibility		
Will students need to speak to participate in some or all of the activities?	☐ Yes ☐ No	☐ Provide augmentative and alternative communication devices, with preprogrammed phrases and words appropriate to the activity (e.g., "your turn," "I win!"). ☐ Teach vocabulary relevant to the activity. ☐ Provide a social communication book with conversation starter phrases (for social reasons and/or for activity purposes).
Are certain social skills expected for participation in the club?	☐ Yes ☐ No	☐ Write social narratives describing the expected behavior and manners of participating in each activity. ☐ Teach turn-taking skills. ☐ Teach waiting skills. ☐ Provide a social Rolodex (names, pictures, and facts/interests of other members) to facilitate conversation. ☐ Provide a peer buddy to assist in social navigation.

Role Variation	
Possible Roles May Include	**Example or Explanation**
Score keeper	Keep score for the group.
Secretary/notes keeper	Take notes on decisions.
Whip	Keep members on task and focused.
Planner / organizer	Organize upcoming events. (By having students with disabilities plan events, you will gain a better understanding of their participation needs while giving them a chance to practice self-determination.)
Assistant	Help others participate in the activities.
Manager (leader's/coach's assistant)	Provide water and towels to the team; provide directions to actors or musicians; offer motivation.
Team statistician	Keep track of relevant statistics (e.g., hits, strikes).
Costume or set designer	Help with choreography, set design, or construction.
Light or sound technician	Design and/or implement lighting or sound themes and choreography for a theater or musical presentation.
Participant	Participate in the activity. (This includes the full range of activities that all students participate in, including trying out, playing on the team, playing an instrument, and so on.)

Clearly, this list of accommodations and possible role variations is far from exhaustive. Instead, student participation is limited only by our creativity. We have found that when we are out of ideas for how to include a student with disabilities in any activity (from academic to extracurricular), all we need to do is ask the student's peers. They always have a list of great ideas that we never even imagined!

Conclusion

Extracurricular participation is an enjoyable and important part of the school experience. In this chapter, we outlined strategies for determining student interest in these activities, developing activities, and providing support for students to participate. The take-away message is simple: It's possible. We are limited only by our own creativity. So get out there and have some fun!

Please be sure to go to the website (http://www.corwin.com/theinclusiontoolbox) to download the forms and resources from this chapter!

9

Academic Access and Participation

Everybody is a genius. But if you judge a fish by its ability to climb a tree, it will live its whole life believing that it is stupid.

—Albert Einstein

When we consider making adjustments to curriculum for students with learning differences in general education settings, the first question often is "But is this fair?" Upon a bit of reflection, it generally becomes quite clear that fair does not mean treating everyone the same. For example, because most students in a classroom do not wear eyeglasses, does this mean that nobody is allowed to wear eyeglasses? Certainly not. Or because most children in class wear size 4 shoes, then all children should wear size 4 shoes? Of course not. Being fair does not mean treating everyone equally. It means taking into consideration the needs of all learners and giving all learners what they need to be successful. One way we do that in inclusive settings is by using adaptations to the materials, schedule, and setting of instruction.

Federal law tells us that students with disabilities must access, participate in, and make progress in the general education curriculum (Individuals with Disabilities Education Improvement Act, 2004) as well as a specially designed education program that addresses their unique needs (Education for All Handicapped Children Act, 1975). To meet all of these requirements, many students with disabilities have adaptations made to the general education curriculum.

Adaptations is an umbrella term covering both accommodations and modifications. Figure 9.1 compares accommodations and modifications.

Adaptations can also be thought of as general or specific (Janney & Snell, 2006). General adaptations are those that can be used by many students and address routine,

---

❖ Box 9.1   What Does the Research Say?

Use of Adaptations

Research reports that the use of adaptations varies widely, often based on the severity of a student's disability and her or his level of inclusion. For example, teachers report using adaptations for students with low-incidence (severe) disabilities 61%–80% of the time (Kurth, Gross, Lovinger, & Catalano, 2012). However, Wehmeyer Lattin, Lapp-Rincker, and Agran (2003) report that adapted materials were available for middle school students with intellectual disabilities during less than 3% of their observations. Others have noted that adaptations are more widely available for students with low-incidence (severe) disabilities than students with high-incidence (mild) disabilities (Dymond & Russell, 2004). And the use of adaptations is greater for students who spend more time in inclusive settings (Soukup, Wehmeyer, Bashinski, & Bovaird, 2007).

Effectiveness of Adaptations

The use of adaptations is associated with a range of positive characteristics, including higher student engagement, fewer student competing behaviors, and less teacher time dedicated to classroom management (Lee, Wehmeyer, Soukup, & Palmer, 2010). Furthermore, teachers report that their students learn more and are better able to participate in class activities through the use of adaptations (Kurth & Keegan, 2012). Curricular adaptations have also been found to improve student on-task behavior and work production (Kern, Delaney, Clarke, Dunlap, & Childs, 2001). Additionally, many educators support the idea of adaptations (Idol, 2006). For inclusion to be successful, the use of adaptations is necessary to meet individual student needs (Cross, Traub, Hutter-Pishgahi, & Shelton, 2004), and adaptations do facilitate access to the general education curriculum (Fisher & Frey, 2001).

Figure 9.1   Accommodations Versus Modifications

	Accommodation	*Modification*
Definition	• Provides access • Does not change the content or mastery criteria of the curriculum	• Provides meaning • Changes the content or mastery criteria of the curriculum
Examples	• Student takes a test in a less distracting location • Test is read aloud to a student with a print disability • Student has extra time to complete an assignment • Student with a physical disability uses speech-to-text software to write an essay	• Student must complete addition problems, rather than algebra problems, in math class • Test is rewritten at lower reading and comprehension level • Student creates a collage about ancient Rome, rather than writing an essay • Student works on social and communication goals in science class, rather than mastering science standards

typical classroom activities. For example, giving students access to graphic organizers, leisure books on a variety of topics and reading levels, dictionaries, and peer tutors are general adaptations that many students can use in a wide range of routines and activities. These general adaptations help all students in the class be more successful and more independent. Specific adaptations, on the other hand, apply to particular students and specific lessons or activities. For example, the materials in a chemistry lab assignment might need to be adjusted for a student with physical disabilities. The lab space is made wheelchair accessible with an adjustable-height workspace, beakers with handles are provided, electric stirrers are provided, and plastic materials are used rather than glass. These specific adaptations have the specific physical needs of a particular student in this particular lab in mind. However, they could be used for all students. For example, if all of the workspaces had adjustable-height desks, all of the beakers had handles, and all of the science lab materials were in plastic containers, the need for extensive specific adaptations is limited! This is the premise behind universal design.

General Adaptations and Universal Design

Today's classrooms are more diverse than ever. Students speak a variety of languages, come from various economic backgrounds, have various proficiency levels in academic skill areas, and have varying experiences with core content matter. Educators, then, cannot realistically design a single lesson plan and expect that all students will be successful with it. Instead, educators must consider this diversity when planning their lessons and anticipate the needs of their students in terms of how instruction is delivered and how students will respond to instruction.

The universal design for learning (UDL) framework addresses this by enabling educators to plan instruction with the needs of diverse learners in mind, rather than make adjustments after the fact for individual students with specific special education needs (Pisha & Coyne, 2001). Within a UDL approach to instruction, general adaptations are available to all students (e.g., all students have the choice to type or handwrite a response) and are considered during lesson planning. Any specific adaptations that may be needed for specific tasks by specific students are also considered proactively for the small percentage of students who need these additional supports (e.g., the provision of a scribe for written work).

BOX 9.2   *Administrator Insight*

Use UDL to meet the needs of all learners at your school. Provide teachers with common planning time, and ask them to focus on identifying different ways to create lessons so that all students are engaged and participating. When observing in classrooms, be sure both general and special education teachers can discuss content and how curriculum is adapted to meet individual student needs. Provide professional development for teaching partners in the area of UDL.

General Adaptations

General adaptations include many different strategies and resources, a few of which are listed here:

- magnification or text enlargement (e.g., books available in different fonts, magnifiers)
- graphic organizers (for all subject areas, including reading, writing, and math)
- slot notes/cloze notes (available for note taking during lectures, reading, etc.)
- peer tutors or paired learning
- audiobooks

- colored overlays or rulers for keeping place while reading
- visuals or pictures supplementing key ideas
- examples embedded in assignments (that students can readily refer to)
- color coding, highlighting, or bolding key words or concepts
- manipulatives or counters
- resource guide or toolkit (that contains examples, steps to be completed, etc.)
- word banks (for reading, writing)
- assignment checklist (including materials to take home from school)
- planner or organizational tool
- alternate responses (e.g., oral, typewritten, pictorial)
- assistive technology (e.g., calculator, word processor, dictation recorder, communication device)
- alternate writing utensils (e.g., weighted pencils, pencil grips, "fat" markers, stamps)
- alternate paper (e.g., paper with raised lines, paper with varied margins, paper with varied line width or length)

Creating Specific Adaptations

With these general adaptations in place, more students are likely to be successful in their general education classrooms without further intervention. A small percentage of students with disabilities, however, may need additional specific adaptations that are focused on their individual needs and support requirements. How does one know what specific adaptations a student requires? This is an important first question to address, as overadapting (creating materials that are "too special") often stigmatizes and isolates the student (Cushing, Clark, Carter, & Kennedy, 2005). And they can be time-consuming to create! Therefore, a first step is to observe the student during typical classroom routines and discover when he or she requires more support.

Ecological Assessment

What is an ecological assessment? Ecological assessment (Macfarlane, 1998; Watson, Gable, & Greenwood, 2011) involves observing the activities the student participates in and noting the required skills to be successful in these activities. Any discrepancies between skills and needs can then be identified and adaptations provided for the student (Downing, 2005).

Who completes an ecological assessment? The process is straightforward, so with a little practice anybody can complete one. This includes teachers, paraeducators, peer tutors, and family members. It is ideal to do this collaboratively so that more than one person completes the assessment or so that the observer discusses the assessment results with others before making adaptations.

How is an ecological assessment completed? When completing an ecological assessment, as demonstrated in Figure 9.2, a series of questions, including the following, are posed and answered through observation and collaboration:

- *Peer inventory/task analysis:* What are peers without special education needs doing in this activity or setting? Completing a step-by-step task analysis of how a peer successfully completes the activity or lesson is often useful.

- *Cues:* What are the naturally occurring cues for performance? That is, how do peers know what to do and when?
- *Student performance:* What does the student with disabilities do at each step? That is, how does this student complete (or fail to complete) each step?
- *Discrepancy analysis:* Is there a discrepancy between what a peer does and what the student with disabilities does? If so, simply write out the difference; this will help identify what supports are needed or what skills must be taught.
- *Adaptations/cues to teach:* If there is a discrepancy, the last step is to consider adaptations that should be put in place or cues to teach the student to respond to, so that he or she may complete each step correctly with the least intrusive level of support.

The first four categories are completed during the observation. The last category can be completed after the observation and can be done collaboratively.

Develop a List of Common Needs: Adaptations Checklist

After observing a student in many different routines and activities, inclusion facilitators generally have a good idea of the student's needs in those common routines. With input from the entire individualized education program (IEP) team, inclusion facilitators can determine the overall supports necessary for students across general education settings and activities. In the following case study, we provide an example of an adaptations checklist completed by an IEP team.

Case Study: Mrs. Simpson Plans Casper's Adaptations

To make sure that Casper has all of the supports in place that are necessary for his success, Mrs. Simpson meets with Casper's general education teachers and his parents to

Figure 9.2	Sample Ecological Assessment for Casper in Ninth-Grade English Grammar Activity

Peer Inventory/ Task Analysis	Cues	Student Performance	Discrepancy Analysis	Adaptations/Cues to Teach
Students take out pencil and paper from backpacks.	Teacher verbal instructions	Casper gets out his AlphaSmart. He does not turn on AlphaSmart.	• Task initiation • Identifying sentence to type	• Provision of AlphaSmart • Peer tutor points to "start" button and reminds Casper to turn on AlphaSmart
Students identify and correct grammatical and spelling errors.	Sentence projected on board, teacher verbal instructions	Casper sits quietly and does not type the sentence.	• Identifying errors • Type responses	• Peer tutor helps Casper navigate to blank page in English 9 file on AlphaSmart. • Give Casper a sentence strip with most errors already corrected and appropriate errors highlighted with choices provided (e.g., "i" or "I")

develop an adaptation plan that will be included in his IEP. They use the form in Figure 9.3 to help guide their discussion. This tool can be used as an attachment to a student's IEP or as a resource sheet for the IEP team to refer to when considering different types of adaptations for students. To use the tool, the following steps are followed:

1. Student-specific needs are identified (e.g., reading comprehension deficits, distractibility).

2. The team selects one or two adaptations to implement for that area of need. For example, a team may select to use graphic organizers and visuals to support a student with reading comprehension deficits.

3. The adaptations plan is shared with the entire team so that all general education teachers, paraeducators, peer tutors, and parents know what to provide for the student's learning throughout the school day.

4. Once the adaptations are identified, they are implemented throughout the day.

5. Student progress is monitored with use of the adaptation; if the student is successful, those selected adaptations are kept in place. If the student is not successful, a different set of adaptations are implemented for the identified area of need.

As seen in Figure 9.3, the team identified several areas of need for Casper, along with one or two adaptations for each area of need.

Figure 9.3 Instructional Accommodations and Modifications

Academic Areas		
Reading		
Area	*Area of Need?*	*Suggested Adaptation*
Decoding print	☒ Yes ☐ No	☒ Add symbols (e.g., writing with symbols) ☐ Add visual cues ☐ Audiobook ☐ Audio directions ☒ Lower-level materials ☐ Text-to-speech software
Comprehending print	☒ Yes ☐ No	☐ Read aloud ☒ Audiobook ☐ Highlight text ☐ Bold key words or phrases ☐ Dictionary
Reading fluency	☐ Yes ☒ No	☐ Read aloud ☐ Audiobook ☐ Extended time
Physical/sensory needs	☐ Yes ☒ No	☐ Large print ☐ Braille ☐ Audiobook ☐ Object representations

Writing		
Spelling	☒ Yes ☐ No	☒ Word processor with spell check ☐ Dictionary ☒ Word bank ☐ Teacher or peer proofreading ☐ Permit drafts of work
Handwriting	☒ Yes ☐ No	☐ Permit oral responses ☒ Word processor AlphaSmart ☐ Pencil grips ☐ Weighted pencils ☐ Dictation
Writing fluency	☐ Yes ☒ No	☐ Note-taking assistance ☐ Word processor ☐ Dictation/oral responses ☐ Record lectures/discussions
Writing organization	☒ Yes ☐ No	☒ Graphic organizers ☐ Provide a model ☐ Provide feedback
Math		
Memorizing math facts	☒ Yes ☐ No	☒ Use of calculator ☒ Use of number charts or lines ☒ Use of manipulatives
Converting word problems into equations	☒ Yes ☐ No	☐ Provide examples ☒ Use of resource guide/word bank ☐ Graphic organizers ☒ Provide formulas
Reading difficulties (word problems)	☒ Yes ☐ No	☐ Read problems aloud ☐ Reduce distracting information ☐ Graphic organizers ☐ Word banks ☒ Provide equations (with fill-in blanks)
Number sense	☐ Yes ☒ No	☐ Manipulatives ☐ Calculator
Testing		
Content of tests	☒ Yes ☐ No	☐ Adapt length, complexity, or content of tests ☐ Format of tests (e.g., multiple-choice rather than open-ended) ☒ Test on prioritized content ☒ Adjust scoring criteria
Delivery of tests	☒ Yes ☐ No	☐ Permit study guides during testing ☐ Provide examples on tests ☐ Permit oral responses ☒ Extended time ☐ Fewer test items ☐ Permit breaks during testing ☐ Test in alternate location ☒ Permit use of tools (e.g., word processor, calculator, etc.)

(Continued)

Figure 9.3   (Continued)

Nonacademic Areas		
Attention		
Easily distracted	☐ Yes ☒ No	☐ Preferential seating ☐ Frequent (positive) feedback ☐ Self-monitoring ☐ Task completion supports (e.g., timer, stopwatch)
Sustaining effort/ attention	☒ Yes ☐ No	☐ Opportunities for choice ☒ Break assignments into smaller parts/segments
Attention to detail	☒ Yes ☐ No	☐ Assignment checklists ☒ Self-monitoring ☐ Frequent feedback ☐ Permit drafts of work before grading
Anxiety		
Anxiety in day-to-day activities	☐ Yes ☒ No	☐ Provide written schedule ☐ Break cards ☐ Cooling-off breaks ☐ Transition warnings
Testing anxiety	☐ Yes ☒ No	☐ Extended time ☐ Test in alternate location ☐ Allow notes/guides on test ☐ Provide study guide
Planning / Time Management		
Organization	☒ Yes ☐ No	☒ Provide written schedule ☐ Break assignments into parts ☐ Provide materials to student (e.g., paper, pencil)
Emotional / Behavioral		
Maintaining appropriate behavior	☒ Yes ☐ No	☒ Token economy ☐ Behavior contract ☐ Provide written schedule ☐ Frequent positive feedback ☒ Break cards (allow three break cards per day) ☐ Cooling-off periods ☐ Progress charts ☐ Home–school communication ☐ Transition warnings
Sensory / Physical Areas		
Visual impairments	☐ Yes ☒ No	☐ Large print ☐ Braille ☐ Audiobook ☐ Object representations ☐ Seat near teacher ☐ Provide materials in specific colors or fonts
Hearing impairments	☐ Yes ☒ No	☐ FM system ☐ Note-taking assistance

		☐ Seat near teacher ☐ Face student when speaking
Physical impairments	☐ Yes ☒ No	☐ Adapted chairs and/or desks ☐ Wheelchair accessible desk ☐ Wedge seat ☐ Mats for stretching
Sensory impairments	☒ Yes ☐ No	☒ Fidgets ☐ Weighted vests ☒ Seat cushion ☐ Wedge seat ☐ Earplugs/headphones
Communication impairments	☒ Yes ☐ No	☐ Communication device ☐ English language learner materials ☒ Add visuals ☐ Graphic organizers
Personnel Areas		
Adult supports (teacher and/or paraeducator)	☒ Yes ☐ No	☐ Academic support ☐ Time management support ☒ Sensory/physical support ☒ Behavioral support
Peer supports	☒ Yes ☐ No	☐ Academic support ☒ Time management support ☐ Sensory/physical support ☐ Behavioral support

In-Advance Adaptations

In-advance adaptations depend on our ability to predict what teachers and classes will be doing ahead of time. Usually, the bulk of our adaptations can be planned and made ahead of time. By knowing what textbooks, curriculum materials, and novels a class will be using, inclusion facilitators can preview that material in the weeks or days before the class uses them and create adapted versions of those texts. It is also a good idea for inclusion facilitators to get teacher editions of the novels, textbooks, and curricular materials. Usually, the curriculum team or even the school library has these on hand.

BOX 9.3   Tech Byte

Many textbook and curriculum developers today include electronic versions of their books and materials; these resources are invaluable when it comes to obtaining pictures and graphs. For example, if students are studying the cell, it might be easiest to simply go to the publisher's website and download the picture of the cell used in the textbook. Not only does this save time, but also the pictures and the "feel" of an adapted book are similar to the original material. If it is not possible to obtain electronic resources from the publisher, ClipArt, Google Images, and even magazines can be excellent resources.

While it may feel time-consuming initially to develop modified versions of textbooks and curriculum materials, major changes to core curriculum (e.g., novels read in a class, textbooks) are relatively uncommon. Once adaptations are created and stored on the computer in the form of electronic (e.g., Word, PowerPoint) documents, they can be easily adapted for other students in the class or for use in future years. In this manner, adapted assignments, novels, and tests are created and banked.

BOX 9.4   Tech Byte

The warehouse created by storing digital versions of your adaptations is a huge time saver. But the time savings multiply when this warehouse is turned into a digital lending library. For example, teachers can use Dropbox (www.dropbox.com) to share adaptations with others. They can even collaborate to divvy up responsibilities. For example, if you adapt *Romeo and Juliet*, I'll adapt *Call of the Wild*. Be sure to check out websites like Tar Heel Reader (www.tarheelreader.com) and other open-source websites to find adaptations that might already be made!

Time Management Strategies for In-Advance Adaptations

- Use the teacher talk sheets (see Chapter 7) to determine upcoming events and topics.
- Get a copy of the curriculum maps/plans for the upcoming semester or school year from all general education teachers.
- Obtain electronic copies of any/all materials from the publisher. This will make adapting worksheets, obtaining images, and so forth much more efficient.
- Obtain copies of the teacher editions of textbooks, curriculum materials, tests, worksheets, and so forth.
- If possible, obtain copies of English language learner versions of the curriculum materials or textbooks. You will find that these have already been adapted from the original, at least slightly.
- Create a bank of materials you have adapted this year. You can then make slight changes, as necessary, to adjust for the needs of different students in following years.
- Reach out to your grade-level or subject-area colleagues. Somebody may have already created an adapted version of pre-algebra, for example. Ideally, you might even be able to split up classes or assignments. For example, the inclusion facilitator at one high school may adapt materials for biology, and the inclusion facilitator at another high school agrees to adapt physics.
- Investigate online resources, such as TeacherVision or Paraeducate. These often have adapted materials that can be downloaded for free or for a small fee.
- Set aside a small chunk of time each day for creating adaptations. This might be before students arrive or after students have left. Typically educators have prep time as part of their contracts (e.g., preparing for IEP meetings, preparing adaptations, preparing assessments). This time is an absolutely essential part of your job. Special education teacher contracts should match general education teacher contracts in terms of student-free prep time.
- Gather adaptation support from other team members. Parents are often great resources for adaptations and can help create adaptations for their children. For example, a parent who was a biology professor at a university created science

adaptations for his son in one high school. Similarly, paraeducators can be excellent resources for adaptations. Often, they know the curriculum and class routines very well and create amazing adaptations for students. Teachers need to review and approve adaptations before implementing them, but by gathering allies and resources, the work of teachers is eased.

- Match paraeducators with classes or activities carefully. For example, match paraeducators who have skills in math with math times/classes.

BOX 9.5 *Administrator Insight*

Do all teachers have grade-level-appropriate textbooks in their classroom? Remove obstacles to curriculum access for both teachers and students by doing the following:

- Ensure that all teachers have grade-level-appropriate general education curriculum materials in their rooms. Intervention curriculum materials or workbooks are not sufficient.
- When piloting textbooks, ask publishers to send the differentiated curriculum, such as those written for English language learners and special education. Pilot these support textbooks at the same time so teachers can evaluate their effectiveness and possibly reduce time spent adapting curriculum.
- Include special education teachers in the budget when purchasing new textbooks and curriculum in general education.

What About "On-the-Fly" Adaptations?

In reality, as the saying goes, "the best laid plans of mice and men often go awry." In other words, the inclusion facilitator may have a solid grasp of upcoming assignments, projects, and tests and has planned accordingly. Yet the unexpected should be expected. A general education teacher may be out sick, and the substitute teacher may implement a totally different lesson or activity. There might be a shortened school day due to an assembly, rendering the typical sequence of events moot. And the list goes on . . .

In these situations, when there are changes to activities, lessons, or materials, inclusion facilitators must make on-the-fly adaptations. Worksheets might need to be adjusted in the moment. Textbooks might need to be made accessible during class time. Writing prompts might need to be simplified on the spot. Having a big toolbox, so to speak, is critical in these moments. Inclusion facilitators might benefit from having a rolling case, a portable filing box, or simply a shopping bag that contains "emergency adaptation" supplies for these moments.

Tools and Strategies for On-the-Fly Adaptations

What are the emergency adaptation supplies an inclusion facilitator should consider having on hand?

- *A label maker for adapting worksheets.* Label makers can be used to white out, and fill in, sections of a worksheet to make it accessible for students with handwriting difficulties. Rather than straining to write on a small worksheet space, the student can simply type her response and tape down the output created by the label maker.

- *Sticky notes.* Sticky notes can be used to sketch out pictures or write words to help students communicate (e.g., "yes" and "no" written on notes), to write responses (e.g., to use as a word bank with words written on notes that students can put in order), to solicit comprehension (e.g., "Who is the story about?" with a camel and a bird drawn or written on the notes), and so on.
- *Highlighter pen or tape.* Important words or definitions can be highlighted. Likewise, examples can be written or highlighted so students know how to solve a problem.
- *Paper clips.* These can be used to attach the adapted work to the original. They can also be used as manipulatives (e.g., as counters to solve addition problems).
- *Small, portable dry-erase board with marker.* Examples can be demonstrated, words can be spelled, and problems worked out and solved all using a whiteboard.
- *Common tools:* Calculator, Wite-Out, highlighters, glue, tape—these can all come in handy for a variety of purposes.
- *Pictures from magazines.* June Downing was a prolific author and inclusion advocate. She suggested that inclusion facilitators develop a filing system of pictures to use on the fly. Pictures of people could go in one folder, animals in another, food in yet another, and so on. As educators and parents are reading magazines, they can simply cut out pictures and file them away. Then when needed, relevant pictures can be pulled out and used to "write" responses, to make choices, and so on.

So What Is a "Good" Adaptation?

There are many tips and strategies for making academic lessons accessible for students with varying learning needs. But how do we know that an adaptation was effective or appropriate? Janney and Snell (2006) and Kurth and Keegan (2012) have outlined some considerations for this important question:

1. *Does the adaptation facilitate social and instructional participation in general education?*
   a. Was the student part of the class/activity while using the adaptation or removed to a seat in the back of the classroom or outside of the classroom?
   b. Was the student using the same or similar materials as peers?
2. *Is the adaptation only as "special "as necessary?*
   a. Is the adaptation nonstigmatizing? Does it draw undue attention to the student's differences?
3. *Does the adaptation promote independence?*
   a. Does the adaptation require a "Velcro" aide from a paraeducator or peer tutor to assist the student with each step, or does it incorporate the student's visual, physical, cognitive, and attentional needs in its design?
   b. Does the adaptation build on the student's strengths and learning preferences?
4. *Is the adaptation age- and culturally appropriate?*
   a. Would it be appropriate for another student of the same age, gender, or culture to use these materials and adaptation? If not, consider a redesign.

5. *Was the student successful in learning or practicing an important skill with the adaptation?*

   a. Does it relate clearly to an IEP goal or a content standard?

   b. Did the student learn the desired skill (measured through data collection)?

Conclusion

In this chapter, we discussed the fact that adaptations can take many forms, including accommodations and modifications, and can be specific or general. Ecological assessments can help the inclusion facilitator decide when adaptations are needed, and adaptations checklists can share those needed adaptations efficiently with the educational team. The Resources Appendix contains various resources for obtaining more information about creating adaptations for students with disabilities, including books, websites, and research articles.

Please be sure to go to the website (http://www.corwin.com/theinclusiontoolbox) to download the forms and resources from this chapter!

10

Supporting Positive Behavior in Inclusive Settings

I never teach my pupils. I only provide the conditions in which they can learn.

—Albert Einstein

When a team is developing an individualized education program (IEP) for a student, they must "consider, when appropriate, strategies, including positive behavioral interventions, strategies and supports" for a student whose behavior impedes his/her learning or that of others" (Individuals with Disabilities Education Improvement Act [IDEA] 2004). Furthermore, IDEA states that before a student with an IEP is disciplined or placed in a more restrictive setting due to his or her behavior, the IEP team must complete a functional behavioral assessment (FBA) to determine the cause(s) of the behavior and then implement a behavior intervention plan (BIP) to address the behavior. The BIP must be reviewed and modified as necessary over time. In this chapter we provide an overview of FBA and BIP, and then jump into practical strategies for implementing positive behavior interventions and plans.

Functional Behavior Analysis

An FBA is the set of activities completed to determine the purpose of a student's problematic behavior. In an inclusive setting, it is especially important to get input from general education teachers, paraeducators, and any others who work with the student

141

❖ Box 10.1   What Does the Research Say?

Exhibiting challenging behavior can negatively impact a person's quality of life (Durand, 1990) and is one of the main reasons students with disabilities are excluded from general education (Reeve & Carr, 2000). The FBA and BIP processes are effective in reducing problem behaviors in students with disabilities (Ingram, Lewis-Palmer, & Sugai, 2005). And positive behavior support strategies, including FBA, can be implemented in general education settings (Heineman, Dunlap, & Kincaid, 2005; Scott et al., 2004) to the benefit of students with disabilities.

When teaching new behaviors to students with disabilities, a range of effective strategies can be implemented in general education settings. First, there are reinforcer assessments (Damon, Riley-Tillman, & Fiorello, 2008) and reinforcement menus (Holt, 1971). Token economy systems are also effective (Matson & Boisjoli, 2009). Break cards, which allow students to temporarily "escape" difficult or nonpreferred tasks, are also effective instructional strategies (Cihak & Gama, 2008). In addition, teaching students to self-monitor their own behavior has been shown to be useful, resulting in improved behavior (Blood, Johnson, Ridenour, Simmons, & Crouch, 2011; Coughlin, McCoy, Kenzer, Mathur, & Zucker, 2012).

(e.g., cafeteria workers, recess supervisors) when completing an FBA. In an FBA, the following are considered and described (see the example in Figure 10.1):

- *Setting events/underlying deficits:* What is happening in this person's life (e.g., are parents going through a divorce, is the home life stressful due to unemployment)? What happened earlier (e.g., change in routine, disturbance at home)? What is this person's quality of life (e.g., can the student effectively communicate, does he or she feel safer when there are few changes, does he or she have the ability to make choices)?
- *Antecedent:* What happened right before the behavior?
- *Behavior:* What was the student's response to the antecedent?
- *Consequence:* What happened right after the behavior?

| **Figure 10.1** | Functional Behavior Analysis Template |

---

1. **Describe the behavior in measurable, objective terms** (i.e., describe so a stranger would know what the behavior looked like, sounded like—to pass the "stranger test" for measurable and objective):

2. **Note the time of the behavior (day of week, time of day) and when the behavior ended (duration).** _____

3. **Hypothesize the function of the behavior.** Use the table below. Place a checkmark to describe the setting, what happened right before the behavior (antecedent), what happened right after the

behavior (consequence), how the student reacted to the consequence, and your hypothesized function of the behavior.

Common FBA Entries				
Setting event/ context	*Antecedent*	*Consequence/ outcomes*	*Student reactions*	*Hypothesized function*
Music	Attempt to communicate	Ignored	Stopped	*Attention* (escape or obtain)
Math	Break time	Redirected	Continued	*Power or control* (escape or obtain)
Computer	Close physical proximity	Verbal reprimand/ warning	Intensified	*Sensory* (escape or obtain)
Reading	Corrective feedback	Time-out	Remorse	*Interpersonal or social* (escape or obtain
Story time	Crowded area	Received item/ activity	Apologized	*Skill deficit* (student does not have a needed skill)
Home economics	Denied access	Sent to office	Cried	*Performance deficit* (student does not consistently complete a known skill)
Group instruction	Difficult task given	Sent home	Different behavior	*Medical or biological* (e.g., toothache, headache)
History	Downtime/ waiting		Moved away	*State of mind or emotional* (e.g., distress, anxiety, sadness)
Free time	Easy task given		Laughed	*Tangible* (escape or obtain)
Hallway	Food presentation		Slept	*Activity* (escape or obtain)
Leisure	Group work time			
Individual (1 to 1)	Individual work time			
Speech	Noisy area			
Science	Peer Interaction			
Gym/PE	Physically assisted			
Centers	Praise			
Writing	Quiet area			
Bus area	Redirection			

(Continued)

Figure 10.1	(Continued)

Choices (offered or not offered)	Request by adult			
Lunchroom	Rest time			
Classroom	Seizure			
Outside or playground	Tangible removal			
Bathroom	Teacher attention to others			
Community-based instruction	Told "no"			
Art	Transition			

Copyright © 2014 by Corwin. All rights reserved. Reprinted from *The Inclusion Toolbox: Strategies and Techniques for All Teachers* by Jennifer A. Kurth and Megan Gross. Thousand Oaks, CA: Corwin, www.corwin.com

BOX 10.2

Administrator Insight

When a student has behaviors that require the team to conduct a functional behavior analysis, it is imperative that staff and families have the support they need during this process. Staff may need support in terms of resources, such as release time to observe a student, assistance from a district behavior specialist, or the listening ear of an administrator who can look out for warning signs that emotions might be inhibiting objectivity in the assessment. The administrator can also support families, who are likely also struggling at home with a student's challenging behaviors, by meeting with them and guiding them to supportive agencies, either through a district parent liaison or community-based agencies.

Behavior Intervention Plan

The information from the FBA is used to develop a BIP. The BIP focuses on teaching appropriate skills to replace the problem behavior with a new, appropriate behavior. The BIP frequently outlines the following:

- What are the problem behaviors (in measurable, objective terms)?
- What are the replacement behaviors that will be taught?
- How will the replacement behaviors be taught?
- What accommodations will be in place to support the student in learning the new behaviors?
- How will progress be measured?

- How long will the BIP be in effect until its effectiveness is reviewed?
- What are reactions and consequences for appropriate (replacement) behavior?
- What are reactions and consequences for the challenging behavior?

It is beyond the scope of this book to go into great detail about these techniques. If you would like to learn more about FBAs and BIPs, please see the suggested readings in the Resources Appendix. In this book, we instead choose to focus on strategies for implementing these techniques in inclusive settings. To do this, let's consider the case of Allison, a new fifth-grade student who has autism and limited communication skills. Allison's behaviors include swearing (various four-letter words), threatening to harm people (e.g., "I'm going to cut your face!"), biting her own hand, and scratching others. Mr. DeMarco completes an FBA and determines that some of these behaviors are attention seeking (swearing, scratching) and other behaviors (biting herself, threatening others) are aimed at escaping stressful or frustrating situations.

Mr. DeMarco realizes how important it is to succinctly and clearly convey this information to the various adults who will be working with Allison, including general education teachers, related services providers, and paraeducators. Because these are busy professionals, he develops a quick guide to Allison's BIP that they can easily refer to, including prevention and reaction strategies, as seen in Figure 10.2.

Figure 10.2   BIP Overview

Student: Allison

Current behavior(s)	Function (why she does it)	→	What student should do or say instead
Swearing	Seeking attention	→	"Look at this!" or "Talk to me!"
Threatening	Stress, needs to end a social interaction	→	"Give me some space" or "I need a break"
Biting self	Expressing stress or frustration	→	"I need help" or "I need a break"
Scratching others	Seeking attention	→	"Look at this!" or "Talk to me!"

Prevention Plan

1. Provide Allison with her escape and attention cards (extra copies of the cards are on the next page; you can print them if she doesn't have them for some reason). Place the cards on her desk.

2. Read social narrative at start of activity.

3. Let Allison decide what she will be working on for this activity (set the deal).

4. Provide frequent positive reinforcement, paired with stickers on her token economy card.

5. Provide all necessary adaptations listed in the IEP so that the work is meaningful and accessible.

6. The paraeducator supporting Allison should walk around the classroom assisting many students; Allison needs personal space.

(Continued)

Figure 10.2 (Continued)

Reaction Plan

Allison's behavior	→	Your reaction
Allison swears	→	1. Ignore swear words. Stay calm and neutral. 2. Prompt Allison to use attention card (look at me, help me, talk to me). 3. When Allison requests attention, give her attention.
Allison threatens	→	1. Ignore threat. Stay calm and neutral. 2. Prompt Allison to use escape or attention card (break, space, help). 3. When Allison requests escape, give her 2-minute escape before giving her any further attention.
Allison bites herself	→	1. Stay calm and neutral. 2. Prompt Allison to use escape or attention card (break, space, help). 3. When Allison requests escape, give her help or escape (depending on which she requests).
Allison scratches somebody	→	1. Model "praying hands." Do not touch her or grab her hands. Stay calm and neutral. 2. Prompt Allison to use attention or escape card. 3. When Allison makes a request, honor it immediately. 4. Provide first aid, if needed.
Allison uses her card without prompting	→	1. Immediately honor her request. 2. Pair this with positive, enthusiastic specific praise: "Thank you for telling me you need [help, space, break, attention]."

Allison should have her cards with her at all times. In case she doesn't, here are copies of the cards that you can print for her.

Allison's Escape Card Point to tell us what you need. • I need a break • I need more personal space • I need to be left alone	**Allison's Attention Card** Point to tell us what you need. • I need somebody to talk to me • I need somebody to look at me • I need help

Reinforcement

Because reinforcement varies from person to person, and even day to day or activity to activity for the same person, it is important to have a good idea of the various items, activities, and experiences a person finds enjoyable. Discovering this can be done in a number of ways, including interviewing people who know the student well, observing the student, and conducting forced-choice observations.

Reinforcer Assessment

A reinforcement assessment is an interview and observation tool that can be used to determine what items, experiences, and activities a student enjoys. Any number of people can complete the assessment, including parents, teachers, paraeducators, siblings, peers, and the student himself or herself. In fact, the more people who complete the reinforcement assessment, the better, since you will have more information and ideas!

BOX 10.3   Tech Byte

Reinforcer and preference assessments exist as apps on iOS and Android devices. For example, the Preference and Reinforcer Assessment by Touch Autism is an inexpensive app for completing preference assessments. This app was created by a Board-Certified behavior analyst and provides step-by-step instructions for completing the assessment. It even makes charts to demonstrate student preferences. The app allows the user to complete assessments for multiple students. For more ideas, check out some of the apps found in the Resources Appendix.

Case Study: Mr. DeMarco Completes a Reinforcement Assessment

To better understand what items, experiences, and activities Allison enjoys, Mr. DeMarco completes a reinforcement assessment based on his observations of her. He asks Allison's parents, her older brother, and two paraeducators who regularly work with her to also complete the assessment. Mr. DeMarco then transfers all of their responses onto one final document as shown in Figure 10.3.

Figure 10.3   Reinforcer Assessment

Child's Name: Allison

Date: January 22

Instructions: Place a checkmark to indicate preferred items or activities.

Social and Sensory Reinforcers

	Adult attention		Hug/squeeze		Private praise
	Attention from specific adults • List preferred adults:		"OK" sign		Applause
			Eye contact		High five
✓	Being left alone		Smiles	✓	Tickles
✓	Time spent with peers • List preferred peers: Connor	✓	Thumbs up	✓	Swinging
			Squeeze ball		Fidget items
✓	Freedom from interference from adults		Jumping	✓	Lotion
✓	Freedom from interference from peers	✓	Vibration		Public praise

(Continued)

Figure 10.3   (Continued)

✓	Brushing		Shake hands		Specific clothing
✓	Takes shoes off frequently		Twirling		
	List others: She likes riding a stationary bike				

Activity Reinforcers

✓	Music • List preferred music/medium: iPod with over-ear headphones	✓	Computer	✓	Making choices
		✓	Puzzle		Watching a TV show
	Playing with toys/items • List preferred toys / items		Outside activities	✓	Inside activities
		✓	Run errands		Socializing
	Interacting with animals (pets)	✓	Snacking, eating		Imaginary play
	Interacting with people • List preferred people		Books		Making lists
			Art	✓	Watching watches airplanes
✓	Going for a walk or run		Balloons		Self-stimulatory
	Wearing jewelry or cosmetics		Free time		Board game
	Completing a job responsibility/list	✓	Structured time		Physical game
	• Preferred computer games/activities: Typer Shark, Fun Time • Social activities: playing simple games (Tic Tac Toe, Trouble board game) • Leisure activities: watching TV with Connor; going on walks List others: Doing simple math problems (single digit); crossing off things from a list when done; erasing the whiteboard				

Areas of Interest

	Animals		Weather		Clothes/fashion
✓	TV program: *SpongeBob*		Toys	✓	Numbers
	Celebrity		Dinosaur		Science
✓	Colors: red is favorite	✓	Math		Shapes
	Movies		Reading		Sports

✓	Song/music genre: hip-hop		Machines	✓	Computers
✓	Places to go: Disneyland	✓	Outdoors		Technology
	Family activities	✓	Transportation: Peterbilt trucks (and logo)		Fantasy
			Tools		Cartoon/anime

Please list the following:

Foods disliked: fruits, vegetables, sweet foods

Noises disliked: any loud, unexpected noise; the air-conditioning hum

Activities disliked: reading, writing, PE, socializing

Places disliked: the gym locker room, crowded hallways

Materials disliked: cotton (scratchy), messy hands

Animals disliked: none

Other dislikes:

Known fears: dark, being alone

Tangible Items

Please list the preferred tangible items, followed by product name/type).

✓	Chips: ANY!		Drinks: soda, milk
✓	Cookies: Oreos, but any		Toys
	Candy		Stickers
	Fruit		Games: Trouble, computer games
✓	Cereal: Honey Nut Cheerios		Meats
	Other: Whiteboards, scented markers, Tic Tac Toe games		

Providing Reinforcement in Inclusive Settings

It is also important to think about how reinforcement can be used in general education settings in nonstigmatizing ways. Because, by definition, each individual chooses his or her own reinforcement, sometimes students might select reinforcement that is not age-appropriate. For example, a 17-year-old student might be very motivated by watching Baby Einstein videos. Or a 6-year-old student might be very motivated to talk about physics. In these types of cases, it's important to provide reinforcement to students, but to do so in a nonstigmatizing manner. How can age-appropriate reinforcement be provided?

- Find private locations at school where students can access noisy or active reinforcement. Students can access these safe locations to engage in activities that would be stigmatizing if done in front of peers. For example,
  - An elementary school student who needs to spin in circles and flap her arms to release energy and relieve stress goes to the nurse's office when needed to engage

in this behavior. If the nurse's office is occupied, she uses the staff bathroom in the school office.

- o A middle school student who loves singing *Little Mermaid* songs as reinforcement is brought to the cafeteria to sing when the cafeteria is empty. When the cafeteria is occupied, she goes to a sports field on campus to sing.
- o A high school student who needs gross motor sensory input as reinforcement and sensory breaks uses a trampoline set up in the weight room. If the weight room is occupied, the trampoline is moved to the coach's office.

- Create safe spaces at school for students who need quiet or alone time reinforcement. Some students need to take breaks, have time to get space from others, or access quiet reinforcement. These are often less stigmatizing because they are quiet and often unobtrusive, but the school needs to provide a safe space that has adult monitoring. For example,

  - o An elementary school student earns the chance to listen to music on her iPod and goes to the library for her earned reinforcement breaks.
  - o A middle school student who masturbates in public is taught to request a personal break and use a private stall in the restroom.
  - o A high school student with emotional regulation difficulties is taught to request a personal break and goes to a teacher who has a prep period to decompress and recompose herself. The teacher on prep is reminded not to interact with the student, but to give her personal space.

In general, remember that delivering reinforcement may bring unusual attention to a student. For example, giving a student a token or something edible will bring attention to the student and might confuse peers. The inclusion facilitator should explain why reinforcement is being provided to a student in a manner that is different from the reinforcement other students receive. This is usually done quickly by simply explaining that everyone is working for something: Some people work for good grades; some people work to feel good about themselves; some people work for money; some people work to make their parents proud. This student is learning about work, so he or she is getting access to something extra, like food or stickers, to help learn about work. And because this is a caring and supportive school, we give students what they need to be successful, and different students will just need different things. Usually, this is easily understood and accepted by peers.

BOX 10.4

Student Choice

Just as a preference assessment was used to determine which items and activities a student finds reinforcing, a similar method could be used to determine which nonstigmatizing spaces a student prefers to use. The inclusion facilitator might find two or three available spaces for safe use of reinforcement, and the student could choose which space he or she feels most comfortable in.

Reinforcement Menus

Once the items, activities, and experiences that are motivating and enjoyable to a student are identified, a reinforcement menu that contains a variety of reinforcements to choose from can be created. Why not just use the same reinforcement, time after time? Because doing so makes that reinforcement lose its power and interest. For example, a young child might beg for pizza for dinner every night. Imagine that the parents concede. Initially, the child will be thrilled—pepperoni pizza every night! But as the weeks and months pass, the child will get tired of pizza and want something else for dinner. Reinforcer menus are like dinner menus: When we plan our dinner or go to a restaurant, there is power and excitement inherent in making a choice of what to eat. After all, variety is the spice of life!

An easy way to create a reinforcer menu is to have a folder or small photo album that contains pictures or descriptions of a student's preferred reinforcers. The student can quickly flip through this book or folder, be reminded of these choices, and select the reinforcer that he or she wants *now*. It is worth repeating that the same student may have different reinforcement preferences on different days, during different activities, or at different times of the day. For students who are not reading, pictures (either photographs, ClipArt, or images found online) can be used to create the reinforcer menu. For students who read, simply writing the choices on a sheet of paper is appropriate.

Case Study: Mr. DeMarco Makes a Reinforcement Menu

Based on his reinforcer assessments for Allison, Mr. DeMarco makes a menu of reinforcing items that she may choose from on a regular basis:

- walk
- use computer
- draw
- go outside
- jump on trampoline
- eat chips
- watch airplanes
- apply hand lotion
- solve single-digit addition problems
- eat cookies
- take shoes off
- listen to music
- erase the board
- drink soda

Then he puts the items into a small picture album that Allison can review before making her choice, as seen in Figure 10.4.

Token Economy Systems

A *token economy system* is the formal term used for a behavior incentive program in which a student earns points or tokens for engaging in specific behaviors, and those tokens or points can be exchanged for a desired reinforcer (Cooper, Heron, & Heward, 2007). For

Figure 10.4 Reinforcer Menu Photo Album

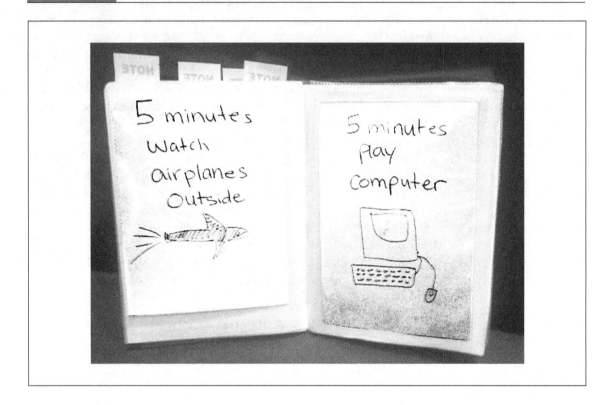

example, a student may earn stars for talking in a quiet voice during class time. Once she has earned five stars, she can engage in a preferred activity such as jumping on the trampoline for 2 minutes.

Here are the basic steps in using a token economy system:

1. Select age-appropriate tokens (e.g., tickets, stickers, plastic chips, coins, tally marks).

2. Identify target behaviors (i.e., the replacement behaviors the student should be learning to use).

3. Select a menu of reinforcers the student can choose from.

4. Establish a ratio of exchange (i.e., will the student earn a token after a specific amount of time? a certain frequency of behaviors?).

5. Assign a price for each menu item (e.g., 5 minutes of computer costs 5 tokens, 2 minutes of computer is 2 tokens; soda is 10 tokens, trampoline time is 5 tokens).

6. Decide if there will be a response cost (i.e., can a student lose tokens?).*

*Remember: Only use a response cost when the value of the item is high and the student has experienced a lot of success over an extended time using the token economy system. Students should always earn significantly more tokens than they lose.

Case Study: Mr. DeMarco Creates a Token Economy System

Using the information gathered regarding Allison's challenging behaviors, replacement behaviors, and reinforcers, Mr. DeMarco creates a token economy system for her.

- *Step 1: Select age-appropriate tokens.* Mr. DeMarco reviews the age-appropriate tokens available for Allison and wants to select a token that is nonstigmatizing, motivating, but also not inherently reinforcing. For example, Allison is really interested in Disney's *The Little Mermaid.* Mr. DeMarco could find an image of Ariel (the mermaid) and use that as a token. However, since Allison loves this image, it acts as a reinforcement (Allison would be happy to look at it). Therefore, Mr. DeMarco realizes this is not an appropriate token. And it's really not age-appropriate anyway! He needs to find a token that is neutral in itself, but that can be exchanged for something that Allison prefers. In this case, Mr. DeMarco decides to use coins, specifically pennies. Many students have wallets and coins, so the use of pennies would not stigmatize Allison.
- *Step 2: Identify target behaviors.* Allison has two challenging behaviors that serve the function of obtaining attention (swearing and scratching). The replacement (target) behaviors include Allison verbally saying, "Come here and talk to me." She has two challenging behaviors that serve the function of communicating a need for a break/ help (threatening and biting). The target behaviors that Allison will earn tokens for are saying, "Come here," and asking for a break/help.
- *Step 3: Select a menu of reinforcers the student can choose from.* Mr. DeMarco previously created a menu for Allison of preferred items that she can select. The menu was placed in a small (4 × 6 inch) photo album. One photograph was placed in each page of the album.
- *Step 4: Establish a ratio of exchange.* Allison will earn two tokens for using the target verbal behaviors "Come here and talk to me," "I need help," and "I need a break." She will also earn one token for each 3-minute period of not engaging in the challenging behaviors (i.e., each 3-minute period without biting, scratching, threatening, or swearing). This ratio is provided to Allison, and her educators, in Box 10.5.
- *Step 5: Assign a price for each menu item.* Mr. DeMarco decides on a price for each item in Allison's reinforcer menu, as seen in Figure 10.5.

BOX 10.5

Token Economy Systems

Behavior	Tokens Earned
Say, "Talk to me" ⇒	2 pennies
Say, "I need a break" ⇒	2 pennies
Say, "I need help" ⇒	2 pennies
3 minutes with no biting, scratching, swearing, threatening ⇒	1 penny

Figure 10.5	Prices for Reinforcer Menu Items

5 min. walk 6 pennies	5 min. singing 6 pennies	5 min. game 6 pennies	5 min. draw 6 pennies
5 min. outside 10 pennies	5 min. trampoline 4 pennies	5 min. computer 6 pennies	8 chips 4 pennies
3 min. watch planes 4 pennies	lotion 2 pennies	4 math problems 2 pennies	2 cookies 8 pennies
5 min. shoes off 3 pennies	5 min. music 5 pennies	erase board 2 pennies	cup of soda 10 pennies

- *Step 6: Decide on a response cost system.* Mr. DeMarco decides to implement the token system for 1 month before considering a response cost. After that month of implementation, he notices how motivated Allison is by the tokens. In fact, she frequently asks for tokens. Given the success of the token economy system, Mr. DeMarco decides to implement a response cost program. He describes to Allison that she may lose pennies for certain behaviors, according to the schedule in Figure 10.6.

Figure 10.6	Response Cost System

Behavior	Pennies Allison pays
Swearing ⇒	2 pennies
Biting self ⇒	1 pennies
Threatening ⇒	3 pennies
Scratching others ⇒	4 pennies

Behavior Support Strategies

A number of specific, effective strategies can be found in the Resources Appendix, including social narratives, power cards, visual schedules, and video self-modeling. Each of these can be easily incorporated into inclusive settings so long as the strategy is age-appropriate for the student. Next, we describe a few additional strategies.

BOX 10.6   *Administrator Insight*

Some behavior support strategies are best applied schoolwide. Resources for schoolwide positive behavioral interventions and supports, including bullying prevention, are available online. The Technical Assistance Center on Positive Behavioral Interventions and Supports publishes research, handbooks, training videos, and many other free resources for K–12 schools at www.pbis.org.

Passes/Break Cards

Often, students need an appropriate means to escape or avoid a difficult situation. A pass can be an effective tool that allows a student to take a break to cool down and recover without resorting to inappropriate or challenging behavior. A teacher can provide a student with a set number of passes for a given day or week, and the student can choose to use them as needed. For example, Andy becomes frustrated and overwhelmed at school. When he feels frustrated or overwhelmed, he throws chairs, pounds on his desk with his fists, or shouts. The team is teaching Andy to identify those feelings before they escalate and allows him five passes per day that he can use at any time, without any question, to remove himself from a situation before it escalates. Andy's pass is seen in Figure 10.7. He is taught to either hand the card to his teacher or simply leave it on his desk and walk out of the room.

Other students may have passes for other reasons. For example, Jason is a student who seems to get lost in the stories in his head. He often appears to be daydreaming and off task. Jason's team created a story pass for him that can be used for 5 minutes at a time, three times a day. Jason was taught to enter the world of his personal stories only when on a pass. Because he subsequently learned to ask to use the restroom as a means to daydream without using a pass, the team also decided to include three bathroom passes per day. Jason's teacher or paraeducator simply initials a box each time Jason requests a restroom or story pass during the day. Figure 10.8 shows this pass. When all of the boxes are initialed, the break is no longer available. Jason is taught to hand this pass card to his teacher to initial before he leaves the room.

Figure 10.7 Break Pass

Students have a predetermined number of passes each day, often 5–10 to use as needed during the day. Each pass can be cut out and given to students at the start of the day to use as needed.

Break Pass	**Break Pass**	**Break Pass**
1. Leave this pass on your desk or give it to your teacher. 2. Go outside or to the "Safe Space" in the gym. 3. Come back to class when you are calm.	1. Leave this pass on your desk or give it to your teacher. 2. Go outside or to the "Safe Space" in the gym. 3. Come back to class when you are calm.	1. Leave this pass on your desk or give it to your teacher. 2. Go outside or to the "Safe Space" in the gym. 3. Come back to class when you are calm.
Break Pass	**Break Pass**	**Break Pass**
1. Leave this pass on your desk or give it to your teacher. 2. Go outside or to the "Safe Space" in the gym. 3. Come back to class when you are calm.	1. Leave this pass on your desk or give it to your teacher. 2. Go outside or to the "Safe Space" in the gym. 3. Come back to class when you are calm.	1. Leave this pass on your desk or give it to your teacher. 2. Go outside or to the "Safe Space" in the gym. 3. Come back to class when you are calm.

Copyright © 2014 by Corwin. All rights reserved. Reprinted from *The Inclusion Toolbox: Strategies and Techniques for All Teachers* by Jennifer A. Kurth and Megan Gross. Thousand Oaks, CA: Corwin, www.corwin.com

Figure 10.8   Story Pass and Bathroom Breaks

These passes can be photocopied, and one card is given to the student per day.

Date:			Date:		
Bathroom Pass 1 ☐	Bathroom Pass 2 ☐	Bathroom Pass 3 ☐	Bathroom Pass 1 ☐	Bathroom Pass 2 ☐	Bathroom Pass 3 ☐
Story Pass 1 ☐	Story Pass 2 ☐	Story Pass 3 ☐	Story Pass 1 ☐	Story Pass 2 ☐	Story Pass 3 ☐

Copyright © 2014 by Corwin. All rights reserved. Reprinted from *The Inclusion Toolbox: Strategies and Techniques for All Teachers* by Jennifer A. Kurth and Megan Gross. Thousand Oaks, CA: Corwin, www.corwin.com

Self-Monitoring

The ultimate goal for all individuals is that we are able to monitor and adjust our own behavior, as needed. Self-monitoring is an effective tool that teaches students to be aware of, and track, their own behavior (Blood et al., 2011). Students are simply taught to either (1) stop and observe their current behavior at a point in time or (2) reflect on their behavior after an activity. For example, during a math class a student is prompted (by an educator or by technology, such as a vibrating watch) to stop every 2 minutes and observe his or her own behavior, or the student can reflect on his or her behavior after math class.

Self-Monitoring During an Activity

The activity is divided into observation periods. For example, a 1-hour math lesson is divided into thirty 2-minute periods. Every 2 minutes, then, the student stops and marks his or her own behavior. In the example seen in Figure 10.9, the a student marks a + if engaged in the target behavior or a − if not engaged in the target behavior.

Figure 10.9   Self-Monitoring During an Activity, Example 1

Instructions: Mark a "+" in the square if you were looking at the teacher. Mark a "−" in the square if you were not looking at the teacher or were talking to your friend.

+	+	−	+	+
−	−	+	−	+
+	−	−	−	+
+	+	+	−	+

Students might also self-monitor during an activity by indicating how many times they engaged in a target activity. This is done by circling the next number each time the behavior occurs. An example is seen in Figure 10.10.

Figure 10.10	Self-Monitoring During an Activity, Example 2

Instructions: Circle the number each time you ask a friend for help during class in the morning (before lunch) and in the afternoon (after lunch).

	Monday	Tuesday	Wednesday	Thursday	Friday
Morning	1 2 3 4 5 6 7 8 9 10	1 2 3 4 5 6 7 8 9 10	1 2 3 4 5 6 7 8 9 10	1 2 3 4 5 6 7 8 9 10	1 2 3 4 5 6 7 8 9 10
Afternoon	1 2 3 4 5 6 7 8 9 10	1 2 3 4 5 6 7 8 9 10	1 2 3 4 5 6 7 8 9 10	1 2 3 4 5 6 7 8 9 10	1 2 3 4 5 6 7 8 9 10

Self-Monitoring After an Activity

Another strategy is to have a student reflect on his or her behaviors after an activity. For example, after a math class a student describes whether he or she engaged in the target behavior. This is illustrated in Figure 10.11.

Figure 10.11	Self-Monitoring After an Activity, Example 1

Instructions: Using a scale of 1–3, rate how well you did in each class.

3 = great

2 = OK

1 = oops

Target	Science	Math	English	History
Wait for teacher to call on you before talking	3	2	2	1
Stay in seat during lecture	2	3	3	3
Take notes during class	1	2	1	2

Students with weaker comprehension skills can simply circle happy or sad faces to reflect on their performance during an activity. An example of this is seen in Figure 10.12.

Figure 10.12	Self-Monitoring After an Activity, Example 2

Instructions: Circle the happy face if you used nice words during class. Circle the sad face if you used mean words when you were talking to your friends in class.

	I used nice words	*I used mean words*
Science	🙂	🙁
PE	🙂	🙁
Math	🙂	🙁
History	🙂	🙁
English	🙂	🙁
Lunch	🙂	🙁
Art	🙂	🙁

Copyright © 2014 by Corwin. All rights reserved. Reprinted from *The Inclusion Toolbox: Strategies and Techniques for All Teachers* by Jennifer A. Kurth and Megan Gross. Thousand Oaks, CA: Corwin, www.corwin.com

Conclusion

This chapter focused on behavioral support strategies that can be implemented in general education settings. We included strategies to share information about student behavior support needs in quick and easy-to-access forms, reinforcement assessment, and a variety of strategies to provide nonstigmatizing reinforcement and self-monitoring. Developing an effective behavior support system for a student requires some trial and error to find a system that works for the student and school staff. Don't be discouraged if your first tool, tokens, or self-monitoring form doesn't work. If you keep fine-tuning the tools you implement, you'll experience success. We believe that when these types of positive behavior strategies are implemented, "behavior" will no longer be a viable excuse to exclude students from inclusive settings.

Please be sure to go to the website (http://www.corwin.com/theinclusiontoolbox) to download the forms and resources from this chapter!

11

Transition Planning

The fewer services your child needs at 21, the better. The more relationships with people without disabilities your child has at 21, the better. Remember, your child is seven going on 21.

—Lou Brown

Preparing our students for new teachers, classrooms, and schools is essential for achieving continued academic success, promoting student social and emotional growth, and building sustainable inclusive education services. Parents, educators, and administrators can work together to prepare resources and plan activities to help all students successfully move to the next teacher or school. This chapter discusses five significant transition periods in a student's school career and highlights ideas and tools to individualize supports so that all students, families, and teachers can start each semester and school year prepared and ready for success. The following transition periods are discussed in chronological order, with the exception of preparing for a new teacher or school, as this happens every academic term for some students:

1. To a new teacher(s) and/or a new school

2. Preschool to elementary school

3. Elementary to middle school

4. Middle to high school

5. Post–high school graduation

❖ Box 11.1   What Does the Research Say?

The Need for Transition Planning

In the *30th Annual Report to Congress on the Implementation of the Individuals with Disabilities Education Act, 2008*, released in December 2011, the U.S. Department of Education provided statistics on high school graduation. In 2005–2006, 56.5% of students with disabilities, 14 to 21 years old, earned a high school diploma. This rate is slightly higher for students receiving special education services for a specific learning disability, 61.6%, and lower for students with intellectual disabilities, 36.7%. Nationally, the average freshman public high school graduation rates, for students who earned a high school diploma in the 2005–2006 school year, were 73.4% (Aud et al., 2012). In addition to lagging behind in high school graduation, students with disabilities struggle to find and maintain competitive employment as adults. In September 2012, the U.S. Department of Labor indicated that only 21.9% of people with disabilities participated in the labor force, compared to 69.3% of people without disabilities (U.S. Department of Labor, 2012).

Focus Areas for Transition Services

As a result of persistent struggles to achieve equality in high school graduation and employment rates for students with disabilities, researchers and educators have proposed schools focus on developing "bridges" for students and families in the transition process. Rusch, Hughes, Agran, Martin, and Johnson (2009) propose transition planning begin in middle school, including teaching students to become self-directed learners; high schools should support students in identifying their interests related to education and employment, ensure students are placed in those settings before high school graduation, and coordinate post–high school support services with families related to education or supported employment. Providing students with instruction in developing self-determination skills (e.g., identifying personal goals; creating, implementing and evaluating plans to achieve goals; engaging in self-reflection) enables students to achieve education and employment goals and has been demonstrated to be an effective model for students across the disability spectrum (Agran, Blanchard, & Wehmeyer, 2000).

Transition and the Least Restrictive Environment

A recent 3-year study of transition-age students in Orange County, California, found that students with severe disabilities, regardless of their IQ or disability labels, were more likely to have integrated, paid employment in their community after high school if they received the majority of their instruction in community-based training, including on-the-job training, and were integrated on a campus (e.g., a college campus) with age-appropriate, nondisabled peers (White & Weiner, 2004). White and Weiner (2004) also note that teacher advocacy for inclusion, initiating community-based training programs on college campuses, and developing jobs for students close to their homes led to a 69.2% employment rate for graduates who were enrolled in a transition program at a local college, compared to a 15% employment rate for students enrolled in a segregated transition program.

Although more research is needed, students who are included in general education classes throughout their school years, receive instruction in self-determination, and are supported by adults with high expectations seem likely to have improved outcomes in adult life (Ryndak, Ward, Alper, Storch, & Montgomery, 2010).

Transitioning to a New Teacher or School

First impressions are important. We believe parents and teachers should play an active role in preparing both the child and the new teacher.

Strategies for Families

Parents can share information with a new teacher and learn about the new teacher's instructional style and classroom in a variety of ways, such as scheduling an in-person meeting, asking to observe the classroom prior to their child's first day, or sharing background information about their child in the form of a letter or presentation. Some parents draft a back-to-school introduction letter each fall and email it to their child's teacher (as seen in Figure 11.1). In this letter they might share information about their child's strengths, unique needs, individualized education program (IEP), and previous successes in school. These introductory letters or emails are also a great way for families to extend an offer to volunteer in classrooms or ask how the teacher prefers to communicate (via scheduled meetings, phone, or email). Other parents have created resource binders or presentations to share with new teachers, paraeducators, and administrators to explain more about their child's disability, specialized health care needs, or learning style.

Figure 11.1	Sample Letter to Teacher from Family

Dear Mrs. Hanson,

Our daughter, Sarah, is in your art class this year. She is very excited to be in your class on Wednesday afternoons and loves to paint, draw, and shape play dough/clay. At the beginning of a new class or school year, we write Sarah's teachers a letter sharing our perspective on her personality, strengths, challenges, and strategies we are currently having success with. We hope this letter will help you get to know Sarah and our family better and be useful to you as you support her in art.

Who Is Sarah?

Sarah is a spunky, kind, and gentle soul. She loves school, shopping, craft projects (especially those involving stickers), Disney movies, dance class, Girl Scouts, and taking pictures on our smartphones. Sarah has a wonderful group of friends from school. Her best friends in Mr. Brown's class are Kylie, Allison, and Paul. Sarah is our oldest child. She has two younger siblings, Mason (third grade) and Zoe (kindergarten). Sarah is healthy and participates in all of our family activities.

Learning Style

Sarah is a visual and hands-on learner. When learning a new skill she'll need to watch you do it, watch her classmates do it, and practice the activity herself with a peer, paraeducator, or you walking her through the steps. After she has completed an activity, she is more likely to remember the steps if she talks about how she made it with a classmate or you. She is able to write simple sentences, 5–7 words long, and reads at the third-grade level. Sarah loves group projects, but she needs to be placed in a group that supports her and understands her so that she actually participates in the project instead of just watching.

Challenges and Strategies

1. Sarah's processing time is slower than that of her peers. She'll need you, a paraeducator, or a peer to check-in with her to make sure she understands directions.
2. Sarah likes to finish what she starts (a little bit of perfectionism passed on by dad). If you are starting on a multi-day project, provide her with a checklist so she knows in advance that you aren't making the finished project in one day and also so she can anticipate when she'll finish.

(Continued)

Figure 11.1 (Continued)

3. Sarah struggles at times with filtering out all of the noise of the classroom and doing her work. It is hard for her to work independently when she is hearing snippets of conversations around the room. She has a pair of earplugs in her backpack and if she looks like she is staring off into space during an independent work time, you can ask if she'd like to use her earplugs today. We do NOT let her use earplugs when we are all talking or someone is giving directions.

Signs of a Rough Day

Sarah has inherited a good dose of stubbornness from both of us, which in addition to her auditory processing challenges can sometimes create the perfect storm. When Sarah is having a hard day (due to frustration, not being able to communicate what she needs, or if she is starting to feel sick), she will not look like her normal perky self. She will not say hello to you or respond to your greetings. She will stare off into space or make comments to peers using a rude tone of voice. Currently we are using this phrase in our house: "It looks like you could use some time to yourself. Would you like to rest in your room or listen to some music?" In Mr. Brown's class he has offered choices such as reading in the bean bag chair, coloring, putting her head down on her desk, or listening to music at her bean bag chair. It is important we offer choices that are appropriate, EASY for her to complete independently, and that allow her some time to herself, such as read a book, look at a magazine, listen to music, or rest in her room. For us, it has been easiest to think about what we would want if we are having a hard day and then combining that with our knowledge of what we know Sarah enjoys. Often she is able to return to an activity in 10–20 minutes. If Sarah is unable to return to classwork, let her know that you understand she needs time to herself and that you'll send home some work to finish up at home when she is feeling better. This is not meant to be a punishment, but we all have to catch up on our work when we take some time off.

Sarah's iPad

Sarah has an iPad in her backpack that she uses at school to access textbooks (via www.bookshare .org), write, create visual presentations, or play games during free choice. She has a collection of art apps that she enjoys tinkering with. If you have any favorite apps that you think would benefit Sarah to use in class or at home, please let us know and we'll get them. Sarah loves her iPad and is happy to work on adapted work using it.

Our Contact Info

Email is the best way to get in touch with us as we check it often when we are at work. We can also be reached on our cell phones.
Matt: dad@email.com
Carly: mom@email.com

We look forward to Sarah starting your class next week and are so excited she has an opportunity to have art in her school day. Please let us know if we can support you in any way (supplies, volunteers, or more strategies to support Sarah).

Thank you for your time.

Sincerely,

Matt and Carly Jones

Strategies for Educators

The inclusion facilitator and previous general education teacher(s) should take some time to talk with the new teacher(s) about the incoming student, preferably before the student arrives. This will help the teacher prepare for the new student and pave the way for a smooth transition. School staff can complete a transition student profile, which details for the new teacher or school information about family needs, student learning style, strengths, and interests (see Figure 11.3). This tool aids the new teacher in learning much of the essential information about a student that isn't always readily understood from an IEP.

Prior to meeting the new teacher, it is also important for parents and teachers to talk about the new teacher with the student. Visiting a new teacher and school before the transition is helpful for students. Teachers or families may want to take pictures of the new classroom, school, and teacher to help the student develop familiarity with the new environment. Some students may need additional support after the first day in learning the routines and expectations of the new teacher. Developing a student's understanding and independence with school routines and expectations may be facilitated by extra support time from a paraeducator or inclusion specialist for the first few weeks of a school year, tailoring visual schedules to include important new routines, or creating personalized "rule books" using photos and short captions with photo albums or computer software so students can review and practice expected classroom behavior.

Older students should be encouraged and supported in participating in transition-related activities. Some of our former middle school students created PowerPoint presentations and shared these with their new teachers and other IEP team members at a new school to help new staff get to know their strengths, interests, needs, and goals. Other students may be equally empowered by leading a transition meeting in the spring or participating in a student-centered planning meeting, discussed in detail in Chapter 6.

BOX 11.2

Strategies to Support Students in Almost Every Transition

- Talk about it and be positive.
- Take pictures or short videos of new people and places.
- Share information about your child or student's strengths, interests, and needs.
- Implement routines and expectations in advance (at school and at home).
- Ensure familiar supplies and support strategies are in place on the first day (e.g., visual schedule, positive behavior support plan, fidgets, planned breaks)

Strategies for Administrators

Administrators, related service personnel, and school office staff also play a significant role in transition, as they may be the first school employees a family has contact with at a school site. School teams should establish general procedures for supporting new students with IEPs so team members can begin communicating and gathering necessary information and supports as soon as possible. A simple process, like the one in Figure 11.2, can assist school staff in understanding and effectively participating in their role in transitioning a new student. Administrators can also allocate release time for teachers to observe new students coming from an in-district school and meet with previous or future teachers to help develop effective transition plans.

Figure 11.2 Enrolling New Students With IEPs

1. The school registrar reviews enrollment information with families; if special education services or an IEP is denoted on paperwork, the registrar asks the family if they can provide the school with a copy of paperwork to expedite scheduling and acquiring appropriate supports. The registrar also informs the family that the principal/counselor or the psychologist/inclusion facilitator will contact them to meet prior to the first day of school. *If this is the day before school starts, see if an informal meeting can be set up immediately.

2. The principal, the counselor, the school psychologist, or the inclusion facilitator meets informally with the family to learn about their student and school history. He or she reviews the IEP with the family and clarifies any information that is unclear. He or she provides a campus tour and answers questions parents might have about the new school.

3. After meeting with the family, this person schedules the student in appropriate class(es) and reviews the IEP for classroom supports and any related services to schedule. He or she makes arrangements for the student to have a peer buddy (elementary) or a peer helper/counselor (secondary) meet with the student on the first day of school to help acclimate to the new campus.

Transitioning to Elementary School

Every transition period in a student's life is significant; however, the transition from preschool to elementary school is important for schools and districts as the process is one of the first experiences a family may have with a school and this first impression may set the tone for the next several years. While this may seem like a lot of pressure to place on a limited period, if schools work to understand family concerns and needs surrounding transition and set up collaborative teams to support both school staff and families, the transition is likely to be successful.

For families, transitioning to elementary school is a departure from a family-centered, center or home-based service system to a student-centered, school-based service system. When surveyed, families of children with and without disabilities entering kindergarten are concerned about a child's separation from family, starting a new school, getting along with peers, and getting along with the teacher. However, families of children with disabilities report significantly more concerns about a child's communication skills, academic readiness, and potential behavior problems in kindergarten (McIntyre et al., 2010). Schools can begin to address these parent concerns prior to the transition meeting through collaboration time between preschool and elementary staff who can meet to observe each other's classrooms and discuss ways to embed important skills for kindergarten readiness in the preschool curriculum. In our experience, when teachers are given this initial collaboration time to prepare for student transitions, teachers are likely to develop a relationship with each other and communicate throughout the school year, outside of formal collaboration time. This relationship between the giving and receiving school staff provides a better understanding of the curriculum and services in each school setting and enables staff to brainstorm or work through challenges prior to transition meetings.

Prior to a transition meeting, school teams and/or families can complete a new student information page, which will help the new teacher(s) and IEP team at the elementary school get to know the student. Transition activities such as observations, school open house, or important school dates such as kindergarten registration should be shared with families in advance. Some families may need accommodations to participate in back-to-school activities, such as a smaller group open house or a 1:1 meeting with a new teacher in a quiet classroom, and the IEP team should assist the family in making these arrangements to help prepare the student and family for the new school.

> **BOX 11.3**
>
> ### Administrator Insight
>
> Consider coordinating with administrators at your feeder schools for release time for key teachers to meet and discuss curriculum and high-need students transitioning in the fall. This helps general education teachers and counselors schedule students in classes that will be a good fit academically, socially, and emotionally. This can also be a good time for teachers to discuss ways to better align curriculum and skills being taught across the grade levels. In addition, it helps prevent at-risk kids, lacking formal 504 plans or IEPs, from falling through the cracks.

Case Study: Mr. DeMarco Prepares for Incoming Kindergartners

Mr. DeMarco is preparing for incoming kindergarten students at Pine View Elementary. In February he receives a list of incoming students from his district's preschool program. He reviews the list of students and potential support needs and makes arrangements to observe the students in the their preschool or during related service appointments. He coordinates with the preschool IEP team to collect new student information from school staff and parents prior to the transition meetings in May. He reviews the form (see Figure 11.3) he has received from Emily's family and makes notes to inform the family that every classroom has an FM amplification system and all teachers wear microphones to help students hear. He also notes that Emily is a student who will likely need support using the restroom at the beginning of the year and with diaper changes if potty training is not completed over the summer. After reading about the parent's communication concerns, he emails the preschool teacher and the speech therapist to learn more about Emily's current communication abilities and goals. He will share information about how the school team supports inclusion at Pine View Elementary, including in-classroom supports and facilitated playgroups.

Transitioning to Middle School

The transition from elementary to middle school is significant for families because it involves the combination of a dramatic change in the education landscape and the arrival of hormones and adolescence. Students and families who have grown accustomed to developing a relationship with one or two kind and loving elementary school teachers have to learn how to develop relationships with five, six, or seven new middle school teachers. In our experience, this transition also tends to invoke negative memories from parents' experiences in middle school, and this causes a lot of parental anxiety about whether their child will fit in and have someone to eat with at lunch and hang out with at a dance, or concerns about bullying.

A smooth transition from elementary school to middle school requires a significant amount of collaboration and honest communication between special education teachers at both school sites. Middle school special education teachers need to observe incoming students during the late winter or early spring. This assists the middle school teacher in identifying supports a student will need to be successful in middle school and also alert the teacher to potential concerns (e.g., overdependence on a paraeducator or a specialized tool that a student needs that is not currently available at the middle school) that will need to be worked out. During this observation, it is important to schedule time to sit down and talk with the elementary special education teacher to learn more about the student and

| Figure 11.3 | Transition Student Profile (Preschool to Kindergarten) |

Student: <u>Emily A.</u>   Age <u>5</u>   Boy ___ Girl <u>X</u>

Consider a student's interests, academic readiness, behavior, communication skills, and learning style in each box below (as appropriate).

<table>
<tr>
<td>

Strengths and Interests

Circle time: singing or listening to stories; matching tactile letters, categorizing objects. Matches colors. Loves playing in kitchen, with stuffed animals, with friends, Candy Land. Favorite movie is *Tangled.* Loves Disney princesses.

</td>
<td>

Challenges

Learning new skills; initiating independent play or free choice; independent academic work; unable to form letters when writing; very active; learning number sense; needs to have structure and consistent expectations.

</td>
</tr>
<tr>
<td>

Social Connections

Friends coming to kindergarten: Benji, Mason, Bella, Casey (comes to playdates every Friday at our house)
Older brother Paul in second grade

</td>
<td>

Supports Needed to Access General Education

In preschool receives occupational and speech therapy as push-in small group; also one session afterschool private speech therapy. Inclusion specialist provides multisensory tools to engage Emily for academic skills; paraeducator or teacher support in small group settings.

</td>
</tr>
<tr>
<td>

Medical Conditions and Needs

Wears diapers; learning to toilet train.
Low hearing in left ear.
Wears glasses (nearsighted).

</td>
<td>

Parent/Family Support or Concerns

Emily is included in everything we do—we want her to be in a gen ed kindergarten class. Improve communication skills. Consistently use the toilet. All staff know Emily's needs and support her. For her to have friends and be happy.

</td>
</tr>
<tr>
<td>

Antecedents to Challenging Behavior

Behavior = crying or yelling.
Didn't sleep well the night before, unable to communicate her needs with teacher or peer, hungry.

</td>
<td>

Student Preferences/Reinforcers

Loves sticker charts and earning time to play with animals. Looking at books, playground. Loves working with her friends and praise. Loves earning stickers to wear on her shirt. Loves looking at her Disneyland photo album. Anything Disney princess.

</td>
</tr>
</table>

family. It is important to be organized with this precious, invaluable meeting time. The transition student profile (Figure 11.4) is a useful framework for this conversation.

Completing an observation prior to a student's transition meeting will also assist the new special education case manager in developing rapport with the student and his or her family. It is essential for the new teacher to be knowledgeable about courses, campus life, and special education services available in middle school. Remember, many parents are nervous about the transition to middle school because they remember their own trying middle school experiences. Be positive and excited about welcoming their child to middle school. Provide parents with your contact information and an information sheet (Figure 11.5) about what to expect in transitioning from elementary school to middle school. Transition meetings are often fast-paced, and providing parents with these resources helps reduce confusion and establish a trend of positive, open communication with families.

Case Study: Mrs. Kelley Prepares for the Middle School Transition

Mrs. Kelley, an inclusion facilitator from Diablo Creek Middle School, observed Anthony in his fifth-grade classroom and at recess. While talking with his fifth-grade special education teacher, Mr. DeMarco, Mrs. Kelley completed a transition profile. During the conversation, she began thinking about recommendations she would make for Anthony's elective courses. She thinks he will be a star in Mr. Dean's industrial technology course. Mrs. Kelley has learned a thing or two over the years and decided to complete the form on her computer this year so she can save time during the summer when she creates Anthony's student profile for middle school. Mr. DeMarco and Mrs. Kelley also use this time to talk with each other about the upcoming IEP transition meeting, brainstorm ideas with each other about appropriate courses, and discuss the difference in intervention styles between the two schools and recommendations for special education services the following year.

At the transition IEP meeting, Mrs. Kelley is able to offer appropriate, meaningful course recommendations for Anthony's family, since she had an opportunity to observe him in his classroom. She also shares the Transitioning to Middle School handout she has prepared, which provides information about the middle school schedule and answers common parent questions (see Figure 11.5).

Figure 11.4 Transition Student Profile (Older Students)

To: Diablo Creek Middle School   From: Pine View Elementary School

CONFIDENTIAL

Special Education Student Profile for Receiving Special Education Teacher

The purpose of this student profile is to provide the receiving teacher with information that may not be reflected on the student's IEP.

Name of Student: Anthony "Tony" Thomsen

Parent(s) Names:	Relationship:	Best contact:
Sarah Jones and Steve Thomsen	~~married~~/divorced	Mom
Address:	**Home phone number**	
Mom: 1234 Walnut Ave, Our Town, CA	510-123-4567	
email	**Cell phone numbers**	
tonysmom@email.com tonysdad@email.com	Mom: 510-223-5555 Dad: 925-111-2222	

(Continued)

Figure 11.4   (Continued)

Best method of contact : cell or email (mom), email (dad).

IEP Information

Next annual: 10/14
Next triennial: 10/16

Special Education Level of Support

Amount of time in general education (average): 5.5 hours
Activities/classes not in general education: speech therapy (misses computer class)

Purpose of Special Education Support:

Tony has an SLD label: severe dyslexia challenges with written language also. Uses support in reading and writing. Has group paraeducator support and benefits from peer supports. Intervention reading instruction provided.

Special Education Services

Support	Frequency and duration		
Paraeducator Support	Language Arts, Social Studies		
SLP	2 × 30 minutes per week		
OT	NA		
Behavior support	NA		
Adapted PE	NA		
Hearing	NA		
Vision	NA		
Mental health	NA		
Other			
Plan		Yes	No
Emergency health care plan			X
Behavior support plan			X
Positive behavior intervention plan			X

Other release of information contacts: none

	Administered at school?	
Medications	*Yes*	*No*
Inhaler for asthma	X	

Academics

Reading level/skills	Math level/skills	Writing level/skills
Likes reading comic books and enjoys listening to small-group novel read aloud (*The Cay*, *The Lightning Thief*). Struggles with decoding polysyllabic words. Needs: vocabulary instruction, decoding, visuals for comprehension support, audio books. **Grade equivalent:** 3.5	Strength area! Enjoying geometry unit. Knows addition, multiplication, and division facts. Algebra 1–2 step problems are mastered. Can be at the top of the class, but doesn't always do his homework. Needs: support for HW completion; word problems need to be read aloud and highlighted. **Grade equivalent:** 6.0	Can be challenging, especially with academic writing. Writes simple structure sentences. Able to write one paragraph independently. Enjoys computers and is using word prediction software. Sends home an email to his mom every day with para support. **Grade equivalent:** 3.0

Describe how student is included in activities (academic, social, field trips):

Tony participates in all class activities. Fifth-grade teacher uses peer tutors during language arts and social studies; peer and Tony take turns reading text. Provide adapted novels or texts for independent reading. Tony has a classroom job: videographer. He videos class projects/presentations, interviews students, and uploads videos to class's YouTube page. This is a big motivator for Tony. He needs to know what the expectations and consequences are at all times—transitions are difficult, and teacher uses a timer for him.

Describe any pull-out from general education or periods of special education classes:

Reading intervention: small group taught by reading specialist. 40 minutes of reading curriculum and 20 minutes of preview and review vocabulary terms and novels from fifth-grade class.

Grading

Language Arts grade is based on adapted novels and texts. Math is graded in standard fashion.

Alternate special education curricula/materials used and levels:

Curricula/materials	In use	Most recent level
Saxon Math	No	
Edmark Reading	No	
Language!	No	
Reading Milestones	No	
Read Naturally	No	
Corrective Reading Decoding	Yes	Book B
Corrective Reading Comprehension	Yes	Book B
Other	SIPPS	Lesson 40

(Continued)

Figure 11.4   (Continued)

Technology Used

Describe the student's use of technology, including but not limited to assistive technology, such as keyboarding, software used at your school that the student likes, preferred websites:

Proficient with video camera, school editing software (Apple iMovie), uploading to YouTube. Proficient with Co-Writer.

Bookshare account set up and in use. Tony has a flash drive with his novels loaded on so he can read at home.

DragonSpeak: piloting this spring; unsure of success.

Student Strengths and Interests

Sports: very active at recess playing soccer, basketball. Favorite football team is 49ers. He is a good advocate for himself once he is comfortable with you. Quick learner with technology. Loves learning new things with school video camera. Cooking projects in living history days were a hit. Has two little sisters and is a good peer tutor with younger students. Likes to be read aloud to. Likes listening to music—into classic rock.

Behavior Concerns

Behaviors that interfere with learning and antecedents:

Typical preteen boy stuff: hooded sweatshirts covering head and eyes on early mornings, sneaking in his headphones during silent reading time. Only concern are transitions: Tony can struggle with moving on from activities he is engaged in.

Interventions and strategies:

Teacher uses a timer for all students; Tony is the timekeeper.

Preferred reinforcers (tangible, activities, breaks):

Teacher uses classwide behavior support system: Tony's on a team and earns points for following class rules, displaying positive character, etc. Tony really likes this and has become more a part of his classroom this year.

Useful Strategies

Describe useful strategies and other information that is not always specified on the IEP, such as visual schedules/checklists, bathroom information, behavior, types of breaks, sensory strategies, reinforcers that work, allergies or food restrictions, etc.

Visual organizers for comprehension (fifth-grade teacher will give template); graphic organizers for writing (uses the hamburger template now) and is more likely to use if other classmates do, too; use of timer for transitions.

Social Information

Names of friends/peers:

Sam, Harry, Chuck, Mason, Jennie, and Elizabeth

Preferred activities for noninstructional time (breaks, lunch, choice, games):

Sports, video projects, setting up for assemblies (loves helping custodian), loves to play Apples to Apples on rainy day recess.

Special areas of interest and activities outside of school:

Plays baseball. Rides a skateboard. Enjoys going to his dad's house on weekends because they do a lot of outdoor activities (camping).

Other things/your personal goals for this student that aren't reflected in an IEP:

Increase confidence sharing ideas in class, especially after a reading activity. Pursue opportunities to increase his technology skills. Participate more in school campus activities, develop more leadership skills. Go to college and be an amazing success!

Figure 11.5	Info Sheet on Transitioning From Elementary School to Middle School

Classes

Sixth graders have little choice when it comes to classes. The main choice to make is between taking 6 or 7 periods during the day. Most students with IEPs require 7 periods, which includes a study skills class.

Electives

Sixth graders take a four-quarter cluster of elective courses that introduce them to the various types of electives they will be able to choose from in the future. They will include at least health and three of the following:

Industrial Technology—Students explore how technology and industrial arts come together.

Computers—Students learn about the many ways computers can help us.

Health—Students learn healthy habits and health information.

Home Economics—Students learn about cooking, cleaning, and organization of the home.

Art Survey—Students learn the basics of different forms of art (watercolor, painting, etc.).

Study Skills—Students with IEPs are encouraged to take part in a yearlong class that focuses on study skills. This class is open to all students at Diablo Creek and includes, but is not limited to, the following instruction:

1. Daily living skills
2. Social/interpersonal skills
3. Organization
4. Study skills

The Schedule

Middle school is broken into separate periods with students changing classroom and teacher each period. After a few weeks most sixth graders learn to enjoy the idea of periods, as it allows for movement each hour of the day. Students begin to learn how to deal with a longer workday as they go through their secondary education.

Paraeducator Support

Paraeducator support is given to any student that needs it (per IEP). However, due to the middle school schedule, different paraeducators will work with your child during different periods. Developing and improving independence is a high priority for students, and we must begin to fade aide support where we can. These times might include elective classes or PE depending on your student's needs. Feel assured that aide support will be given when needed and agreed on in an IEP.

Social Life

Middle school is a place and time when students desire independent socialization with peers. This can be a hard time for young adults who see themselves on the fringe of their social world. Clubs, dances, sports, or even in the hallway are all places students socialize in middle school. Your child will be encouraged to join a club and, if needed, be supported in that club. Your child will also be more than welcome at dances throughout the year.

Commonly Asked Questions

1. **Will my child be in general education classes? How will the class be adapted to fit what he or she needs?** Beginning in middle school, the inclusion staff focuses increasingly on modifications and accommodations your child may need to successfully participate in and learn in academic classes. Generally, a modification is a significant change to the course curriculum,

(Continued)

Figure 11.5   (Continued)

while an accommodation is a change that does not alter the content, such as extra time or audiobooks. The differences between each and the needs of your student will be more fully explained at the individual transition meeting.

2. **How will my child be graded?** If a child is taking a modified class, the student's grade is generally on an A, B, C, Pass, Fail basis.

3. **How will my child keep track of all those classes?** Students in middle school use planners to track their assignments, due dates, and tests. Students will spend the first part of sixth grade learning to use their planners and enter information as accurately and independently as possible. Many teachers have email accounts or school voice mail systems and are more than willing to speak with you about any questions or concerns you have. As always, your inclusion specialist is likely the best place to start for questions about classes and can be reached by email or voice mail.

4. **What if my child and I can't keep up with the homework?** Many parents find that the homework load and academic rigor of classes is significantly higher than in elementary school. Not to worry; this is true for all students. Practice making short- and long-term plans to finish homework and assignments with your child, and use the planner. It is a good idea to buy folders for each class to keep work and assignments in. It is also a good idea to have a dedicated homework folder, with one section of "work to do" and another of "work to turn in." This way your student will know where to look for homework to do and where to find assignments that need to be submitted.

5. **Will my child get a locker?** All students will be assigned a locker. If your child is unable to use a traditional locker (for PE or classes), you may use a key lock with permission from the inclusion teacher and middle school staff.

Transitioning to High School

Preparing a student for life after high school is a key responsibility for inclusion facilitators working in secondary schools. Students with IEPs must have an individual transition plan (ITP) developed no later than their 16th birthday (Individuals with Disabilities Education Improvement Act [IDEA] 2004). The ITP provides a roadmap for students to reach their postsecondary goals in the areas of education/training, employment, and independent living. Although not all high school students have a formalized transition plan such as an ITP, planning and preparing for life after high school is addressed through general education resources such as counseling guidance for course selection and meeting course requirements for enrolling in colleges or universities, resources available in a career center, internship opportunities, standardized testing for college admissions (e.g., SAT or ACT), or vocational courses. Inclusion facilitators are critical links for students and their families to these activities and assisting them in navigating the resources available in the community.

Inclusive Community-Based Instruction

High schools are diverse environments with an incredible variety of academic classes and instructional opportunities that exist both inside and outside the traditional classroom walls. With a little creativity, inclusion facilitators can utilize existing courses or school environments to develop community-based instruction activities that enable students to address domestic or vocational skills in an inclusive setting.

Course Catalog

Inclusion facilitators should become familiar with the various academic and elective courses available during the academic year. Many electives, such as home economics, health, nutrition, and cooking, naturally lend themselves to students learning essential life skills. Technology-based elective courses, with adaptations as necessary, can support students in learning to use computers or mobile devices for work, communication, and entertainment. Cross-age tutoring electives may be appropriate for students with interest in a helping profession or with goals to learn how to navigate the community with greater independence. Many schools also have a teacher assistant (TA) course, whereby students can apply to support their favorite teacher, or work in the office, the kitchen, or the library, for one period a day.

For students with more significant support needs, it is critical that inclusion in these elective courses is supported with either instructional adaptations or support from peers or educators. While these classes may be fun, with a little bit of planning they can also enable students to learn functional skills, such as cooking, cleaning, reading, writing, following multistep directions, or communication skills.

Developing Instructional Opportunities

Some students have instructional needs or interests that do not fit in neatly with the current course offerings at a high school. With a little creativity, however, inclusion facilitators can carve out inclusive opportunities for community-based instruction. Here are some strategies for developing these opportunities:

- *Utilize student interests to create new opportunities.* For example, a student who loves playing basketball might be an assistant for the basketball coach and learn how to become a team manager or athletic assistant.
- *Schedule students with faculty who share interests.* Teachers sometimes need to have processing time, just as much as students do. If you think a student might be a good match for a class, club, or extracurricular activity that a particular faculty member advises, find a way for the student to connect with that teacher on a regular basis. This might mean that a student takes a physical education course with the teacher who is also a baseball coach or enrolls in the homeroom class of the robotics club teacher. This will allow the student and teacher to get to know one another and develop a relationship that might lead to opportunities such as working out with the baseball team or being a TA for an advanced robotics class.
- *Develop internships and volunteer positions.* Many high school students pursue volunteer activities or internships during a work-study period or outside of the school day. Design internships in the school cafeteria for students to learn cooking skills, internships in the school finance office for students to practice counting and money math skills, or volunteer positions in the local library.
- *Remember, it's never too early to start.* Many people think of community-based instruction and planning for adult life as a task that begins in high school. However, with inclusive schooling, a wide range of opportunities exists for students to develop vocational skills that are age-appropriate and inclusive. Young children can take lunch counts to the office, be a "line leader," be responsible for cleaning up their workspace, and so on. These are all valuable vocational learning skills for all students, and inclusive settings happen to offer a lot of such opportunities.

What Does IDEA Say?

In addition to designing meaningful instruction, we also have federal guidelines to address postsecondary goals in IEPs. The 2004 revisions to the federal Individuals with Disabilities Education Improvement Act clarified required components and services related to transition. The law requires all IEP teams to do the following:

- Create an ITP that is in effect by the time the student is 16 years old.
- Invite the student to attend his or her IEP meeting and participate in developing the transition plan.
- Develop measurable postsecondary goals, based on appropriate assessments, addressing education/training, employment, and independent living skills (if appropriate). These goals must be updated annually.
- Develop annual goals in the areas of education/training, employment, and independent living skills (if appropriate) to help a student reach postsecondary goals.
- Provide transition services such as instruction, community experiences, related services, and any skills related to independent living.
- Identify a course of study during high school that is multiyear and will assist the student in achieving postsecondary goals.
- Receive parent consent to invite and coordinate services with agencies who provide postsecondary services.

A student's ITP must be updated annually alongside his or her IEP.

Developing an ITP

ITPs are developed based on appropriate assessments of students' skills and needs in the domains of education/training, employment, and independent living skills. Special education teachers are skilled at assessment, yet the assessments involved for an ITP do not follow the usual evaluation protocol of a standardized assessment such as the Woodcock Johnson III Test of Achievement. To develop a meaningful ITP, these assessments are likely to be interviews with a student and his or her family, interest inventories, or surveys, in addition to standardized assessments such as a high school exit exam or an academic achievement test. Some middle schools and high schools incorporate interest inventories or student interviews in their general education curriculum as a way to assist students in preparing a course of study for high school. Information gathered from these general education assessments are important to include in an ITP and assist an inclusion facilitator in efficiently preparing for the meeting. Resources for obtaining free transition assessments for students with all ability levels are included in the Resources Appendix.

Case Study: Mrs. Simpson Completes a Transition Interview

Mrs. Simpson is meeting with Jeff, a 10th grader, to help him prepare for his IEP meeting and to develop his ITP. Together they complete the transition interview questions (see Figure 11.6). Mrs. Simpson drafts ITP goals based on Jeff's answers, her observations of Jeff over the course of the school year, and a conversation with his parents about his future plans. The team agrees to the following goals for Jeff's ITP:

Postsecondary Goals

1. *Education/training:* Upon high school completion, Jeff will attend a 4-year university to pursue a degree in science.

2. *Employment:* Upon high school completion, Jeff will work part-time while attending university; after receiving his degree, he will obtain full-time employment in the science/biotechnology field.

3. *Independent living:* Upon completion of high school, Jeff will live in student housing while attending college.

Annual Goals

1. *Education/training:* By next year, given access to the Internet, Jeff will research the admissions requirements for a minimum of three universities he is interested in attending and identify high school course requirements, components of the personal statement, number of recommendation letters required, and annual tuition (including housing).

2. *Employment:* By next year, given access to the Internet and following school Career Day, Jeff will research two to three science careers and identify the degree requirements, typical job responsibilities and duties, and average salary for a person in that position.

3. *Independent living:* By next year, given access to and instruction in how to use an alarm clock, Jeff will wake up for school independently and arrive to school and be in his first-period class before the final warning bell.

Figure 11.6	Postsecondary Transition Interview Questions

Education/Training

1. After you finish high school, you can do more school. Some people go to college; some go to vocational school to learn how to do a job. What type of school would you be interested in?

   I want to go to a 4-year university. Maybe USC or UC Berkeley.

2. What would you be interested in learning more about?

   Maybe science. I've been really into the projects we've been doing in science about alternative energy. I also love art.

Employment

3. Have you ever had a job (taking care of a dog, taking out the garbage, etc.)?

   I take care of my dog at home. But I've also had an afterschool job part-time helping out with afterschool programs through Parks and Rec. I also help coach the summer football camp.

4. What kind of job would you like to have after high school? Part-time, full-time?

   Full-time job. I guess if I don't make it to the NFL, it'd be cool to have a job where I could use my art or something in science. Not sure what type of job I'd like to have.

5. Will you need special training for that job/skills?

   I have to think of a job first!

(Continued)

Figure 11.6	(Continued)

Independent Living

6. Where would you like to live after high school (dorm, apartment, house, etc.)? Would you like to live by yourself or with others?

   Dorm! Then apartment with friends.

7. Do you have chores at home now? (Identify type and accountability for completing.)

   We're all responsible for cleaning our own rooms. I also help my mom out with babysitting my little sister and driving my mom around town to run errands.

8. Do you cook at home?

   Sometimes. Nothing fancy. My dad is teaching me how to BBQ and I learned a lot of stuff in Foods class in middle school.

9. How do you get to places you need to go? After high school, what type of transportation do you think you would use to get around town (bus, car, subway, bicycle, etc.)?

   My mom has to wake me up for school every morning because I don't have an alarm clock. I just got my driver's license and am saving money for a car. I hope to have a car when I go to college. But I also ride my bike or take the bus with friends.

10. Do you have any experience saving your money or making a budget to buy the stuff you want? What experience do you have banking?

    Well, I don't usually have any money, because I go out to lunch a lot, but I'm trying to save some money right now for a car. My mom helped me make a budget and I have to set aside $20 a week.

11. What do you like to do for fun or in your spare time?

    Play football, draw, listen to music, hang out with friends.

Educating Parents

After years of navigating the IEP process, many parents are surprised to learn a new acronym, ITP, when their child enters high school. Inclusion facilitators play an important role in educating parents about the ITP process and assisting them in connecting with coordinating agencies (e.g., vocational rehabilitation) and services in the community. Many states have transition planning guides available through the state department of education that teachers can use to help educate parents about developing an ITP and preparing for a student's life after high school. It is helpful for inclusion facilitators to develop a brief resource sheet for parents highlighting local agencies and contact information. Some schools and states set aside financial resources to provide staffing hours to create tools related to transition and organizing transition services such as supported employment, internships, or college tours. Check with your school or local special education agency to see if these tools exist in your district before reinventing it.

Case Study: Mrs. Simpson Reviews Coordinating Agency Information

At the start of every school year, Mrs. Simpson updates the contact information for her parent transition checklist (see Figure 11.7). She develops this resource as part of her responsibilities as her school's work and internship coordinator for students with IEPs. She then provides these resources to all of the inclusion facilitators in her district. At annual IEP/ITP meetings, Mrs. Simpson reviews this checklist with her students' families and provides guidance on accessing services from each agency. When she met with Jeff's family for his IEP/ITP meeting, they reviewed the checklist together and identified completed actions and discussed what action the team needed to take in the current school year.

Figure 11.7	Parent Transition Checklist

Transition Case Manager:	Mrs. Simpson	**Phone #:** 925-555-1177
Regional Center Case Manager:	N/A	**Phone #:**
Vocational Rehabilitation Case Manager:	Mr. Jones	**Phone #:** 510-123-4567

Action	Contact agency	Date
1. Obtain Social Security Number	Social Security Office 5500 Apple Dr. Our Town, CA 91234 510-234-5678	Birth
2. Obtain state identification card	DMV 1111 Jefferson Blvd. Our Town, CA 91235 510-345-6789 *make online appointment	12/2010
3. Obtain bus pass	Our Town Transportation www.ourtowntt.bus	12/2010
4. Register for Selective Service	Post Office 5510 Apple Dr. Our Town, CA 91234 *form in lobby	
5. Register to vote	School, Library, City Hall School voter registration Sept. 15–30	

6. Apply for entitlement programs
  a. Supplemental Security Income (SSI)
  b. Medical assistance
	Social Security Office
	5500 Apple Dr.
	Our Town, CA 91234
	510-234-5678	

7. Attend parent meeting on transition	Our Town SELPA 1000 Education Dr. Our Town, CA 91235 Fall: Nov. 3 (Constitution Room) Spring: TBD	
8. Vocational assessments (formal and informal)	Mrs. Simpson	10/2014

(Continued)

Figure 11.7 (Continued)

9. Develop transition plan	Mrs. Simpson and IEP Team	11/2014
10. Make application to Department of Rehabilitation (DVR)	DVR 999 Government Blvd. Regional, CA 92345 *online application: www.dvr.regional	
11. Contact regional center (if applicable)	Local Regional Center Susan Smith 510-554-1111 333 East Road Our Town, CA 91234 *www.regionalcenter.ourtown	
12. Develop long-term plan for financial support and advocacy	ARC, People First, private attorney	
13. Apply for guardianship or conservatorship	ARC, private attorney	
14. Obtain information and visit potential residential placements	Local regional center	
15. Obtain information and visit potential vocational placements	Local regional center, DVR	
16. Review and update transition plan prior to graduation	Regional center, DVR, parent, student, teacher, etc.	
17. Placement upon graduation	Regional center, DVR	
18. Vocational resume (employment/ work experience history)	Mrs. Simpson	
19. Leisure skill connections	Parks Department, Special Olympics, People First, etc. Our Town Rec Center and Guide www.recnow.ourtown	

Implementing ITPs

Successfully implementing and monitoring transition goals in inclusive classrooms requires knowledge of general education activities related to transition (e.g., career day, SAT/ACT testing calendar, guidance counselor planning), prescheduling students in meaningful courses, and collaborating with general education teachers and counselors to address students' transition needs. In addition, it requires ongoing communication between home and school, as some transition needs, such as applying for Supplemental Security Income, require parental support or involvement. An IEP goal matrix can be a helpful tool for planning how to address a student's ITP goals in the context of his or her course schedule and schoolwide activities.

Case Study: Mrs. Simpson Plans for Jeff's ITP Goals

Following Jeff's IEP/ITP meeting, Mrs. Simpson develops a goal matrix to identify when and how Jeff and the team are going to address his ITP goals (see Figure 11.8). Mrs. Simpson begins by reviewing the school calendar and recording the general education activities that are going to occur during the school year, including a college fair, career day, and appointments with the guidance counselor available to all students. In addition, Harvard High School requires all students to compile a portfolio of their work related to academics, assessments, and personal planning for life after high school. The school provides two block periods each school year for students to use the library and to obtain help from mentor teachers to complete research and document their progress. In addition, Jeff is also enrolled in a daily Study Skills class, where he is able to receive additional tutoring in his academic subjects and also complete assessments related to college and career interests. This year, Mrs. Simpson is also collaborating with an English teacher and a counselor to plan a tour of the local university. Finally, Mrs. Simpson coordinated with Jeff's parents to support his independent living skills goal of using his alarm clock. Mrs. Simpson and Jeff reviewed the instructions during a study skills class one day, and she will check in with his mom once a week for the first month to monitor his progress with using the alarm clock. In addition, Mrs. Simpson will closely monitor attendance records to ensure Jeff is improving in this area of independent living.

Figure 11.8 ITP Goal Matrix

Activity/Time/ Class	ITP: Education/ Training Research three universities, ID course requirements, application needs, tuition	ITP: Employment Research two to three science jobs, degree required, job responsibilities, salary	ITP: Independent Living Use alarm clock, to wake up and arrive to school on time
College Fair October	X		
Career Day March		X	
Freshman Portfolio Workdays	X	X	
College Tour November	X	X if able to tour science lab	
Appointment with guidance counselor	X	X	X
Study Skills class	X	X	X
Appointment with special education teacher	X	X	X
Communication between home and school	X	X	X

Conclusion

Preparing students for school and life transitions is a collaborative, ongoing process for families and school staff. IEP teams from preschool to high school benefit from using tools such as observation, student profiles, interviews, and sharing information among team members to assist a student and his or her family in transitioning to a new classroom or schools.

Please be sure to go to the website (http://www.corwin.com/theinclusiontoolbox) to download the forms and resources from this chapter!

PART III

Expanding Inclusive Practices

Part III of this book focuses on the strategies and activities that may be completed to maintain, strengthen, and expand existing inclusive programs. Typically, these activities are used in the years following initial implementation of inclusion, when the inclusion facilitator is comfortable with and confident in his or her role and has established collaborative relationships at his or her school site.

Starting an inclusive program is a lot of work, and we don't expect everyone to complete every important piece right away. We believe that the strategies and activities in Part III are important, but not critical, to inclusive practices. We suggest that inclusion facilitators who are interested in enhancing, and expanding, their inclusive program focus on this part of the book.

12

Co-Teaching

As you navigate through the rest of your life, be open to collaboration. Other people and other people's ideas are often better than your own. Find a group of people who challenge and inspire you, spend a lot of time with them, and it will change your life.

—Amy Poehler

When students with disabilities are included in general education classrooms on a consistent basis, energy that was previously spent on advocacy for one student or a small group of students to be included can now be spent on implementing supports all students can benefit from. Co-teaching harnesses the resources of both special and general education to create classrooms where two educators work together to plan, instruct, and assess students in a class. In this chapter we share strategies for selecting a co-teaching partner, co-teaching on a daily basis, and resolving conflict in the co-taught classroom.

Co-Teaching Models

Murawski (2012) describes five commonly used approaches to providing instruction in a co-taught classroom. Some teaching partners may find they prefer certain models or discover they rotate through many of the models each week depending on the nature of the content they are delivering. No model is the "right" way to implement co-teaching, but each model offers ways for both teachers to provide meaningful instruction in the classroom. Regardless of which model you implement, it is important to always be aware of student groupings and ensure that both teachers actively teach all students, which prevents students being grouped by ability or disability label, or creating an environment where there is a classroom within a classroom.

❖ Box 12.1   What Does the Research Say?

Roots of Co-teaching

Co-teaching can trace its roots back to the 1950s in general education, when general education teachers worked together, providing "expert" lectures to large groups of students. The concept of team teaching has continued to evolve since that time and has taken different forms, such as two elementary teachers sharing a room with a divider or two secondary teachers teaming to provide content, such as a history and English teaching together (Friend, Cook, Hurley-Chamberlain, & Shamberger, 2010). The No Child Left Behind Act of 2001 and the reauthorization of the Individuals with Disabilities Education Improvement Act of 2004, with their mandates for students to receive instruction from highly qualified teachers in the least restrictive environment, have also contributed to a renewed interest in co-teaching as a model for providing special education services to students with disabilities in general education settings (Murawski & Dieker, 2004; Villa, Thousand, & Nevin, 2013).

Types of Co-teaching

Co-teaching can take many forms, depending on the preferences of the co-teachers, the needs of the students, and the design of the lesson. Murawski (2012) defines five types of co-teaching (presented in the main text of this chapter). There are many different ways that co-teachers can teach and work in a classroom together. Teacher teams might alternate between these different types of teaching, and take on different roles within the types of teaching, on different days or with different lessons.

Benefits to Teachers

When teachers are interviewed about their beliefs related to co-teaching, many report positive outcomes such as gaining increased content area knowledge or skills in classroom management and developing adaptations (Austin, 2001). Administrator support of co-teaching is essential due to the time needed for collaborative planning.

Benefits to Students

In co-taught classrooms, teachers report using differentiated instruction and assessment, including more hands-on activities and visual supports such as graphic organizers (Cramer, Liston, Nevin, & Thousand, 2010). Teachers also report being able to better meet the needs of all learners in a co-taught classroom (Downing & Peckham-Hardin, 2008).

One Teaches, One Supports

In this model, one teacher assumes primary responsibility for delivering instruction to the whole class, while the other teacher may perform supportive functions such as observing students, facilitating behavior management, handling class materials, setting up the classroom activity, or walking around the classroom and assisting students who may need support to participate in the activity. This is a common approach to implement when teachers are new to co-teaching. As teaching partners become more comfortable with each other, it is a good idea to incorporate other models into instructional delivery as this ensures that each teaching partner assumes the role of "teacher" on a regular basis and appropriately utilizes each teacher's knowledge and skills.

Station Teaching

In this approach, the class is divided into heterogeneous groups that rotate through multiple instructional centers. Each teacher facilitates instruction at a center or may rotate to all stations to instruct students in the activities. The use of centers-based instruction is common in elementary classrooms but can also be adapted for secondary classroom instruction, such as during science labs or writer's workshop.

Parallel Teaching

In this model, each teacher provides instruction to half the class. Both groups may work together inside the same classroom or in different settings. Students may be working on the same assignment with each teacher, or each teacher may be facilitating different activities; for example, one teacher may be supporting a group of students who are starting a homework assignment, while the other teacher is providing a review lesson.

Team Teaching

In this approach, both teachers are in front of the classroom providing the content of the lesson. Teachers may implement this in a variety of ways, depending on the content and their interests. One teacher may lecture while another teacher models note taking or demonstrates examples, or the teachers may divide the lesson with one teacher instructing for the first half of class and the other teacher doing so for the second half. Of all the co-teaching models, team teaching is perhaps the most advanced, as it requires teaching partners to utilize each other's strengths fluidly and for both teachers to be knowledgeable and comfortable with the content.

Alternate Teaching

In this approach, one teacher works with a majority of the class while the other teacher provides instruction, such as preteaching, review, or enrichment, to a smaller group of students. The large group is not engaged in new instruction, so students in the small group can return to the large group when finished.

Starting a Co-Teaching Relationship

If you're interested in co-teaching at your school, take some time to develop relationships with general education teachers by providing support to students in classes, and assess what is needed (training, planning time, schedule changes) to effectively implement co-teaching at your school. Then work with your administrator to garner support for the model before taking the next steps in finding a partner and planning your new class together.

Finding an Interested Ally

Co-teaching is sometimes referred to as a "professional marriage" as it requires constant communication, negotiation, and the commitment of two teachers to be successful (Murawski & Dieker, 2008). Ideally, you will have an opportunity to select your own co-teaching partner. If this is the case, consider approaching a teacher who you feel aligns with your values, teaching style, and interests. This is a teacher you should have some prior experience working with (e.g., as members of the same individualized education program (IEP) team, on a school or grade-level committee) or a teacher who enthusiastically includes students with disabilities in his or her classroom. Talk with the teacher about your interest in co-teaching and providing supports to all students in a particular class and find out if he or she might also be interested in pursuing a team approach to teaching. Identify what each of you would need to make co-teaching a reality for the next semester or school year. Be honest with each other and consider starting small, co-teaching maybe for 45 minutes a day in an elementary school or for one section of a class each day at the secondary level, so you can be successful.

Before you begin teaching together, it is important to meet to discuss your ideas and concerns about co-teaching and then plan what and how you are going to teach. Villa et al. (2013) have developed a set of guiding questions for co-teaching partners to consider related to the following:

- personal strengths and concerns about co-teaching
- rules for operating as a team
- logistics of co-teaching setup and administrative duties
- instruction
- communication
- managing student behavior
- evaluation

For each of these topic areas, consider questions related to who, what, when, where, and how. For example, who will be responsible for planning content? How will we adapt materials to ensure all students can access the curriculum?

Finding Planning Time

We recommend setting up a regular weekly meeting time with your partner throughout the school year. You might be lucky and have a common prep period that you can use, or you may have to be creative and carve out time before or after school or meet once a week for lunch. Regular meetings allow co-teachers to communicate, share ideas and strategies, and plan on a regular basis. If your administrator is supportive and resources are available for substitutes, consider requesting release time once or twice a year, and use that time to create a lesson planning guide for several units, identify routine activities and different co-teaching models to use to present content, and establish timelines for developing lesson materials and assessments.

Case Study: Mrs. Simpson and Mr. Reynolds Co-Teach Algebra 1

Last year, Mrs. Simpson provided daily, push-in support to students in Mr. Reynolds's Algebra 1 class. Mrs. Simpson usually observed while Mr. Reynolds taught the class. She would also take notes on lecture days and rove around the room to support students with their homework during independent work time. Mrs. Simpson felt comfortable doing this, as it had been several years since she was in a math class and she hadn't previously worked with Mr. Reynolds. At the end of the school year, the two teachers made plans to work together again in the fall. Mr. Reynolds asked Mrs. Simpson to consider having a more active role in content area teaching, which made her feel excited and nervous. In August, the two teachers met and determined that they would use a combination of co-teaching models. They would take turns being in front of the whole class, with Mr. Reynolds providing introductory lessons and Mrs. Simpson leading daily reviews. In addition, they would spend 2 days a week using parallel teaching, both leading a different group in homework and review exercises. Mr. Reynolds and Mrs. Simpson also requested from their principal a half-day of release time so they could create a semester-long calendar of instructional topics and identify any possible adaptations students would need to access the curriculum. Throughout the semester the two teachers worked well together and did a daily check-in at the beginning of the period and checkout at the end of the period to quickly plan for instruction or troubleshooting, as they did not share common planning time.

Day-to-Day Implementation of Co-Teaching

Co-teaching on a daily basis requires ongoing communication and coordination. Our lives at work and home are busy, so it is important for co-teachers to maximize their planning time, respect each other's time by being responsible and reliable, and demonstrate patience when things don't work according to plan.

Deciding on Teaching Arrangements

We recognize that it is highly unlikely for most co-teaching partners to have planned every detail of each lesson together, so we recommend teachers begin with working together to plan for class routines. Consider identifying which co-teaching models you will use to provide instruction on a weekly basis and within classroom routines that occur during the beginning, middle, and end of class. Both teachers should have teaching and lesson preparation responsibilities each week and not always perform the same role in the classroom.

In new co-teaching relationships there is a tendency to rely on the "one teach, one support" model of co-teaching, with the general education teacher being solely responsible for content and the special education teacher modifying materials and providing supports to a few students on a regular basis. This situation almost naturally occurs, as general education teachers tend to be experts in the content while special education teachers are experts in strategies and adaptations. While this model may utilize both teachers' strengths, it does not help either teacher stretch and gain new skills. Student outcomes are likely to improve if a variety of co-teaching and instructional approaches are used in the classroom (Murawski & Dieker, 2008). As co-teaching partners, discuss ways in which both teachers can present content, regardless of who is the content "expert." One way to do this is to begin with having one teacher teach the big ideas and the other teacher be responsible for leading review lessons, leading guided practice, or overseeing independent practice (Brown Beyers, Howerter, & Morgan, 2013). This will help the teacher with less content knowledge increase her or his familiarity with the content while still providing meaningful instruction in the classroom. General education teaching partners can help their special education partners take on more of the content delivery role through sharing content-specific resources, providing encouragement, and preparing content lessons in advance so teaching partners have a chance to review and adapt as needed.

BOX 12.2   Tech Byte

Lesson planning in the "cloud" allows co-teaching partners to share ideas and lessons from anywhere with internet access. Tools such as Dropbox (www.dropbox.com) and Google Drive (drive.google.com) allow teachers to share documents, spreadsheets, and presentation files, for free! Evernote (www.evernote.com) allows teachers to digitally store favorite websites notes, videos, images, and files, with a searchable database to help you find your content. Teaching partners can share select folders or resources.

Collaborative Planning

Finding a regular time to lesson plan with your co-teacher is important and necessary for a lasting co-teaching relationship. Common planning time is often filled with department or schoolwide obligations, so co-teachers should consider what planning can be completed independently and digitally in order to maximize face-to-face meeting time. One strategy is to divide lesson planning, with one teacher mapping out a week's lessons and then emailing the draft plans to the other teacher to review and then add activities, identify adaptations that may be needed, and suggest student-specific goals (Villa et al., 2013). When this process is complete online, teachers can meet in person to discuss the lessons, divide preparation and teaching responsibilities, and plan for specific student needs. Figure 12.1 shows an example lesson plan co-teaching teams could use to collaboratively plan lessons. For additional lesson planning templates, see the Resources Appendix.

BOX 12.3   *Administrator Insight*

Administrator support of co-teaching is essential to its success. In addition to providing common planning time for co-teachers, administrators are in a unique position to help teachers build their capacity for co-teaching. Often, time is set aside only for lesson planning, and important conversations about co-teachers' roles and expectations are forgotten until challenges arise. Meet with co-teachers and assist them in developing a framework for what co-teaching looks and feels like, for both teachers and students at your school.

When evaluating lesson plans and strategies, we suggest partners keep the following question posed by Murawski (2012, p. 8) readily available: "How is what we are doing together substantively different, and better for students, than what one of us would do alone?" If our lesson plans are not different when teaching together, then we likely aren't fully capitalizing on the resources and capacity both teachers bring to the classroom on a daily basis, and our students are missing out on the opportunity for dynamic and varied classroom instruction. If teaching partners agree to consider this question at the beginning of the semester, it might also help them negotiate changes to lesson plans with each other later on when there are disagreements about instruction.

Case Study: Mr. DeMarco Collaboratively Plans a First-Grade Math Lesson

Mr. DeMarco co-teaches a first-grade math class with Mrs. Penn. At the end of each week, she sends him a draft of the lesson calendar for the upcoming week. Since both teachers have a copy of the curriculum and the digital resources, Mrs. Penn identifies which topic the class will cover each day, but does not identify the standards or lesson objectives, as this is included in the curriculum materials both teachers review prior to their lesson planning meeting. Mr. DeMarco then reviews Mrs. Penn's draft and adds ideas for activities, co-teaching strategies, and any adaptations that might be needed to support specific-student goals. The teachers eat lunch together on Friday and discuss their plan for math class for the next week. On Monday, they check in with each other at the end of recess to make any final adjustments to the plans for the week.

Figure 12.1	Co-Teaching Lesson Planning

Week of February 16th

Day	Lesson (main ideas/goals)	Activities and co-teaching model	Materials and adaptations/student-specific goals	Notes and reminders
Monday	Practicing addition facts to 20	1. "I have, who has" facts game (team) 2. Large group practices math facts; small group for enrichment (alternative teaching)	Game cards Worksheet (WS) 12-1 James and Pam work with facts to 10 Jesse's WS adapted for counting with pictures	District benchmark assessment next week! Collect Jesse's behavior data.
Tuesday	Fact families	1. Linking cubes (team) 2. Independent practice (both teachers circulate)	WS 12-2 James and Pam work with facts to 10 Jesse: counting mats for independent work time and write numbers	
Wednesday	Using addition to subtract	Whole-group video model (1 teach; 1 support)	WS 12-3 James and Pam practice fact families more during independent work time Jesse: use objects to model adding	
Thursday	Subtraction facts	Ten frames mat (parallel)	WS 12-4 Jesse: count out markers for demonstration; count 10 frames peer buddy; records and writes number sentence	
Friday	Spiral review	Fun Friday centers (station)	Math game boards, dice, clipboards, math craft	Mrs. Penn supports Jesse's group; Mr. DeMarco circulates around class

Plans for Problem Solving

Co-teaching can be an incredible experience, but it can also be challenging and messy. Although conflict naturally occurs in personal relationships, dealing with conflict at work, especially in a classroom setting with a colleague, is hard. Before we engage in conflict resolution with our co-teaching colleague, we often find ourselves engaging in a "vent and reflect" process with our trusted mentors or colleagues. This is not an official collaborative problem-solving strategy, but something that works for us in our line of work. First, we allow ourselves a few moments to explain the situation and vent. Then we often remark, "Maybe I should just go back to my little island (i.e., classroom) and teach by myself. It would be far easier." At this point in time our trusted friend usually concurs that "Yes, it would be easier to teach by ourselves, but . . ." and it's the "but" that gets us every time. When we remind ourselves of the reasons for co-teaching and the opportunities for learning and inclusion that our students may otherwise not have, we are ready to engage in problem solving.

Resolving conflict with a co-teacher requires both teachers to try to remove concerns that might be clouded by ego and instead identify the problem, potential barriers, and possible solutions that would resolve the problem and ultimately have the greatest benefit for the students. If you're unable to resolve a conflict with your teaching partner, it is a good idea to seek out assistance from an administrator who may be better suited to facilitating a conversation between you and your partner and support you in resolving the conflict.

Conclusion

Co-teaching requires communication, patience, flexibility, and a commitment between two teachers to function as a cohesive team in their instruction and management of their classroom. If your school has a solid foundation for including students with disabilities already in place, we feel that this can be a great strategy to implement to increase support services and access to differentiated curriculum for all students.

> Please be sure to go to the website (http://www.corwin.com/theinclusiontoolbox) to download the forms and resources from this chapter!

13

Peer Supports

Docemur docendo—He who teaches, learns

Inclusive schools are rich in natural supports for students with disabilities. Peers, in particular, are powerful and effective natural supports in these settings. This chapter outlines a number of strategies for implementing and maintaining peer support programs in inclusive settings.

❖ Box 13.1   What Does the Research Say?

Many schools are embracing the use of peer supports as effective, natural supports to help students with disabilities succeed and participate in general education (Carter, Cushing, Clark, & Kennedy, 2005). The benefits of peer supports are numerous, including higher levels of social interaction (Carter, Hughes, Guth, & Copeland, 2005), contact with the general education curriculum (Carter, Cushing, et al., 2005), and as alternatives to reliance on paraeducators (Carter, O'Rourke, Sisco, & Pelsue, 2009).

Benefits to Peers

Peer supports (peer tutors and cross-age tutors) report learning about people with disabilities, having higher expectations of peers with disabilities, developing friendships with peers with disabilities, and enjoying the experience of tutoring a peer (Copeland et al., 2004).

Benefits to Tutees

Tutees, or students with disabilities, benefit from peer supports in many ways, particularly in increased social interactions and increased functional academic skills (Copeland et al., 2004), and have improved access to the general education curriculum (Cushing, Clark, Carter, & Kennedy, 2003).

What Are Peer Supports?

Peer supports, who can be cross-age tutors or peer tutors, are students who provide academic, communication, and social support to students with disabilities in general education settings. Peer supports are actively involved in the classroom, working side by side with a student with a disability in all class activities. Peer supports might read to a student, act as a scribe, provide adapted materials, provide prompts to a student, model and facilitate communication and social interactions (when appropriate), and attend special events such as field trips. Peer supports do not replace a teacher or act as a disciplinarian; the role of the general education teacher is still important. Peer supports can come primarily from two groups: Cross-age tutors are generally older than the tutee, and peer tutors are generally about the same age as the tutee.

BOX 13.2

Reflections From Peer Supporters

I have become confident in tutoring and helping other students. I have also noticed that . . . it pays off in different areas. This year, I have become a lot better in being myself around my classmates I don't know or just met, instead of shy like I have always been. I can stand up in front of my class, and present something how I would in front of family or friends. . . . I look at myself now and know that I am different, and I have my share of thanks to give to peer tutoring. (C. S., eighth-grade peer tutor)

    Being a peer tutor has had a huge impact on my perception of people with disabilities. Through this course I've learned that people with disabilities are just as capable as everyone else when it comes to school work. I've also learned that people with disabilities don't need to be waited on hand and foot. They're independent, capable, and extremely intelligent people! (E.Y., ninth-grade peer tutor)

Cross-Age Tutors

Cross-age tutoring is most common in elementary schools. A cross-age tutor may be an older student attending the same elementary school or a middle or high school student who comes to the elementary school to provide tutoring to a student in an elementary classroom. In some instances, teachers of young children work with the teacher of older students to set up a classwide cross-age tutoring program. For example, Mrs. Johnson, a kindergarten teacher, and Mrs. Kirby, a fifth-grade teacher, schedule time once per week for all of the fifth-grade students to read to the kindergarten students. While this approach is common and beneficial to all students, cross-age tutoring is focused more specifically on students with disabilities. A tutor is assigned to assist a student with disabilities in a specific activity during the school day.

    A cross-age tutoring program, then, generally requires collaboration between teachers at elementary and secondary schools. An elementary school teacher can initiate this by seeing if the neighborhood secondary school (middle or high school) has a cross-age program already in place. If so, the elementary teacher simply needs to communicate with the teacher in charge of cross-age tutors at the secondary school and let that teacher know she is interested in having a cross-age tutor. If no cross-age tutoring program exists at the secondary school, then the elementary school teacher needs to work with the secondary school to develop one. While this may seem like a daunting task, it is often easier than one might expect. This is because most secondary schools already have elective class periods in place whereby students can elect to be assistants one class period per day (e.g., working in the library, taking notes or materials from the office to classrooms, copying materials, sorting mail). Therefore, there is very likely already a pool of potential cross-age tutors. Finally, if you are in a situation in which there are no assistants or cross-age tutors, you need to work with the secondary school to develop a one-credit tutoring class (how to do this will be outlined in the next section: Peer Tutors).

Who can be a cross-age tutor? The simple answer is anyone. Research has documented that students who are struggling academically themselves might benefit a great deal from being tutors. Students who are interested in helping careers, including becoming special education teachers, would also make great cross-age tutors. In addition, students with disabilities can be cross-age tutors themselves. This can provide a great boost to self-esteem and a chance to practice communication and academic skills in different environments.

Setting up a cross-age tutoring program requires a series of steps, including recruiting students, providing information and training to cross-age tutors, obtaining parent permission for their child to be a cross-age tutor, and, if needed, to travel to an elementary school, and matching cross-age tutors with students. Next we present two case studies, which further explain how to establish a cross-age tutoring program.

Case Study: Harvard High School Cross-Age Tutoring Program

Recruiting Tutors

Ms. Leopald, the school counselor at Harvard High School, coordinates the cross-age tutoring program. Each year, she recruits students to be cross-age tutors for the following school year so that students will have the opportunity to sign up for the course before the school year begins. Recruitment can take place by nomination (i.e., asking teachers to nominate cross-age tutors), by inviting specific students to enroll, and through flyers. Ms. Leopald decides to recruit with flyers, which she sends out to all students (see Figure 13.1).

Figure 13.1 Cross-Age Tutor Interest Survey

Name: _____ Grade (next year):_____

Do you like working with younger students? Do you enjoy teaching children? Would you be interested in being a cross-age tutor, working with an elementary school student one class period per day for a semester? ( ) Yes ( ) No

If yes, describe why you would like to be a cross-age tutor:

Have you ever taught or played with a child who has a disability?

What days/times after school, before school, or during lunch are you available for a cross-age tutoring information session in the next two weeks?

Please return this to Ms. Leopald in the office by November 15.

Cross-Age Tutoring Information and Training Sessions

Once students have indicated an interest in signing up to be cross-age tutors, Ms. Leopald meets with them to provide more information and enrolment permission forms. She informs students that there will be three to four training sessions. The training sessions will cover important topics such as information on various disabilities, inclusion, prompting, reinforcement, strategies to model and facilitate communication and socialization, problem solving (e.g., what to do if the student has a seizure), and working with teachers and paraeducators. The first information session meets during lunch. Students bring their lunches, and Ms. Leopald provides some popcorn. At the meeting, she describes cross-age tutoring. An agenda, such as that in Figure 13.2, is used to guide her discussion.

Additional meetings may be scheduled, as necessary, to provide more training and practice with various instructional methods, such as prompting students, maintaining confidentiality, and problem solving.

Cross-Age Tutoring Permission (With Travel From Another School)

Before students can enroll in the course, parents must approve their child's enrollment. Ms. Leopald develops a permission form, as seen in Figure 13.3, for students who will travel to an elementary school from Harvard High School.

Figure 13.2   Cross-Age Tutoring Information Meeting Agenda

1. Cross-age tutor elective course
    a. What is a cross-age tutor?
    b. What will I do as a cross-age tutor? What do teachers and paraeducators do when I'm a cross-age tutor?
    c. What are the assignments I need to do for this class?
        i. Attendance
        ii. Journal writing
        iii. Unit assignments
        iv. Final project
2. What is inclusion?
3. Expectations
    a. Behavior and attitudes
    b. Role models
    c. Ways to provide support
    d. Confidentiality (privacy)
4. Forms to complete
    a. Parent permission slips
    b. Information sheet

Copyright © 2014 by Corwin. All rights reserved. Reprinted from *The Inclusion Toolbox: Strategies and Techniques for All Teachers* by Jennifer A. Kurth and Megan Gross. Thousand Oaks, CA: Corwin, www.corwin.com

Figure 13.3	Parent Permission Form for Cross-Age Tutors, Example 1

Dear Parent or Guardian,

Your son/daughter (<u>Robert</u>) has expressed an interest in being a cross-age tutor. I would like to notify you that your child has been accepted into this program and, with your permission, hope they will join the Cross-Age Tutoring Program.

As a cross-age tutor, your child will assist elementary school students with disabilities at (<u>Pine View Elementary School at 1948 Apple Lane</u>). The duties of a cross-age tutor include:

- teach students with disabilities academic skills, such as reading, writing, or math
- provide role models for students with disabilities and facilitate social interactions
- provide role models for behavior
- increase awareness and sensitivity about disability and inclusive education
- learn skills in mentoring, teaching, and disability awareness

Cross-age tutors will travel to <u>Pine View Elementary School (6 blocks from Harvard)</u> for one class period per week during Fall or Spring semester. Cross-age tutors will complete journals and assignments throughout the semester. If you have questions about the cross-age tutoring program, please call <u>Ms. Leopald at 123-456-7890</u> or come by Harvard High School's office.

_____ I hereby give permission for my child (<u>name</u>) to enroll in the Cross-Age Tutoring Program for one period per day during:

_____ Fall semester _____ Spring semester

_____ I allow my child to walk to Pine View Elementary School:

_____ With other cross-age tutors _____ With adult supervision

_____ I do not give permission for my child (<u>name</u>) to enroll in the Cross-Age Tutoring Program at this time.

Cross-Age Tutoring Information Sheet

Finally, once students have been selected, parent permission has been granted, and cross-age tutors have received information and training, it is time to match cross-age tutors with students! Ideally, tutors and students will be matched based on mutual interests, the strengths of the tutor, and the availability of the tutor. Ms. Leopald uses a survey, as seen in Figure 13.4, to determine the strengths and preferences of each tutor; she then works with Mr. DeMarco at Pine View Elementary School to match tutors and tutees. Ms. Leopald provides Mr. DeMarco with a weekly attendance sheet, and students are required to check in at the school office at Pine View upon arrival and departure. Ms. Leopald, Mr. DeMarco, and the general education teachers where tutors are placed communicate via email to ensure the program runs smoothly throughout the year.

Case Study: Pine View Elementary Cross-Age Tutoring

In situations where cross-age tutoring is not possible (e.g., schools are not within walking distance, no cross-age tutoring program can be developed at a secondary school), older elementary students can be recruited to be cross-age tutors for younger children with disabilities. In this instance, the teacher of the older student must give permission for the student to leave his or her class and be a cross-age tutor for a set

Figure 13.4   Cross-Age Tutor Survey

1. What age of students do you prefer to work with ( ) K–2nd grade ( ) 3rd–5th grade
2. What areas/activities would you feel most comfortable teaching?
3. What areas/activities would you NOT feel comfortable teaching?
4. What periods are you available to cross-age tutor?
5. What are your hobbies?

Copyright © 2014 by Corwin. All rights reserved. Reprinted from *The Inclusion Toolbox: Strategies and Techniques for All Teachers* by Jennifer A. Kurth and Megan Gross. Thousand Oaks, CA: Corwin, www.corwin.com

amount of time each week, and parents must also give permission. In addition to the recruitment and informational tools Ms. Leopald uses, Mr. DeMarco, the inclusion facilitator at Pine View, has developed a permission form for older elementary students to be cross-age tutors for younger elementary-aged students, as seen in Figure 13.5.

Once Mr. DeMarco has received parent and teacher permission, he matches elementary students with primary student tutees. In addition to considering common interests of the students, he often tries to match older students with tutoring students in classrooms of their former teachers, as this reduces the amount of time it takes for a tutor to feel comfortable working in a classroom.

Figure 13.5   Parent Permission Form for Cross-Age Tutors, Example 2

Dear Parent or Guardian,

Your son/daughter (<u>Chelsea</u>) has been nominated by his/her teacher to be a cross-age tutor. I would like to notify you that your child has been accepted into this program and, with your permission, hope they will join the Cross-Age Tutoring Program.

As a cross-age tutor, your child will assist younger students with disabilities. The duties of a cross-age tutor include:

- teach academic skills, such as reading, writing, or math
- provide role models for students with disabilities and facilitate social interactions
- provide role models for behavior
- increase awareness and sensitivity about disability and inclusive education
- learn skills in mentoring, teaching, and disability awareness

As a cross-age tutor, you child will be excused from (<u>Art</u>) once per week to work with a child in (<u>first grade</u>). If you have questions about the cross-age tutoring program, please call Mr. DeMarco at 123-456-7890.

_____ I hereby give permission for my child (<u>name</u>) to enroll in the Cross-Age Tutoring Program for one hour per week.

_____ I do not give permission for my child (<u>name</u>) to enroll in the Cross-Age Tutoring Program at this time.

BOX 13.3   Tech Byte

Remembering to provide reinforcement or specific feedback is often difficult for many of us; peers who have less experience with instruction might find this especially difficult. The i-Prompt app can be down-loaded for free for this purpose. The teacher can type in what a peer tutor should do (e.g., "gather data," "provide reinforcement"). The phrase the teacher typed in will scroll across the screen on a given time schedule, providing the peer supporter with a visual (and silent) reminder that he or she should say or do something.

Peer Tutors

Peer tutors typically work as tutors at their own school, with students who have disabilities and are about the same age as them. Peer tutors, like cross-age tutors, generally sign up to be peer tutors as an elective class. Setting up a peer tutoring program requires a series of steps, much like cross-age tutoring. These steps include developing a one-credit elective class, recruiting students, providing information and training to peer tutors, and matching peer tutors with students who have disabilities.

Developing a Peer Tutoring Elective Course

A peer tutoring elective course is created following the same process as developing any new course in a district. Before you begin the process of establishing a new course, ask your school counselor or administrator for a list of all district-approved courses, not just the courses currently being taught. In our experiences, we have found previously adopted tutoring courses which have not been offered for a variety of reasons, such as lack of personnel time, the teacher who created the course accepted a different position, or school staff simply being unaware the course existed as an option. If the class does not exist, then it will be necessary to collaborate with district and school personnel to create a new class. Typically, a peer tutoring course is set up as a one-credit elective. Depending on the school district, this process may be completed over the course of one summer or may be an ongoing process over the course of an entire school year. While you are in the process of establishing a formal course, your administrator may allow you to recruit and train peer tutors using an elective course such as Teaching Assistants (TAs). A creative solution such as providing peer support trainings to student TAs enables teachers to establish a peer support program quickly and will likely help the teacher recruit the necessary students to establish a new class.

BOX 13.4   *Administrator Insight*

When establishing a new peer tutoring course, give faculty and students an opportunity to participate in training. This may be meeting with a local school with an established peer tutoring program to obtain start-up guidance or a regional training. Showcase the work of peer tutors at faculty and parent–teacher association meetings, and don't forget the end-of-term pizza party to reward students' hard work!

Case Study: Developing a Peer Tutoring Course at Harvard High School

After utilizing student teaching assistants as informal peer supports for a few years, Mrs. Simpson approached her principal about creating a peer tutoring course, which would enable students to receive transcript recognition and provide an opportunity for a formal training program. As part of the course approval process, Mrs. Simpson created a course description for the school registration catalog and an outline of the course program, as seen in Figure 13.6. The course information was also shared with prospective students.

Figure 13.6	Peer Tutoring Course Information

Course Description

This course is designed for students who have a strong interest in and enthusiasm for helping others. Tutors may support students in general education classes (one period per day) or in our afterschool homework club (5 hours per week). Tutors will receive training before they are matched with a tutee. Tutors are required to attend four meetings each semester with the peer tutoring coordinator, in addition to completing a reflective weekly journal and semester project.

Target Students

Tutors: Students of all ability levels and backgrounds. Priority will be given to students who are below proficient and could also benefit from participating in a class twice a day, as both a student and a tutor (e.g., 10th-grade student is assigned as a tutor for a student with a disability in a U.S. History class, so he or she would participate in a U.S. History class twice a day).

Tutees: Students with disabilities, students in intervention and support classes. (Students may also request a tutor in the afterschool program if they have a grade of a C or below in a class.)

Training

Students will participate in two training sessions each semester (for a total of 8 hours). This will be divided into two half-day training sessions to occur during school hours (one during the first full week of school, one after Progress Report 1).

Students will be given training in the following areas:

1. Tutoring strategies
2. Communication and problem-solving skills
3. Ability awareness

In addition, tutors will meet with the coordinator four times a semester (lunchtime meetings) to debrief tutoring sessions, problem-solve with other tutors, and learn new skills and strategies.

Course Requirements

Students will receive credit in each of the following areas for this course:

1. Attendance
2. Weekly reflective journal

3. Participation in lunchtime meetings (four times each semester)

4. Semester project

Students will NOT be able to be a peer tutor if they do not attend and participate in the training sessions.

Copyright © 2014 by Corwin. All rights reserved. Reprinted from *The Inclusion Toolbox: Strategies and Techniques for All Teachers* by Jennifer A. Kurth and Megan Gross. Thousand Oaks, CA: Corwin, www.corwin.com

Recruiting Peer Tutors

Recruiting peer tutors can be done with the same methods as recruiting cross-age tutors using flyers, posters, announcements, discussions in faculty meetings, and even in PTA newsletters. Who can be a peer tutor? Any student who shows interest can be a peer tutor. Some schools, such as Harvard High School, give preference to students who are below proficient in state testing; others require peer tutors to maintain a certain grade point average; and some schools require that students have good school attendance. Certainly, a number of factors can be considered when recruiting and selecting peer tutors, and these will vary by student population, school needs, and student interest in the peer tutor program. The resources listed on our book's companion website have fantastic strategies for recruiting peer tutors; the websites and books are absolutely worth investigating if you are planning a peer tutoring course.

Providing Information and Training to Peer Tutors

As was true with cross-age tutors, peer tutors need information on disabilities, inclusion, prompting, reinforcement, strategies to model and facilitate communication and socialization, collaborating with teachers and paraeducators, and problem solving. Peer tutoring training typically takes place over several days and may include role-playing, watching videos, reading case studies, and engaging in group discussions. The inclusion facilitator and/or a coordinator of the peer tutor program will likely be involved in these trainings.

Matching Tutors and Tutees

Tutors and tutees should once again be matched based on preferences, areas of strength, and mutual student interest in working together. Practical considerations, such as course schedules, also need to be considered. The coordinator of the peer tutoring program may complete this process; however, a team effort might be most effective. That is, various teachers, school counselors, and even administrators can provide input about individual students, review peer tutor applications, and match students.

Case Study: Harvard High School Peer Tutor Survey

The peer tutoring coordinators at Harvard High School created a peer tutor survey, shown in Figures 13.7 and 13.8, which is used to match students with and without disabilities in the program. Peer tutors and tutees (students with disabilities) both complete the survey. The first version of the survey is for peer tutors (Figure 13.7), and the next version is for the tutees (students with disabilities), which they complete with support, as necessary, from family, teachers, and friends.

Figure 13.7   Peer Tutor Survey

Name: _____ Grade: _____
Periods that I am NOT available: _____
Hobbies:

_____   _____

_____   _____

My favorites . . . (books, movies, TV shows, music, sports teams)

Something unique about me that would help me relate to a peer (for example, sibling has a disability, family has moved a lot, parents are divorced, languages I speak):

_____

_____

_____

An area in which I do not think I could support someone in at this time:

_____

_____

_____

Academic strengths and academic challenges:

Source: Adapted from tool created by Cara Messmore and Megan Gross (2009).

Figure 13.8   Tutee Survey

Name: _____ Grade: _____
Hobbies:

_____   _____

_____   _____

My favorites . . . (books, movies, TV shows, music, sports teams)

_____

Something unique about me that would help me relate to a peer tutor (for example, family has moved a lot, parents are divorced, languages I speak):

_____

_____

_____

A class/area that I would most like a peer tutor for is/are:

_____

_____

_____

A class/area that I would not want a peer tutor for is/are:

_____

_____

_____

Academic strengths and academic challenges:

_____

_____

_____

Source: Adapted from tool created by Cara Messmore and Megan Gross (2009).

Conclusion

Peer supports are an excellent way to provide all students with an opportunity to access and engage with the general education curriculum and develop positive peer relationships. Additional resources for developing cross-age and peer tutoring programs are provided in the Resources Appendix. These resources provide great sample training lessons and course syllabi.

Please be sure to go to the website (http://www.corwin.com/theinclusiontoolbox) to download the forms and resources from this chapter!

14

Student-Led IEPs

The greatest lesson learned from the civil rights movement is that the moment you let others speak for you, you lose.

—Ed Roberts, Autistic Self-Advocacy Network

Self-determination is being increasingly recognized as an important skill and outcome in the life of a student with disabilities. For too long, professionals and caretakers have made decisions for people with disabilities. Self-determination means, simply, that people (including people with disabilities) have control over what happens in their own lives. It involves skills such as setting goals and learning how to follow through to make those goals a reality. Certainly, self-determination is something that all humans are working on each day, and the degree of self-determination a person has depends on her or his age. In this chapter, we consider two aspects of self-determination that the inclusion facilitator can focus on in the school setting: student-led individualized education programs (IEPs) and ability awareness.

Rationales for Student-Led IEPs

Legal

The Individuals with Disabilities Education Improvement Act (IDEA, 2004) requires that students participate in the IEP "whenever appropriate." Students must be invited to the meeting whenever postsecondary goals are to be considered or when they reach age of majority (in most states, 18 years old). In sum, IDEA advocates for the student's participation and presence on the IEP team.

> ### ❖ Box 14.1   What Does the Research Say?
>
> Traditionally, an IEP meeting consists of adults talking about students. Sometimes students are invited to attend the meeting. Yet the IEP is for and about the student, therefore it should reflect the student's input. Furthermore, when leading their own IEP, students learn more about their disability, strengths and needs, and how to advocate for themselves (Barrie & McDonald, 2002). Student-led IEPs occur when a student takes an active and leading role in an IEP meeting, identifying strengths, needs, and preferences; developing goals; and monitoring progress (Eisenman, Chamberlin, & McGahee-Kovac, 2005). A growing body of research indicates a number of positive outcomes associated with student-led IEPs, including benefits to students directly and to other team members as well.
>
> #### Benefits to Students
>
> A number of positive outcomes are associated with student participation and leadership in their IEP meetings, regardless of student age or disability label (Test et al., 2004). Specifically, participation in meetings is associated with improved academic outcomes for elementary school students (Barnard-Brak & Lechtenberger, 2010), more active involvement in the IEP (Danneker & Bottge, 2009; Martin et al., 2006), greater motivation to achieve transition goals (Benz, Lindstrom, & Yovanoff, 2000), improved self-determination skills (Williams-Diehm, Wehmeyer, Palmer, Soukup, & Garner, 2008), and knowledge of their rights (Mason, McGahee-Kovac, Johnson, & Stillerman, 2002). Teachers have further reported improvements in choice-making, self-advocacy, self-awareness, and self-reflection when students lead their own IEPs (Hapner & Imel, 2002).
>
> #### Benefits to Education Team Members
>
> Professional team members, including teachers, administrators, and related services personnel, report that student participation in the IEP progress is valued but that students are simply not as involved as they should be (Mason, Field, & Sawilowsky, 2004). Team members, including teachers and parents, report that student-led IEPs result in parent pride, improved climate of the meetings, and streamlining the meeting (Eisenman et al., 2005).

Moral/Ethical

It is also clear from a moral or ethical standing that students should be involved as much as possible in the IEP team, beginning even with young children and those children with more significant support needs. Imagine if one were to wait to invite a child to a meeting until it was legally required to do so: The child may have never participated in a legal discussion of himself or herself, taken an advocacy role, or even known that his or her teachers and parents gathered on this annual basis to talk about the student. How would it feel to have this experience? In sum, the mantra "nothing about us without us!" which is used in the disability community to communicate that decisions affecting people with disabilities should not be made without them (Charlton, 2000), is quite applicable here.

Strategies for Parents

In this section, we suggest activities that parents might complete to assist their child in developing and leading the IEP. However, we do not intend that *only* parents complete these activities. The activities we highlight here could also be completed by educators with parent permission. Likewise, parents could complete the activities in the Strategies for Educators section with the assistance of educators. In fact, this type of home–school collaboration would be ideal for all of the following activities.

BOX 14.2

Common Core Connections

There are many opportunities to work on Common Core State Standards (CCSS) in the student-led IEP process. Here are a few examples of goals that might be addressed:

- *Writing*: CCSS English-Language Arts standards for Grades K–12 include writing goals, which can be demonstrated in preparation for a student-led IEP. For example, a student may prepare a written summary of his or her needs, strengths, and progress when addressing writing standards (Grades 9–10 standards), including CCSS.ELA-Literacy.W.9–10.2a, *Introduce a topic; organize complex ideas, concepts, and information to make important connections and distinctions; include formatting (e.g., headings), graphics (e.g., figures, tables), and multimedia when useful to aiding comprehension*, and CCSS.ELA-Literacy.W.9–10.2b, *Develop the topic with well-chosen, relevant, and sufficient facts, extended definitions, concrete details, quotations, or other information and examples appropriate to the audience's knowledge of the topic.*
- *Listening and speaking*: CCSS English-Language Arts standards for Grades K–12 include listening and speaking goals, which can be demonstrated in the context of a student-led IEP. For example, CCCSS.ELA-Literacy.SL.5.1, *Engage effectively in a range of collaborative discussions (one-on-one, in groups, and teacher-led) with diverse partners on grade 5 topics and texts, building on others' ideas and expressing their own clearly.*
- *Math*: A variety of mathematics goals can be included in the preparation for a student-led IEP. For example, a student may calculate the percentage of goals met or, in early grades, determine how many goals were written (e.g., the previous IEP contained six goals) and how many were met. This addresses CCSS.Math.Content.1.OA.D.7, *Understand the meaning of the equal sign, and determine if equations involving addition and subtraction are true or false.* In this example, the student can determine if the number of goals written is equal to, or less than, the number of goals met.

Facilitate Attendance and Participation

To prepare students for substantive input in the IEP, parents might consider starting early. For example, preschoolers may come to their IEP meeting and just play during the meeting. This helps children be accustomed to the meeting atmosphere. By the time a child reaches elementary school, perhaps he or she sits in at most of the meeting and tells a little bit about his or her preferences and goals for himself or herself. This helps the student build communication, self-reflection, and self-advocacy skills. By late elementary school, the student may be attending the entire meeting and even leading some or all of it. His or her participation through middle and high school will then be focused on sharpening self-advocacy and self-awareness skills.

Teach Disability Label

This participation is predicated on the student knowing about his or her disability, IEP document, and IEP meeting. Telling your child that he or she has a disability may be

---

BOX 14.3   Tech Byte

- Use PowerPoint templates to create outlines of IEP information that students can fill in while learning about and preparing for their IEP meeting (see the I'm Determined website for templates for various grade levels: www.imdetermined.org).
- Use free speech-to-text software (e.g., Dragon Dictation) so that students can dictate information about themselves in preparing for an IEP meeting.
- Use camera phones or video equipment (e.g., FlipCams) to record student progress on IEP goals. Students can watch these films to reflect on their progress. Some students may even want to edit these films to show clips of their progress during their IEP meetings.
- e-Portfolios can be created, often using free apps (e.g., Google Apps), for students to record their progress on IEP goals. Many such apps exist, including ePortfolio California (www.eportfolioca.org), Evernote (www.evernote.com), and eBackpack (www.ebackpack.com).

---

uncomfortable for some parents. Some parents may worry that their child will feel less self-worth due to having a disability. Others may worry about the stigma associated with disability and how that may impact self-esteem for themselves, their child, their extended family, and their circle of friends. Still other parents may worry that their child will use the disability label as a "crutch," thus diminishing his or her capacity. And parents may have a variety of other concerns. It is important, then, to know your child and how best to describe the disability in terms he or she will understand and in a manner that values his or her inherent worth and builds self-esteem.

So how do parents (and sometimes teachers) broach the subject of disability? Despite the concerns, this information is often liberating for a child. For example, when told he had an emotional behavioral disorder, one child exclaimed, "So that's why sometimes I feel like a volcano!" Before he learned about his disability label, he didn't understand why his emotions were difficult to process and control. He had felt like he was a "bad" kid, and now he understood that his needs and learning styles were simply different from other children's.

Tactics for describing disability to a child with a disability can range from heartfelt conversations; to showing a movie or reading a book that includes a character with a similar disability and starting by asking, "Do you see yourself in this character?"; to writing short social narratives or comic strips defining a disability. Again, of course, the options are quite limitless and depend on the age and abilities of the child.

Case Study: Disability Label Social Narratives

Sally is a 7-year-old with trisomy of chromosome 21 (Down syndrome). She is becoming aware that she is somehow different from the other students in her second-grade class; she has more adult attention than her peers, she wears glasses whereas many of her peers do not, and she feels like often people don't understand her when she speaks. To alleviate her confusion in an age-appropriate manner, Sally's parents write a simple social narrative describing Down syndrome (see Figure 14.1).

Case Study: Casper's Parents Describe Asperger Syndrome

Casper is a 15-year-old with Asperger syndrome. He has never been told about this label, his IEP, or even why he has extra supports in class such as extra time and assistance

| Figure 14.1 | Sally's Disability Label Social Narrative |

My Name is Sally. I have Down syndrome.	Some kids wear glasses to see better, so they can learn at school and play at recess. I wear glasses, too!
	Some kids talk loud, and some kids talk quietly. Sometimes people don't understand me. When somebody says, "What?" I just tell them again!
	Having red hair is part of who I am. Having a brother is part of who I am. Having Down syndrome is part of who I am. My parents love me very much. My friends think I'm a lot of fun. My brother loves me, too!

with math. Casper loves science—computers in particular. To help him understand Asperger syndrome while incorporating his interests, talents, and vocabulary, his parents describe Asperger syndrome in the form of a social narrative (see Figure 14.2).

Assist in Identifying Strengths, Needs, Rights, and Preferences

Parents play an important role in helping their children identify and understand their learning and support strengths, needs, and preferences. Students who are learning to lead their IEPs may "interview" their parents to gain their input. In this manner,

| Figure 14.2 | Casper's Disability Label Social Narrative |

What is Asperger syndrome?

Asperger syndrome is invisible. No one can see it. It is one of the things that make me who I am. Asperger syndrome affects the way my brain works. The brain is like a computer that is always on and keeps people living and learning. Asperger syndrome causes my brain to sometimes work differently than other people's brains.

Having a brain with Asperger syndrome is like having a computer with an Asperger Operating System, while most other people have a Plain Operating System. Asperger syndrome makes me experience the world in a certain way. Sometimes it's the same as most people, but sometimes I experience the world differently.

Asperger syndrome is another way of thinking and being.

Why do I have Asperger syndrome?

No one knows why I have Asperger syndrome. Scientists are not sure what causes it. They are trying to find out why some people have it and others don't. Asperger syndrome is a mystery. But they do know some things about it.

Scientists know that:

Asperger syndrome is not a disease.

It is nobody's fault that I have it.

It does not mean that I have a problem or that I am better than others. It is just another way of thinking and being.

Many other people at my school, in my town, and in the world also have Asperger syndrome.

Asperger syndrome is another way of thinking and being.

students can gain a variety of perspectives in helping to understand their needs. Students could ask parents the following:

- What do you think are my greatest strengths?
- In what areas do you think I need to have support (help)?
- Can you think of a time when I did a great job on a project at school? What helped me do well on that project?
- Can you think of a class that I need more help in? What kinds of help do you think might be best for me?
- How do you think that I learn best?

Parents can provide further support for their child in understanding their learning needs by providing a copy of any previous IEPs, highlighting previously identified strengths and needs. This is also a good time to discuss student rights as they relate to the IEP. The discussion of rights may vary by age and student ability, but it will be important to highlight a few key points, including the student's

- right to privacy,
- right to be safe and protected at school and at home,
- right to be treated fairly and respectfully, and
- right to an appropriate education.

Case Study: Sally's IEP and Student Rights

In an effort to teach Sally about her IEP and student rights, her parents and teachers collaborate to create a document describing her IEP and rights in age-appropriate terms (see Figure 14.3).

Case Study: Casper's Parents and Teachers Define His Rights as a Student

To assist Casper in understanding his IEP and rights as a student receiving special education services, Casper's parents and teachers developed a written statement outlining the IEP (see Figure 14.4).

Strategies for Educators

Collaborate With Families and Obtain Permission

Before beginning the process of involving students in participating in, or leading, their IEPs, educators must be sure to get permission from parents and sometimes from

Figure 14.3 Sally's Student Rights

IEP!	Me!	Help!	Learn!
My IEP tells my teachers what I need to learn and how I learn best.	I go to my IEP meeting. My mom, dad, Ms. Clark, Mrs. Davis, and Mr. DeMarco also go to my IEP meeting.	I have the right to be safe at school. I can tell people if I need help.	I have the right to learn at school!

| Figure 14.4 | Casper's Student Rights |

What is an IEP?

An IEP is an individualized education program. It is a program that makes sure you have an education that meets your learning needs (helps you learn best).

Who sees my IEP?

First, you can see your IEP. Your parents also see your IEP. Your teachers, school psychologist, parents, speech therapist, and usually the principal will also see the IEP. All of these people help write the IEP every year. These are the people who are legally required to be on your IEP team.

Who will not see my IEP?

Your friends, other teachers at school, yard supervisors, and most other people you know will never see your IEP. Usually, your brothers and sisters also do not see your IEP, unless you want them to. Only the people who are legally required to be on your IEP team will see or even know about your IEP. Your IEP is confidential; you get to decide who, outside of your IEP team, can know about your IEP.

What are my rights?

Your IEP is confidential, meaning that is a private document and meeting. You have the right to keep it confidential and keep information about your disability private. You also have the right to have an appropriate education; this means the right to an education that will best work for you and help you learn. You have the right to be treated fairly at school; fairness means that everyone gets what they need, not that everyone is treated the same. Your right to be treated fairly means that you will have extra time to complete tests and homework, and the right to use a word processor for writing. You have the right to be treated with respect; if you feel that an adult or student is not treating you with respect, you have the right to tell an adult whom you trust what is happening. This adult will help you feel safe and respected. This adult could be a parent, a teacher, a coach, or a counselor.

school administrators as well. Educators may set the stage for this by speaking with families about the individualized lessons related to IEPs and disability during initial IEP meetings, transition meetings, and back-to-school events or parent-teacher conferences. To remind families about the lessons, Mrs. Simpson sends a letter to families 2 weeks before beginning instruction (see Figure 14.5).

Once permission is obtained, educators can begin to meet with students and provide instruction related to disability, the IEP, and planning for participation in the IEP meeting. Parents and educators will create (ideally together) a disability label social narrative, as illustrated previously with Sally and Casper. In this case, Mrs. Simpson provided a rough draft that parents added to or edited, based on their preferences and knowledge of their child.

Delivering Instruction

How does this instruction work in an inclusive setting? Some inclusion facilitators in secondary settings teach a study skills class, which is open to all students (with and without IEPs), so that educators can provide students with assistance in organization, working on assignments, and studying for exams. This can be an ideal time to deliver instruction to students about disabilities. Other times, teachers meet with students before school, after school, during lunch, or at other times during the school day that are mutually agreed upon.

| Figure 14.5 | Letter to Families About Disability Awareness |

Dear Families,

I will be starting a Disabilities Awareness unit with your child in 2 weeks. Attached to this letter you will find information outlining the lessons. The lessons will focus on the following:

1. Learning styles: Everyone learns differently; everyone has strengths.
2. Disability labels: What is the label? Who knows about it?. See the attached disability social narrative for your child. Please provide any input by writing on this, or calling, or emailing me to discuss it.
3. Having an IEP: what it says, who can see it, how I can help create it. See the attached IEP and Student Rights document. Once again, please provide your input!
4. Accommodations to help you learn.

I am very excited to offer this curriculum to our students. It should help students gain skills to advocate for themselves as well as understand better how they learn and what services are available to them.

Sincerely,

Mrs. Simpson

How should instruction be provided—individually or in a group? Because of the confidential nature of an IEP and disability status, this instruction should generally be provided individually between the student and the teacher. There are times when small-group instruction can be useful, such as when broadly discussing student rights, learning styles, and learning needs. However, the educator must be mindful to ensure that the student's status as a student with a disability is never disclosed or suggested during small-group instruction.

Case Studies: Determining Instructional Delivery

Case Study: Sally

Mr. DeMarco decides to meet individually with Sally during transition times in her second-grade classroom. Mr. DeMarco speaks with Sally's classroom teacher and determines that when the students are transitioning from reading instruction to silent reading will be an ideal time for instruction on disability issues. Mr. DeMarco and Sally move to the library (a quiet, confidential space) for instruction.

Case Study: Casper

Casper's special education teacher, Mrs. Simpson, reviews Casper's class schedule, looking for a time when the two will have time for approximately five or six 30- to 45-minute meetings in the next 3 weeks (in preparation for Casper's IEP meeting). Mrs. Simpson determines, in consultation with Casper and his parents, that Casper will be free to meet after school 1 day per week on Wednesday afternoons. Mrs. Simpson also determines that Casper will be able to use his study skills class meetings on Fridays, as typically there is not much pressing work to do in this class on Fridays due to homework policies over the weekend. Mrs. Simpson teaches the study skills class and decides that once she gets the class started on Fridays, the paraeducator, Mary, can skillfully take charge while Mrs. Simpson meets privately with Casper.

Instructional Topics

Educators, in collaboration with families, may choose to provide specific instruction to students on a variety of topics in preparation for participating in or leading their own IEP. These topics may include ability awareness, goal setting, and self-determination or self-advocacy activities.

Ability Awareness and Wheel of Me's

When learning about disability labels, some students may not be sure how having a disability defines (or fails to define) who they are. In part of an informative interview, Norman Kunc describes how a disability label has impacted him (Giangreco, 2004, p. 34):

> If I had to describe myself to you now I'd say that I have an undergraduate degree in humanities and master's in family therapy. I got divorced, now I'm remarried and I live with Emma and two step-kids. I like classical music and jazz. Having cerebral palsy is one small aspect of who I am: it's part of who I am, but it's not the defining characteristic that makes me who I am. . . . The fact is that a very small part of my life gets blown up into a very big part. Unfortunately, too many people see me as nine-tenths disability, one-tenth person.

This interview highlights the need to place the person before the disability and to place disability in perspective. A Wheel of Me's is a tool to help students describe who they are as a *whole* person. The Wheel of Me's activity can also be a useful tool in preparation for a student-led IEP. In fact, some students may wish to share it at an IEP meeting when describing their strengths and preferences. Some students may need educators to guide them in identifying all of their characteristics, strengths, and preferences. Here are some sample questions for developing ability awareness:

- Who are the people in your family?
- What do you like to do after school?
- What are you good at (or what do people say that you are good at [if the student cannot think of this on her or his own]?
- What are your favorites . . . ? (Think of school subjects, out-of-school activities, foods, music, movies, television shows, things to learn about, and so on)
- Who are your friends?
- What are things that you wish or hope for?

The information is transferred to a pie chart. Each "slice" of the pie contains a piece of information about the student. A disability is one slice of the pie; without that slice, the person wouldn't be complete or the "real" version of themselves. But it's also just one slice—each slice is equally important in defining who the person is as a whole person. Sally's Wheel of Me's is depicted in Figure 14.6.

Student Self-Determination

Recently, a young man named Brian, who uses a wheelchair for mobility, was attempting to enter his high school. Students enter through a series of swinging doors. This school is not equipped with an automatic door opener. Brian attempted to open several

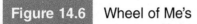

Figure 14.6   Wheel of Me's

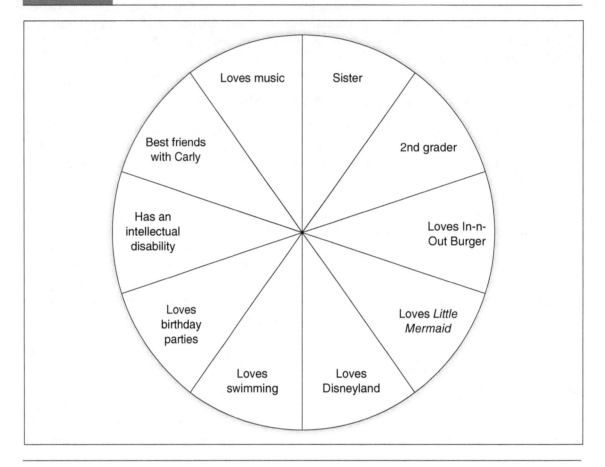

Copyright © 2014 by Corwin. All rights reserved. Reprinted from *The Inclusion Toolbox: Strategies and Techniques for All Teachers* by Jennifer A. Kurth and Megan Gross. Thousand Oaks, CA: Corwin, www.corwin.com

doors, but each time he was unable to open the door wide enough, for a long enough time, so that he could enter. Meanwhile, a steady stream of students was walking by and entering the school. This brief scenario represents a teachable moment for all students involved. On the one hand, it would have been thoughtful for a peer to simply hold the door open so Brian could enter. On the other hand, Brian could have said, "Hey, please hold that door for me," to any number of passing peers. By knowing one's support needs, and being able to advocate for them, students demonstrate self-determination skills such as the following (Wehmeyer & Field, 2007):

- choice making
- decision making
- problem solving
- goal setting (and attaining)
- self-management
- self-advocacy
- self-awareness
- self-knowledge

Inclusion facilitators can facilitate teaching self-determination in a number of ways. Educators can help students learn their own strengths and needs, and therefore participate in developing their own IEPs, by reflecting on student learning preferences and support needs.

BOX 14.4   *Administrator Insight*

Many students learn self-determination skills through participation in school-based co-curricular or extracurricular activities such as student leadership council, student government, lunchtime clubs, sports, or project-based learning. Are students with disabilities also represented in these diverse student groups? How might faculty and peers support students with more severe disabilities in participating in these activities on your campus? Provide access and opportunities for all students to have a voice on your campus.

Case Study: Mr. DeMarco Teaches Self-Determination

Sarah is a fifth grader who has an intellectual disability. She is learning about self-determination and her IEP. To begin, Mr. DeMarco prepares a series of questions to discuss with Sarah. With some students, Mr. DeMarco gives the questions to the students as a handout to complete independently and then discuss with him and parents; with other students, Mr. DeMarco completes three worksheets (see Figures 14.7–14.9) with them.

Figure 14.7   Self-Determination Worksheet

Things that HELP me learn		Things that make it HARD FOR ME to learn	
Check if TRUE		Check if TRUE	
X	Using pictures	X	Reading
	Working with friends		Writing
X	Taking breaks		Teacher lecturing
	Working with teachers	X	Math
	Writing in my agenda	X	Needing to be quiet
	Having notes	X	Staying in a chair
X	Using manipulatives or objects		Staying in one place for a long time
X	Having a schedule		When the room is noisy
	Having more time		Working with other people
	Working alone		When the room is quiet
	Having modified assignments	X	Having lots of things to do at once

(Continued)

Figure 14.7 (Continued)

	Being allowed to leave class early or come late		Typing
x	Typing instead of writing		Handwriting
	Taking tests in a quiet area	x	Being bored
	Having less homework	x	Leaving or missing parts of class

Everyone learns in a different way. Put a check mark next to all of the things that are true for the way you learn.

When I'm learning something new, it's best for me if I

x	See it (pictures)
_____	Hear a teacher talk about it
_____	Can try doing it
_____	Something else:

When I'm taking a test, it's best for me if

_____	I can use tools on the test (book, study guide, calculator)
x	Somebody helps me read the questions
_____	I have extra time
x	I can take the test someplace else
_____	Something else:

When I'm doing work in class, I prefer to

_____	Work alone
x	Work with a friend
_____	Work with an adult
_____	Something else:

When I am doing an assignment, I get stressed out if

x	There is a lot of reading
x	There is a lot of math
_____	I have to do research
_____	Something else:

When I have an assignment to do, I usually

_____	Get started right away

_____ Wait until the last minute

x Wait until somebody helps me

_____ Something else:

I know best what I need to do when

_____ I have it in writing

_____ I hear the teacher say it

_____ Somebody reminds me about it

x Something else: I have it in my schedule

When I'm working on an assignment, it helps me if

x An adult helps me get started and think of ideas

_____ An adult helps me edit when I'm done

x An adult helps me along the way

_____ Something else:

When I'm taking a test, it helps me if

x There are fewer choices on the test

_____ I have a little extra time on the test

_____ The words on the test are explained to me

_____ Something else:

Put a check mark by the statements that seem to be *mostly* true about you:

Socially

I would rather be alone than in a group.

_____ Yes   x   No

I have difficulty making new friends.

_____ Yes   x   No

It is easier for me to talk about something than to take turns in a conversation.

_____ Yes   x   No

I have specific interests and activities. For example, I am really interested in trains, and this is the only thing I like to talk or think about.

x   Yes   _____ No

If yes, please say what your interest is: Disney

(Continued)

Figure 14.7 (Continued)

It is sometimes hard for me to tell if other people are being funny or sarcastic.

_____ Yes x No

Something else that is true about me socially:

Math

I sometimes put numbers in the wrong place.

x Yes _____ No

I sometimes forget what step to do in a long math problem.

x Yes No

In word problems, I don't always know if I should add, subtract, multiply, or divide.

x Yes _____ No

I have a hard time remembering math facts.

_____ Yes x No

I have a hard time remembering math formulas.

x Yes _____ No

I like to use a calculator in math.

x Yes _____ No

I use a resource guide in math.

x Yes _____ No

Something else that is true about math for me:

Math is my favorite class

Organization

Sometimes I forget to do my homework.

_____ Yes x No

Sometimes I forget to bring my homework back to school.

_____ Yes x No

I often lose things and forget where I put them.

_____ Yes x No

My bedroom is messy.

_____ Yes x No

My locker and/or backpack is neat and organized.

     x   Yes   _____   No

I write down everything in my planner without reminders.

    _____   Yes   x   No

Being neat and organized is really important to me.

     x   Yes   _____   No

Usually I work slowly.

     x   Yes   _____   No

Having extra time helps me keep organized.

     x   Yes   _____   No

Something else that is true about my organization:

Spelling and Writing

It is easier for me to

     x   Type   _____   Write by hand

My handwriting is messy.

    _____   Yes   x   No

My handwriting is neat, but the spacing is wrong and other people can't read it.

     x   Yes   _____   No

I have lots of good ideas to write about, but I have a hard time remembering them to write them down.

     x   Yes   _____   No

I like to write more about

    _____   Facts   x   Opinions

I have awesome spelling.

    _____   Yes   x   No

Something else that is true about my writing:

Reading

I love to read.

     x   Yes   _____   No

(Continued)

Figure 14.7 (Continued)

Reading is hard for me. Sometimes the letters like *b* and *d* look the same to me.

x   Yes   _____   No

I know a word one time, but forget it the next time I see it.

x   Yes   _____   No

Sometimes when I read, I skip words or lines on a page by accident.

x   Yes   _____   No

It is hard for me to remember everything I read.

x   Yes   _____   No

When I read, I don't know what a lot of the words mean.

x   Yes   _____   No

It is easy for me to "read between the lines" to infer things when I read.

_____   Yes   x   No

Something else that is true about my reading:

I love reading Disney books

Tests

When I take a test, I like to use a resource guide to help me remember things.

x   Yes   _____   No

When I take a test, I get stressed out.

_____   Yes   x   No

When I take a test, I like to have a little extra time to finish it.

x   Yes   _____   No

I would rather take the test

x   In my classroom   _____   In a different, quiet place

When I take a test, it is easier for me to

_____   Bubble it in myself   x   Have somebody fill in bubbles for me

Something else that is true about me when I take tests:

Attention

It is easy for me to pay attention in class.

_____ Yes   x   No

It is hard for me to shift my attention from one person to another.

x   Yes   _____ No

I know what to do in class better if I

x   See It   _____ Hear It

I have a hard time following directions.

_____ Yes   x   No

I get distracted by noises or what other people are doing.

x   Yes   _____ No

Adults are always telling me, "Pay attention!"

x   Yes   _____ No

Taking breaks helps me pay attention.

x   Yes   _____ No

Something else that is true about my attention:

Sensory Sensitivity

I don't like loud, unexpected noises like alarms.

x   True   _____ Not True

I don't like it when people touch me unexpectedly.

_____ True   x   Not True

I don't really like people to sit close to me. I would rather have a little more space.

_____ True   x   Not True

I like the way some things feel, like the walls or carpets, but I don't like the way some other things feel.

x   True   _____ Not True

I like to fidget with objects.

x   True   _____ Not True

Fidget breaks (like the trampoline) help me focus.

x   True   _____ Not True

Something else that is true about my sensory needs:

Figure 14.8   Understanding My Strengths and Weaknesses

Everybody has strengths (things they are good at or things that they like) and weaknesses (things that are harder or things that they don't like).

Things you are good at	*Things you need help with*
• Talking • Drawing • Reading picture books • Having ideas to write about • Working with other people • I like to have breaks when I'm working • Word banks • Talking calculator • PE running	• Listening to the teacher for a long time • Reading • Being quiet • Sitting down for a long time • Noisy places hurt my ears

Figure 14.9   Planning for the Future

What are some of your goals for when you are older?

School

1. Classes I want to take in middle school:

   Art, PE, cooking, social studies

2. Grades I want to earn:

   Only A's

Work

1. Do you want a job in high school?

   No

2. Where do you want to work in high school?

   I don't want to work in high school

3. What kind of work do you want after high school?

   I want to work at Disneyland

Friends

1. Do you want friends (more, different, fewer) in middle school?

   More friends and to keep my friends I have now

2. What do you want to do with your friends?

   Watch movies, go to their houses, go swimming

Other Goals for the Future

1. Go to college in New York

2. Have my own apartment

3. Work at the gift shop in Disneyland

Goal Setting

Setting short- and long-term goals (age-appropriate to the student) is another part of the process of leading, or participating, in the IEP. Goal setting includes deciding on a goal, creating an action plan for accomplishing the goal, and then self-monitoring progress toward the goal and action plan (Lee, Palmer, & Wehmeyer, 2009). Students may need assistance determining short- and long-term goals. For some students, a goal may be to earn a passing grade in a difficult class. This may be a short-term goal, but it is also an important step in the long-term goal of graduating high school.

Educators and parents can help students identify goals in the following ways:

- Ask students (individually or in a small group) what they want or need to do (now and in the future).
- Review formal goals developed by others (e.g., the student's previous IEP goals) and determine which of the goals are relevant and important to the student today.
- Brainstorm with the student (or a group of students) desired long-term outcomes (e.g., having an apartment, working as a professional football player, going to college). Students can then research skills or qualifications needed to achieve this goal and, with assistance from educators and families, devise short-term goals to achieve the necessary skills or qualifications.
- Ensure that students consider goals in a variety of domains, including social skills, vocational skills, organizational skills, academic skills, communication skills, study skills or habits, self-determination or self-advocacy skills, and independence skills.

Once goals are developed, educators and/or families can help students decide the timeline for the goal. Is this something that can be accomplished in a month? If not, are there steps toward the goal? For example, if a student sets a goal to earn a passing grade in Biology, the first step in achieving this goal may be to write down all homework in the student's agenda. This could be accomplished by the end of the week. The next goal may be to complete all homework; this could also be accomplished by the end of the week. An additional goal may be to take notes during class, to study for exams weekly, and so on. Often, students may not realize the necessary steps toward accomplishing goals that are important and motivating to them, thus failing to meet their goals. This identification of steps or subgoals can be thought of as the action plan—the things the student and people supporting the student will do to help the student reach his or her goal (Lee et al., 2009).

Last, students self-monitor their progress toward the goal. Lee and colleagues (2009) suggest framing self-monitoring in the form of "I" questions, for example, "Did I turn in my homework today?" Students can answer this question in the form of a yes or no response. They may also note the quality of their work. For example, when reflecting on their homework completion, they could note how many minutes they worked on the homework assignment, how much effort they put into the assignment, or what key concept they practiced in the homework assignment.

Case Study: Jeff Sets Goals and Monitors His Progress

Jeff is a high school student with a learning disability. He has a goal to pass his science class. He uses the self-monitoring plan seen in Figure 14.10 to track his progress toward this goal (adapted from Lee et al., 2009).

Figure 14.10 Goal Setting and Self-Monitoring Progress

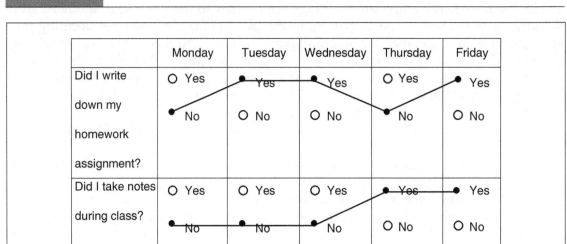

	Monday	Tuesday	Wednesday	Thursday	Friday
Did I write down my homework assignment?	○ Yes / ● No	● Yes / ○ No	● Yes / ○ No	○ Yes / ● No	● Yes / ○ No
Did I take notes during class?	○ Yes / ● No	○ Yes / ● No	○ Yes / ● No	● Yes / ○ No	● Yes / ○ No

Strategies to Prepare for the Meeting

Students should engage in a number of activities prior to the meeting to ensure their full and meaningful participation once the meeting begins. These include reviewing previous IEP documents, preparing information to share during the meeting, scheduling the meeting, setting goals, and monitoring progress toward existing goals.

Evaluate Any Previous IEP

To begin, students should review their previous IEP (if there is no previous IEP, discuss with the student why he or she is being considered for special education services). This is often best done by taking the time to sit down with a student and go through the document page by page, explaining that each page is required by law for every student receiving special education services, but that the content of the pages is different for each student, because different things are important for each student and family. The general content of each page should be discussed, with great attention paid to describing goals, accommodations, and services. Some students will be able to then proceed to read the IEP on their own; other students may require an adult to read the IEP to them. In general, however, it is a good idea to read the IEP with a student page by page so that the student has a chance to ask questions and understand that the purpose of this document is to help the student learn, be happy, and be successful at school.

Case Study: Mrs. Simpson Reviews Casper's IEP With Him

Mrs. Simpson and Casper agree to meet after school for 20 minutes to review his current IEP. Casper has not seen his IEP before, so Mrs. Simpson is aware that she will need to take her time explaining the document to him and expects that this first meeting may involve simply reviewing the purpose of the IEP. The following day, the two meet again for another 20 minutes to review the contents of the IEP. Mrs. Simpson clarifies again that the IEP is a document about and for Casper and that he should be comfortable, and familiar, with its contents. She reads each page carefully, drawing attention specifically to his goals, services, and accommodations. She asks Casper regularly if there are any words he's not familiar with or if he has any questions or concerns about the IEP. Finally, a few days later, Mrs. Simpson and Casper meet again to debrief about the IEP. She asks him a series of questions now that he has seen the IEP document. She has the IEP available so they can look through it while thinking about these questions:

- What is your general impression of the IEP written for you?
- How did you feel when you read it?
- Are there parts of the IEP that you agree with?
- Are there parts of the IEP that you disagree with?
- If you went to your next IEP meeting, what would you want to make sure people knew and got right?
- When you think of your goals, are they good/important goals for you? Would you want to change anything about them?
- When you think of your accommodations, are they good/important/helpful to you? Are there any that you would want to change? To delete? Are there different accommodations you can think of that would be more helpful?
- Write a summary of each goal, and write one or two sentences saying how you think you are doing on the goal.

Certainly, there are a variety of activities that can be completed with students before the meeting to help them become experts on their own IEPs. Rather than re-creating these resources here, we would like to direct you to some excellent free online resources. These are materials that can be downloaded and used immediately during instruction. A favorite is the "I'm Determined! Understanding and Preparing for My IEP" from the I'm Determined website (www.imdetermined.org/files_resources/105/im_determined_understanding_and_preparing_for_my_iep.pdf). It contains sample discussion items and questions that can be used to help a student fully understand his or her current IEP. Other materials are presented in the Resources Appendix.

Preparing Information to Share During the Meeting

Students who lead their own IEP meeting will need to prepare information for the meeting, in addition to understanding the components of the IEP document. This information can include brief descriptions of the student's needs from his or her perspective, a meeting agenda, and a presentation to use during the meeting to guide the discussion.

Describing My Disability

Students should be able to indicate their IDEA disability label and describe in a few sentences their strengths and needs. The "One Pager" tab on the I'm Determined website (www.imdetermined.org) has a great one-page template students can download and use to concisely state their interests, preferences, strengths, and needs. It also has sample videos of students describing themselves in these terms, which can serve as great models to show students.

Students should also prepare a presentation about themselves that can be included in the IEP meeting. Figure 14.11 is an example slide from a student's self-advocacy presentation. The I'm Determined website has free downloadable PowerPoint templates for this purpose in the Student Involvement section. Templates are available for preschool, elementary, and secondary students. In addition to describing oneself, the presentation can be used as an agenda. For example, the I'm Determined template can be expanded to include a slide reminding everyone to sign in, invitations for specific participants to report progress (e.g., "Mrs. Smith, please describe how I'm doing in math"), and all other components that are required in a meeting. Many speakers use PowerPoint slides as an organizational tool during a lecture; this can certainly help students with disabilities (and frankly the entire IEP team!) to stay on topic and on track during the meeting!

Strategies During the Meeting

During an IEP meeting, students with disabilities can play a variety of important roles. As noted above, students may act as managers in terms of setting and managing the agenda, asking clarifying questions, commenting, and ensuring a strengths-based perspective. For example, students could be prompted (by the PowerPoint slide, verbally, or with a small note) to ask, "Are there any questions?" following each speaker. This may also help students formulate questions they might have. Some students may indicate "I agree" or "I disagree" with statements made by IEP team members as a further mechanism for participating. Students may also ask, "Can you say that a different way?" if the statement was unclear, used jargon, or lacked a strengths-based description of the

| **Figure 14.11** | Student IEP and Self-Advocacy Presentation Slide |

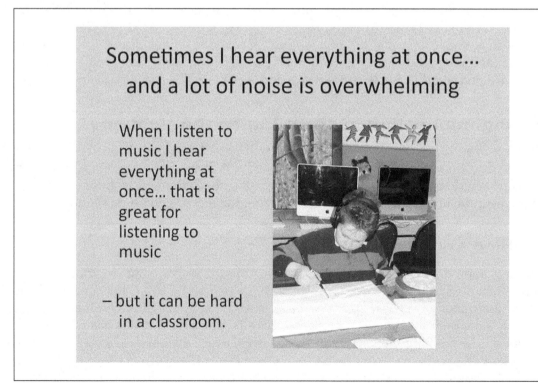

Source: © Leah Kelley, Thirty Days of Autism (2013).

student. Finally, it's important to have a plan in case the meeting gets too heated or the student gets too uncomfortable or overwhelmed during the meeting. Make a plan ahead of time so that the student can easily leave if needed. You might give the student a note that can be handed to you in such a situation, determine a hand signal, or other means so that the student knows there is a safe way to leave the meeting if needed for any reason (McGahee-Kovac, Mason, Wallace, & Jones, 2001).

Case Study: Mr. DeMarco Has a Back-up Plan

Before Sally's IEP meeting begins, Mr. DeMarco and Sally spend time learning about the meeting, discussing the contents of her IEP, and planning for her participation during the meeting. Mr. DeMarco acknowledges to Sally that it is possible that she will want to leave the meeting before it is over, and that is OK. He gives her a "break card" and tells her that he will be sitting next to her during the meeting, and if she needs to leave to take a break, or to leave altogether, to just give Mr. DeMarco this card. The card, about 3 × 5 inches in size, is printed on yellow paper, and reads:

I need a break.

I will go to the library for a break during the meeting.

I will come back when I can.

Mr. DeMarco emphasizes that the card might not be needed, but if it is, Sally can use it any time during the meeting.

Strategies After the Meeting

After IEP meetings conclude, it is a good idea to debrief with students. Praise students for their participation and accomplishment in this important activity. Ask students if they would like to share their reactions with you or their family (McGahee-Kovac et al., 2001). Students will then begin the practice of progress monitoring goals, as discussed previously.

Conclusion

Student participation in the IEP meeting and document development is essential for all students, regardless of age or disability label. Key to this participation is the ancient Greek aphorism "Know thyself." Strategies that educators and families can engage in to help students know their needs, preferences, interests, and strengths are critical in this important endeavor!

Please be sure to go to the website (http://www.corwin.com/theinclusiontoolbox) to download the forms and resources from this chapter!

15

Inclusive Related Services

The physical therapist would come up to me and say, "Walk up the stairs." And I'd say, "Why? They don't go anywhere." But she'd say, "Never mind, walk up the stairs." So, I'd walk up the stairs and nearly kill myself getting up there. When I got to the top the physical therapist would say, "Good! Now walk back down the stairs."
I'd say, "Wait a minute! If you didn't want me up here in the first place, why did you ask me to walk up here?"

—Norman Kunc (quoted in Giangreco, 1995)

Related services are a collection of support services to assist a student in accessing and making progress in his or her special education program in the least restrictive environment. They include services like transportation, counseling, behavior analysts, social workers, and therapies such as speech and language, occupational, physical, vision, and orientation and mobility. The providers under the related services umbrella may also vary from district to district and state to state. Traditionally, students who receive related service therapies are pulled out of their classroom and meet with a therapist for a limited amount of time each week to address specific individualized education program (IEP) goals related to the therapist's field. The activities during this time may be unrelated to the rest of the student's day or require a student to practice a skill outside of a natural context, which was the experience of Norman Kunc as a child, as he described in the quote at the start of this chapter. An inclusive, or push-in, model of therapy brings whatever services a student needs to the student. A therapist in this model may provide direct services in a general education classroom, playground, gym, or community-based instructional setting. In this chapter we discuss the legal framework for related services in the least restrictive environment and provide strategies for integrating related service therapies into a student's day.

❖ Box 15.1   What Does the Research Say?

Providing related service therapies in inclusive settings, using a team approach among educators and therapists, has been advocated since the passage of PL 94-142 in 1975 (Giangreco, 1986a). The literature on inclusive related services promotes the use of a variety of service delivery models, including role release, a process in which a therapist trains a core group of team members to implement interventions on a daily basis, co-teaching, or direct services in inclusive settings, depending on the needs of a student identified by a collaborative team (Giangreco, Prelock, Reid, Dennis, & Edelman, 2000; Giangreco, York, & Rainforth, 1989; York, Giangreco, Vandercook, & Macdonald, 1992).

Outcomes for Students

While there is limited research on the outcomes for students who receive inclusive related services, there is some research based on single subject design or case studies demonstrating benefits to students (Kellegrew & Allen, 1996). Giangreco (1986b) found that when therapy is provided in the natural setting of a student's classroom, the student demonstrates an increase in skill development compared to direct therapy services that are provided in a separate room. In addition, students receiving therapy services in their classroom setting experience increased instructional time (Rainforth & York-Barr, 1997).

Preferences and Practices of Educators

Research from the past 20 years on integrating related services into the classroom has focused on defining the roles of therapists in inclusive classrooms (Giangreco, 2000; York et al., 1992), strategies for professional collaboration (Giangreco et al., 2000), and ways to provide therapy to students who are fully included (Giangreco et al., 1989). Classroom teachers indicate a preference for inclusive occupational therapy and speech therapy and report that this leads to students' IEP goals being addressed throughout the day, rather than only in therapy sessions, and that all students in the classroom receive help as needed (Downing & Peckham-Hardin, 2007). Therapists report enjoying working with other members of the IEP team, but need support to make collaboration effective (Rainforth & York-Barr, 1997) and prevent the "watering down" of therapy or performing the role of a classroom aide instead of a therapist (Ehren, 2000).

Rationales for Inclusive Related Services

Legal

The provision of related services to students with disabilities was included in the first federal law regarding special education, PL 94-142, in 1975. Since that time the definition of related services has expanded. The most recent reauthorization of IDEA, §300.34. provides an in-depth, although not exclusive, definition of related services:

> transportation and such developmental, corrective, and other supportive services as are required to assist a child with a disability to benefit from special education, and includes speech-language pathology and audiology services, interpreting services, psychological services, physical and occupational therapy, recreation, including therapeutic recreation, early identification and assessment of disabilities in children, counseling services, including rehabilitation counseling, orientation and mobility services, and medical services for diagnostic or evaluation purposes. Related services also include school health services and school nurse services, social work services in schools, and parent counseling and training.

IDEA, §300.320, also defines how related services should be stated in a student's IEP:

(4) A statement of the special education and related services and supplementary aids and services, based on peer-reviewed research to the extent practicable, to be provided to the child, or on behalf of the child, and a statement of the program modifications or supports for school personnel that will be provided to enable the child—

(i) To advance appropriately toward attaining the annual goals;

(ii) To be involved in and make progress in the general education curriculum in accordance with paragraph (a)(1) of this section, and to participate in extracurricular and other nonacademic activities; and

(iii) To be educated and participate with other children with disabilities and non-disabled children in the activities described in this section.

These guidelines are important because they require IEP team members to consider how related services assist the student in making progress toward goals and how they enable a student to participate and progress in the general education environment.

Ethical

Related service providers and IEP team members have a responsibility to follow the guidelines set forth in IDEA and yet, in doing so, it is easy to write legally compliant statements that a student cannot participate in general education for therapy services because he or she needs instruction in a "small-group setting" or a statement that the therapy session would be disruptive to the general education environment. We recognize there are a few related services, such as those related to providing personal care assistance with toileting or health-related monitoring, which should be provided in a private setting; however, the majority of the students we serve have related services that can and should be provided in general education.

Practical

Rainforth and York-Barr (1997) have identified three benefits to integrating therapy into a student's day:

1. Teachers and therapists work together as a team to identify intervention strategies that are taught throughout the day.
2. Therapy is embedded in a student's day and does not remove a student from the general education environment.
3. When therapy is provided in the context of real life, students gain new skills in a meaningful environment, which reinforces the continued use of these skills when a therapist is not present.

If we want our students to develop and use communication, movement, motor, and social skills in a variety of environments, it makes sense to provide this instruction in those environments on a regular basis.

When students receive related services in a traditional pull-out model, their daily and weekly schedules become complex and fragmented. Students are required to leave the classroom to receive therapy services, which results in missed instructional time and possible stigmatization from peers because they are gone at different times of the day (McLeskey & Waldron, 2007). Students with more than one related service provider may leave their grade-level classroom multiple times a day and visit more than one therapy room or special classroom. This requires students, often those with the most significant disabilities, to learn behavior expectations and procedures for multiple professionals and navigate several extra transitions a day. This just doesn't make sense!

Strategies for Related Service Providers

Providing therapy services in an inclusive environment, successfully, requires IEP team support, therapists communicating and collaborating with teachers to meet students' therapy needs, and coordinating a schedule that works for both the students and the adults.

BOX 15.2   Tech Byte

There's an app for that! More therapists are integrating technology into services with their students. Find recommended apps for your therapy field through a Google search or checking out your association's webpage. App websites for occupational therapists and speech-language pathologists are listed in the Resources Appendix.

Communication and Collaboration

When developing inclusive related services for students, it is important for IEP teams to discuss the type of services a student needs that are educationally relevant and necessary (Giangreco et al., 2000). While a student may benefit from intensive one-to-one therapy, the goal of related services in an education setting is to provide the supports necessary for a student to make *progress* in his or her special education program so the student can attain IEP goals, access general education, and participate with nondisabled peers (IDEA §300.320). In this spirit, IEP teams should discuss whether a student would benefit from related services that are flexible and enable a therapist to provide direct services in a classroom or general education environment and provide consultative services to the IEP team, such as making appropriate curricular or environmental modifications and supports, and training teachers, paraeducators, and peers how to implement interventions across the school day. Since some therapists providing related services are contract employees and required to bill a district for a specific set of hours, it is important for the IEP team to document and describe what type of and where the inclusive related services may take place. For example, the team might write "OT services 60 minutes weekly to include direct services in the classroom during independent, small-group, or whole-group instruction and consult with teacher and team." The team should also prioritize and write collaborative goals and then identify which team members will work together to provide the instruction and supports necessary to meet that goal.

To effectively deliver therapy in inclusive settings, therapists need to be familiar with the general education curriculum and classroom routines. Therapists need to meet with classroom teachers on a regular basis so they can plan activities in advance, discuss the roles of each educator in the classroom, and have a conversation about how to tailor lessons and the therapist's time to support students' IEP goals. Viewing the curriculum with a therapy lens, the therapist can then prepare any modifications or instructional activities a student needs to access the curriculum and connect to the student's IEP goals. This ensures the therapist is meeting the needs of her or his caseload and is not "watering down" therapy (Ehren, 2000). We recognize it can be difficult to schedule in-person meetings, especially when related service staff is itinerant or responsible for large caseloads. In these cases, we recommend setting up a communication system, such as email, phone calls, or texting that, works for both the therapist and classroom teacher.

Initiating Inclusive Related Services

Related service providers who are new to inclusive education, or find themselves with extremely large caseloads, may need to build an inclusive model a few students at a time. This gives them time to learn about the general education curriculum, develop relationships with classroom teachers, and set up a successful inclusive related services delivery model.

We have worked with related service professionals who have been creative in carving out inclusive therapy opportunities. Figure 15.1 presents some examples of general education activities that lend themselves to inclusive related services. Related service providers

Figure 15.1 Ideas for General Education Activities to Provide Inclusive Services

Related service provider	General education environment or activities	Examples of IEP goal areas to target
Speech-language pathologist	Literacy centers: students work independently or in small groups on reading and writing activities Lunchtime club History	Phonological awareness Vocabulary development Comprehension Speech fluency Lead articulation activity center Pragmatic language Conversations Oral presentations
Occupational therapist	Writer's workshop or literacy centers Free choice play (early elementary) Community-based instruction	Handwriting Sensory needs Typing Games addressing fine and gross motor skills Use assistive technology device to complete job tasks
Physical therapist	Physical education Passing periods Class lectures	Stretching Flexibility Range of motion Navigating campus safely (using walker, wheelchair)
Adaptive physical education	Physical education	Building strength and endurance
School psychologist/ counselor	"Fun Friday" activities Recess club	Working in a group Emotional regulation Social skills

collaborate with general education teachers and special education case managers to identify instructional routines or activities in which the therapist could work with a student on a focused skill and IEP goal area in a class assignment during independent seat work, lead a small group of students with and without disabilities, or facilitate conversations or play. While the therapist works in the classroom, on the playground, or with a club, teachers and peers are also able to learn effective strategies for supporting students that could be used across a student's schedule.

Case Study: Dan Provides Physical and Occupational Therapy

Dan is an occupational therapy (OT) and physical therapy (PT) provider working in secondary schools. Recently, he and the school's inclusion facilitator met and planned strategies to deliver PT and OT in the general education classrooms. This revolutionary idea was difficult to imagine at first, but almost immediately the possibilities became clear, and exciting! Dan took the lead; he brought the equipment that had once been stored in his classroom space and spread it around the school. Exercise therapy balls found new homes in social studies classrooms. Therapy mats were moved to gyms and English classrooms. Therapeutic seating discs made their way to math classes. Soon these resources were available where the students already were, rather than in a space that students had to travel to.

Dan found useful times and mechanisms for providing therapy. During English classes, while the teacher was reading a novel aloud, Dan sat on a therapy mat to work on stretching with Jessica, who has cerebral palsy. Jessica was able to listen to the book, along with her class, while getting out of her wheelchair and stretching her muscles. During social studies, Dan worked with Jeff to use adaptive equipment to write and improve handwriting. At lunch, Dan helped Matt learn to open his food containers.

As these brief examples illustrate, inclusive related services benefit everyone. Students with disabilities benefit in that they are not forced to miss instruction in one area to get instruction in another. The therapist benefits as well. He is able to learn what skills are actually needed in the student's lives. Dan can then target his therapy to skills that are truly useful and directly relate to the day-to-day needs of students. Special education teachers and paraeducators benefit from learning some skills that can be implemented in the classroom when the therapist is not there. Also, peers benefit. Having equipment available decreases stigma associated with its use. And with permission and supervision, a truly universally designed setting can be created where peers can be permitted to use these tools themselves, thus learning what strategies help them learn, too.

Scheduling

Administrators and special education case managers should include related service providers in conversations about the master school schedule and ensure that therapists are able to push-in to classrooms. Therapists may find that designing flexible therapy service times, such as a block schedule, or seeing students for one extended session a week, may help them develop a schedule that allows for co-teaching, direct therapy services, observation and consultation, and time for evaluations.

BOX 15.3   *Administrator Insight*

When building your master schedule, include related service providers and teacher leaders in the conversation. Many related service providers are itinerant, and for inclusive related services to work, their particular scheduling needs should be considered. For example, a therapist may be interested in pushing in to support students during English language arts (ELA) activities but is available at your school site only in the mornings. If time for ELA is set aside for the afternoon periods or block, the therapist may have to resort to pull-out services to meet her or his IEP-dictated service minutes.

Case Study: Developing an Inclusive Therapy Schedule

Samantha, a speech-language pathologist assigned to Pine View Elementary School, creates her therapy schedule at the beginning of the year, as shown in Figure 15.2. She begins the school year with a caseload of 60 students. She sees all of her students at least once a week, most for a 1-hour block. She has chosen to see her students in these blocks so that she has time to participate in literacy centers and projects, and co-teach lessons as they focus on language-specific goals. In addition, some of Samantha's students with pragmatic language goals participate in a lunch group, with peers to facilitate conversations and play games in a natural setting. Once a month, she collaborates with the kindergarten team to develop and teach language activities during the Wacky Wednesday celebration at school. This allows her three other Wednesday mornings a month and all day Friday to observe students, conduct evaluations, participate in IEP meetings, or write IEP documents. Samantha knows that sometimes she will need her Fridays to make up time that might have been lost earlier in the week due to IEP meetings or to spend additional time in the classroom of a student who is struggling and needs additional support. This type of scheduling arrangement can be easily matched in a secondary setting. In secondary schools, the therapist would work around class periods and schedule times to provide any group or individual services during a class period.

Minimizing the Impact of Pull-Out Related Services

Sometimes therapists are not able to provide fully push-in, inclusive services for a variety of reasons, including protecting the dignity of a student who has goals that are best addressed in a private setting (such as self-care goals). When related service providers deliver services under a pull-out model, it is important to work with the general education teacher, the special education case manager, and the family to identify times during a student's day that would be least disruptive for the student. In an elementary school classroom, a general education teacher may recommend a period of time reserved for independent work or daily silent reading after lunch. It is important for the general education teacher to maintain a consistent schedule and be conscientious of when students are receiving pull-out instruction when planning lesson activities. At the secondary level, pull-out during elective or study skill classes may be more ideal. Students with significant needs at the secondary level, who receive therapy services from three or more providers, may benefit from having one period a day scheduled for related services, leaving the rest of the day open for inclusion in general education classes.

Figure 15.2 Related Services Inclusive Therapy Schedule

Figure 15.2 Related Services Inclusive Therapy Schedule

Time	Monday	Tuesday	Wednesday	Thursday	Friday
8:10–9:10 am	Kindergarten A	Kindergarten B	Evaluations/Wacky Wednesday last week	Kindergarten C	IEP meetings/evaluations
9:15–10:15 am	1st grade A	1st grade B	1st grade C	3rd grade C	IEP meetings/evaluations
10:15–10:30 am	Recess	Recess	Recess	Recess	Recess
10:40–11:40 am	2nd grade A	2nd grade B	2nd grade C	3rd grade B	IEP meetings/evaluations
11:45 am–12:15 pm	3rd grade A	3rd grade B	K and 1st grade lunchtime social language group	3rd grade A	IEP meetings/evaluations
12:15–1 pm	Lunch	Lunch	Upper grades lunch bunch	Lunch	Lunch
1:05–2:05 pm	4th grade A	4th grade B	Lunch and evaluations	4th grade C	IEP meetings/evaluations
2:05–3:05 pm	5th grade A	5th grade B	Early release—professional development	5th grade C	IEP meetings/evaluations

BOX 15.4

Finding a Time and Place for Therapies

In this chapter, we've focused on how therapists can provide information and strategies to teachers. However, the collaborative relationship is always a two-way street. Teachers can give great strategies and help therapists think of real-world applications for therapy. For example, a student might have an OT goal to hold scissors appropriately and cut out various objects. This standard goal has limited real-world applications, and it might be challenging to think of when or how this goal could be worked on in general education settings. Ecological inventories, as discussed in Chapter 9, can help identify when and where a student needs specific skills. It might become obvious that cutting out materials is best worked on during lunch, to open up food packets. Besides, imagine the motivation of learning to hold scissors to open a bag of chips versus cutting out a bunch of triangles. There is sure to be greater improvement made by the student in the real world than the therapy world!

Utilizing Peer and Paraeducator Supports

When therapies are provided to students in the general education environment, the therapist is able to model intervention strategies for peers and paraeducators, who can later support the student in using these strategies throughout the day. For example, during free choice time, the speech-language pathologist facilitates communication and turn taking for a group of students playing a game. She models and directs peers to use picture cards with the words "Your turn" to help cue a student to pick up the dice and take his turn. The students can later use this card when playing as a group without adult support. In a secondary classroom, an occupational therapist might be observing a paraeducator reviewing flashcards with a student. The therapist notices the student does not seem to be looking at the cards before making a choice and offers suggestions for how to change the array of cards to help the student focus and make an accurate choice. If therapists had not been in the classroom in either scenario, students would have lacked meaningful modes of participation, communication, or instructional supports.

Strategies for Educators

Successful inclusive related services are built on a foundation of teamwork between therapists and teachers. It is important for teachers to remember that therapists' schedules have a variety of constraints and to honor the time of each professional by maintaining communication, including therapists in planning, and developing a consistent instructional schedule that allows therapists to contribute their particular skills to the classroom. Teachers can help pave the way for an effective collaborative relationship by welcoming therapists into their classrooms and remembering that the therapists are there to support students, not "fix" them.

Collaboration to Share Goals and Strategies

Developing a plan for how IEP goals are going to be addressed in the general education environment is essential. This may be addressed through an inclusive instructional plan (see Chapter 5) developed by the IEP team or through informal conversations between teachers and therapists. During conversations between teachers and therapists, it is helpful to document agreed-upon schedules, ideas for integrating therapy into the classroom, and the roles of each team member in implementing IEP goals. Team members can then refer to this document to help them establish a routine in the classroom and then later evaluate the effectiveness of integrating therapy into the classroom, making adjustments as necessary.

BOX 15.5

Common Core Connection

In addition to traditional literacy and mathematics, the Common Core State Standards emphasize skill development in speaking, working in collaborative groups, and using technology for writing, research, and developing multimedia projects. Related service providers can be an asset to their colleagues and students by offering strategies and designing therapy sessions that support students in developing these skills.

Case Study: Sarah's IEP Team Creates a Related Service Instructional Plan

A related service instructional planning tool, such as the one in Figure 15.3, was used by Sarah's fifth-grade IEP team to clarify the roles of each team member in implementing interventions and working on IEP goals in the classroom. Sarah's classroom teacher, Mr. Brown, met briefly with each therapist the first week of school and discussed his classroom routines and offered recommendations for ideal times for therapists to push in to the classroom. Once therapists identified a time that would support Sarah's acquisition of therapy-related goals and their schedule, they discussed with Mr. Brown how to integrate therapy into the instructional routine and identified ways for each team member to contribute to Sarah's progress. In addition, the team recognized the importance of including her peers and determined some ways to involve them in supporting Sarah in making progress toward her goals. The team also identified times to provide consultation to Mr. Brown and Sarah's special education team.

Implementing Therapy Interventions in the Classroom

Classroom teachers are responsible for the instructional planning of their classroom and play a significant role in the success of inclusive related services through their implementation of therapy-specific strategies into classroom routines and instruction. Teachers should ask therapists for clarification and support when needed to successfully incorporate strategies into their instructional planning. Therapists can aid this by offering some flexibility with consult time and observe during a lesson that may not be on their typical schedule so they can provide a teacher with useful feedback and strategies. Mutual respect of professionals' time and expertise will lead to student progress and further develop the collaborative relationship.

Strategies for Parents

Parents are the only member of the IEP team who will work with every single therapist, educator, and medical professional a student receives services from during his school years.

Figure 15.3 Related Services Instructional Planning Tool

Student: Sarah   **Teacher:** Brown

Therapy schedule: SLP: Wed. book club (10–11); OT writing workshop (Thurs. 9–9:30); PT 2nd week of school every day PE (2–2:20), 2 x month Fri. (11:30–12:15); consult at end of therapy session and during times as needed during the year.

Goals	Therapist	Teacher	Paraeducator	Peers
Listen to class novels or nonfiction texts and respond to comprehension questions with 85% accuracy and use augmentative and alternative communication (AAC) to make comments, requests, and ask questions	SLP: set up vocabulary on software; push in during Language Arts for weekly book club and facilitate small-group conversation about novel the group is reading; model and facilitate use of AAC to participate in conversation about novel	Acquire audio or digital copies of books; front load book club (and comprehension questions) to Sarah so she has time to type and save her answers; teach comprehension strategies; provide SLP with book club lesson/novel in advance	Read aloud passages as Sarah references text to find answers; scribe answers into AAC when Sarah is fatigued; use comprehension strategies taught in class	Teach peers to pause and allow wait time for Sarah to use her AAC to respond; ask Sarah to use her AAC to read aloud important sections of text; teach peers and Sarah how to make flashcards on AAC for group to study with
Select an activity and ask a peer to participate during independent work or free time	OT: develop a collection of partner/free time activities Sarah can access in the classroom SLP: following book club provide Sarah with cues for activity choice and working with peers	Give Sarah a 30-min. heads-up before free time so she can plan which activity she wants to do and be prepared to ask peers	Facilitate working with peers as needed during this time	Assist Sarah with setting up her AAC to the game tab; respond to Sarah's questions during independent work time
When frustrated or upset, initiate a calming activity or request a break	OT: provide Sarah and classroom with a box of stress relievers, chart of options for when upset and rehearse using; teach whole class how to recognize and regulate emotions SLP: develop vocab for requesting a break on AAC and facilitate use as needed during book club	Keep classroom stress relief kit in accessible location; encourage use by whole class; be knowledgeable of Sarah's mood and cue her to take a break when needed	Be knowledgeable of Sarah's mood and cue her to take a break when needed; remind all students to use the stress relief box when needed	Teach peers to access the stress relief box when they need it

(Continued)

Figure 15.3 (Continued)

Transition within and between classrooms in power wheelchair without bumping into objects or people	PT: practice safe transitions as alternate to PE for 2nd week of school to practice safe transitions, then during workshop push in to support Sarah in classroom activity transitions and transition to lunch; teach staff how to guide Sarah and chair during transitions	Consider time needed for Sarah to transition to next activity/classroom (allow for early or late arrivals); cue Sarah to clean up activity a few minutes before rest of class; check for accessible access for field trips	Know how to use Sarah's chair (what to do in case of power failure, manual mode, etc.); use PT cues throughout day to support safe transitions	Keep backpacks on classroom hooks to prevent Sarah running over them
Use email to communicate with friends and family	SLP: at end of book club teach Sarah how to email teacher what her group discussed OT: push in during writing and teach Sarah how to use predictive text software, organize contacts to send email	Send email to Sarah on weekly basis; adapt written assignments so Sarah can respond via email; respond to Sarah's emails; send OT writing activities in advance	Observe OT and SLP and utilize strategies during other classroom writing activities with Sarah	Encourage students to email Sarah

Establishing Priorities

Parents have the right to request that the IEP team consider inclusive related services and to participate in making this a reality for their child. In our experience, we have seen parents act in an integral role in enabling inclusive related services by asking the team how therapy could be provided in a student's class, prioritizing goals with the team, agreeing to discontinue goals that may no longer be age-appropriate or essential for secondary students, and following through with using therapy strategies at home and in the community.

Conclusion

Establishing inclusive related services requires conversations at the IEP team level, at the school site level to align master schedules and establish time for collaboration, and sometimes at the district level to address concerns regarding caseload size and itinerant staffing. Starting inclusive services with one or a few students on a therapist's caseload may be the best place to start while working out systemic issues surrounding caseloads and site staffing levels. Therapists, teachers, and parents must work together to ensure therapy-specific strategies are implemented consistently throughout a student's day at home and school.

Please be sure to go to the website (http://www.corwin.com/theinclusiontoolbox) to download the forms and resources from this chapter!

16

Concluding Thoughts

When you know better you do better.

—Maya Angelou

As we write this book, we recognize the challenges and limitations individual teachers, parents, related service providers, and administrators face as they advocate for inclusive education in their classrooms and schools. Our hope is you've found some strategies and tools to help you organize for inclusion and do inclusion well, whether you're working at including one student, one classroom, one school, or one district at time. We know from personal experience that the road to inclusive education is still currently the road less traveled and at times tests our endurance. But we also know it is the road worth taking.

In this book, we've provided you with a toolbox containing resources, strategies, and ideas to help you on your journey. Like any toolbox, the skilled worker will pick and choose the right tool for the job. We view our toolbox in a similar manner; you, as the inclusion facilitator, can peruse ideas, tools, and strategies, and use (or modify) those that are applicable and important for your situation. Be sure to refer to the accompanying website for templates and resources you can use throughout your journey—you are free to use the tools in whatever way you need to in your situation. We simply encourage you to think carefully about the tools you select, keeping the following big ideas in mind:

1. *Placement in general education is a starting place, not an end.* Getting in the door is a huge accomplishment, but be sure to make meaningful learning happening once the student is the general education setting.

2. *Bring in supports and services; focus on outcomes.* Once the student is in the door, make sure that those people who are providing instruction are skilled and confident to do so, that a focus on positive outcomes in all domains is envisioned and supported, and that those supports and services a student needs to be a successful learner are provided.

3. *Be flexible.* There is no one right way to support a student's inclusion. Create for yourself a big toolbox, and be ready to pull out the right tool for the job. And remember, the fun (and challenge) of teaching is that often the first tool or strategy we try isn't the right one. It's okay to put that tool back and try something else. This is easier to do with a bigger toolbox, so keep working and building your skills and resources!

Fuel for the Journey

If you start out alone on your inclusive education journey, and it will be a journey, take the time to find other professionals or families who can support you, inspire you, and remind you to persevere while overcoming barriers to inclusion. You may find your support system in your school, home, university, or online. We have become fans of social media to help us stay inspired and energized, and to give us ideas. Facebook and Twitter are great for this. Some of our favorite websites include the following:

- The Inclusive Class
- Kids Included Together
- PrAACtical AAC
- Think Inclusive
- Paula Kluth
- TASH

As we conclude this book, we thank you for going on this journey with us, and hope that you find this book to be a useful resource in supporting the full and meaningful inclusion of all students. As time goes by we know that you'll find Maya Angelou's quote to be true: As you know better, you do better. There is no one way to do inclusive education right and you'll find over the years that inclusion can and does look different for different students and in different schools. You'll make mistakes and hit bumps in the road, just like we have, and we hope that you'll pick this book back up and find a new strategy to help you begin on your journey again.

Food for Thought

We would like to leave you with some food for thought and final inspirations to sustain you on this endeavor.

> When inclusive education is fully embraced, we abandon the idea that children have to become "normal" in order to contribute to the world. . . . We begin to look beyond typical ways of becoming valued members of the community, and in doing so, begin to realize the achievable goal of providing all children with an authentic sense of belonging.
>
> —Norman Kunc

> It wasn't that I didn't know the answers to the algebra and calculus questions that bothered me. It was that I didn't even know what algebra and calculus were.
>
> —Nancy Ward, reflecting on a segregated education

Regardless of how good of a swim instructor you are, you can't teach a person to swim in the parking lot of a swimming pool.

—Norman Kunc

An optimist: Someone who figures that taking a step backward after taking a step forward is not a disaster, it's more like a cha-cha.

—Source Unknown

References

Agran, M., Blanchard, C., & Wehmeyer, M. L. (2000). Promoting transition goals and self-determination through self-directed learning: The self-determined learning model of instruction. *Education and Training in Mental Retardation and Developmental Disabilities, 35*, 351–364.

Allport, G. W. (1954). *The nature of prejudice.* Cambridge, MA: Addison-Wesley.

Aspy, R., & Grossman, B. G. (2007). *The ziggurat model: A framework for designing comprehensive interventions for individuals with high-functioning autism and Asperger syndrome.* Shawnee Mission, KS: Autism Asperger.

Aud, S., Hussar, W., Johnson, F., Kena, G., Roth, E., Manning, E., . . . Zhang, J. (2012). *The condition of education 2012* (NCES 2012–045). Washington, DC: U.S. Department of Education, National Center for Education Statistics. Retrieved from http://nces.ed.gov/pubsearch/pubsinfo.asp?pubid=2012045

Austin, V. L. (2001). Teachers' beliefs about co-teaching. *Remedial and Special Education, 22*, 245–255.

Barnard-Brak, L., & Lechtenberger, D. (2010). Student IEP participation and academic achievement across time. *Remedial and Special Education, 31*, 343–349.

Barrie, W., & McDonald, J. (2002). Administrative support for student-led individualized education programs. *Remedial and Special Education, 23*, 116–122.

Benz, M., Lindstrom, L., & Yovanoff, P. (2000). Improving graduation and employment outcomes of students with disabilities: Predictive factors and student perspectives. *Exceptional Children, 66*, 509–529.

Billingsley, B. S. (2007). Recognizing and supporting the critical roles of teachers in special education leadership. *Exceptionality: A Special Education Journal, 15*(3), 163–176.

Blood, E., Johnson, J. W., Ridenour, L., Simmons, K., & Crouch, S. (2011). Using an iPod Touch to teach social and self-management skills to an elementary student with emotional/behavioral disorders. *Education and Treatment of Children, 34*, 299–322.

Broer, S. M., Doyle, M. B., & Giangreco, M. (2005). Perspectives of students with intellectual disabilities about their experiences with paraprofessional support. *Exceptional Children, 71*, 415–430.

Browder, D., Spooner, F., Ahlgrim-Delzell, L., Harris, A. A., & Wakeman, S. (2008). A meta-analysis on teaching mathematics to students with signifiant cognitive disabilities. *Exceptional Children, 74*, 407–432.

Browder, D., Wakeman, S., Spooner, F., Ahlgrim-Delzell, L., & Algozzine, B.. (2006). Research in reading instruction for individuals with significant cognitive disabilities. *Exceptional Children, 72*, 392–408.

Brown Beyers, N., Howerter, C. S., & Morgan, J. J. (2013). Tools and strategies for making co-teaching work. *Intervention in School and Clinic, 20*(10), 108.

Bugaj, S. J. (2000). Avoiding the pitfalls of failing to implement an IEP: Tips for secondary school principals and guidance counselors. *NASSP Bulletin, 84*(613), 41–46.

Bullard, H. R. (2004). 20 ways to . . . ensure the successful inclusion of a child with Asperger syndrome in the general education classroom. *Intervention in School and Clinic, 39*(3), 176–180.

Bunch, G., & Valeo, A. (2004). Student attitudes toward peers with disabilities in inclusive and special education schools. *Disability & Society, 19*(1), 61–76.

Burstein, N., Sears, S., Wilcoxen, A., Cabello, B., & Spagna, M. (2004). Moving toward inclusive practices. *Remedial and Special Education, 25*, 104–116.

Carrington, S., & Elkins, J. (2002). Bridging the gap between inclusive policy and inclusive culture in secondary schools. *Support for Learning, 17*(2), 51–57.

Carter, E. W., Cushing, L., Clark, N., & Kennedy, C. (2005). Effects of peer support interventions on students' access to the general curriculum and social interactions. *Research & Practice for Persons With Severe Disabilities, 30*(1), 15–25.

Carter, E. W., Hughes, C., Guth, C., & Copeland, S. R. (2005). Factors influencing social interaction among high school students with intellectual disabilities and their general education peers. *American Journal on Mental Retardation, 110*, 366–377.

Carter, E., O'Rourke, L., Sisco, L. G., & Pelsue, D. (2009). Knowledge, responsibilities, and training needs of paraprofessionals in elementary and secondary schools. *Remedial and Special Education, 30*, 344–359.

Carter, E. W., & Pesko, M. J. (2008). Social validity of peer interaction intervention strategies in high school classrooms: Effectiveness, feasibility, and actual use. *Exceptionality, 16*, 156–173.

Causton-Theoharis, J. N., & Malmgren, K. W. (2004). Increasing interactions between students with severe disabilities and their peers via paraprofessional training. *Exceptional Children, 71*, 431–444.

Cawley, J., Hayden, S., Cade, E., & Baker-Kroczynski, S. (2002). Including students with disabilities into the general education science classroom. *Exceptional Children, 68*, 423–435.

Charlton, J. I. (2000). *Nothing about us without us: Disability oppression and empowerment.* Berkeley: University of California Press.

Chopra, R. V., Sandoval-Lucero, E., & French, N. K. (2011). Effective supervision of paraeducators: Multiple benefits and outcomes. *National Teacher Education Journal, 4*(2), 15–26.

Cihak, D. F., & Gama, R. I. (2008). Noncontigent escape access to self-reinforcement to increase task engagement for students with moderate to severe disabilities. *Education and Training in Developmental Disabilities, 43*, 556–568.

Claes, C., Van Hove, G., Vandevelde, S., van Loon, J., & Schalock, R. L. (2010). Person-centered planning: Analysis of research and effectiveness. *Intellectual and Developmental Disabilities, 48*, 432–453.

Collins, B. C. (2012). *Systematic instruction for students with moderate and severe disabilities.* Baltimore, MD: Paul H. Brookes.

Cook, B. G. (2001). A comparison of teachers' attitudes toward their included students with mild and severe disabilities. *Journal of Special Education, 34*, 203–213.

Cook, B. G. (2004). Inclusive teachers' attitudes toward their students with disabilities: A replication and extension. *Elementary School Journal, 104*, 307–320.

Cooper, J. O., Heron, T. E., & Heward, W. L. (2007). *Applied behavior analysis.* Upper Saddle River, NJ: Pearson.

Copeland, S. R., Hughes, C., Carter, E. W., Guth, C., Presley, J., Williams, C. R., & Fowler, S. E. (2004). Increasing access to general education: Perspectives of participants in a high school peer support program. *Remedial and Special Education, 25*, 342–352.

Coughlin, J., McCoy, K. M., Kenzer, A., Mathur, S. R., & Zucker, S. H. (2012). Effects of self-monitoring strategy on independent work behavior of students with mild intellectual disability. *Education and Training in Autism and Developmental Disabilities, 47*(2), 154–164.

Courtade, G., Spooner, F., & Browder, D. (2007). Review of studies with students with significant cognitive disabilities which link to science standards. *Research & Practice for Persons With Severe Disabilities, 32*(1), 43–49.

Cramer, E., Liston, A., Nevin, A., & Thousand, J. (2010). Co-teaching in urban secondary school districts to meet the needs of all teachers and learners: Implications for teacher education reform. *International Journal of Whole Schooling, 6*(2), 59–76.

Cross, A. F., Traub, E. K., Hutter-Pishgahi, L., & Shelton, G. (2004). Elements of successful inclusion for children with significant disabilities. *Topics in Early Childhood Special Education, 24*(3), 169–183.

Cushing, L. S., Clark, N. M., Carter, E. W., & Kennedy, C. H. (2003). Peer supports and access to the general education curriculum. *TASH Connections, 29*(10), 8–11.

Cushing, L. S., Clark, N. M., Carter, E. W., & Kennedy, C. H. (2005). Access to the general education curriculum for students with severe disabilities: What it means and how to accomplish it. *Teaching Exceptional Children, 38*(2), 6–13.

Dabkowski, D. M. (2004). Encouraging active parent participation in IEP team meetings. *Teaching Exceptional Children, 36*(3), 34–39.

Damon, S., Riley-Tillman, T. C., & Fiorello, C. (2008). Comparing methods of identifying reinforcing stimuli in school consultation. *Journal of Educational and Psychological Consultation, 18*(1), 31–53.

Danneker, J. E., & Bottge, B. A. (2009). Benefits of and barriers to elementary student-led individualized education programs. *Remedial and Special Education, 30*, 225–233.

Dore, R., Dion, A., Wagner, S., & Brunet, J.-P. (2002). High school inclusion of adolescents with mental retardation: A multiple case study. *Education and Training in Mental Retardation and Developmental Disabilities, 37*, 253–261.

Dotger, B., & Ashby, C. (2010). Exposing conditional inclusive ideologies through simulated interactions. *Teacher Education and Special Education, 33*(2), 114–130.

Downing, J. (2005). *Teaching communication skills to students with severe disabilities* (2nd ed.). Baltimore, MD: Paul H. Brookes.

Downing, J. (2010). *Academic instruction for students with moderate and severe intellectual disabilities in inclusive classrooms.* Thousand Oaks, CA: Corwin.

Downing, J., & Eichinger, J. (2008). Educating students with diverse strengths and needs together: Rationale for inclusion. In J. E. Downing (Ed.), *Including students with severe and multiple disabilities in typical classrooms: Practical strategies for teachers* (pp. 1–20). Baltimore, MD: Paul H. Brookes.

Downing, J., & Peckham-Hardin, K. D. (2007). Inclusive education: What makes it a good education for students with moderate to severe disabilities? *Research & Practice for Persons With Severe Disabilities, 32*(1), 16–30.

Downing, J., Ryndak, D., & Clark, D. (2000). Paraeducators in inclusive classrooms: Their own perceptions. *Remedial and Special Education, 21*(3), 171–181.

Downing, J., Spencer, S., & Cavallaro, C. (2004). The development of an inclusive charter elementary school: Lessons learned. *Research & Practice for Persons With Severe Disabilities, 29*(1), 11–24.

Drecktrah, M. E. (2000). Preservice teachers' preparation to work with paraeducators. *Teacher Education and Special Education, 23*(2), 157–164.

Durand, V. M. (1990). *Severe behavior problems: A functional communication training approach.* New York, NY: Guilford Press.

Dymond, S. K., & Russell, D. L. (2004). Impact of grade and disability on the instructional context of inclusive classrooms. *Education & Training in Developmental Disabilities, 39*(2), 127–140.

Education for All Handicapped Children Act, PL 94-142, U.S. Statutes at Large. 899. 777–796 (1975).

Ehren, B. (2000). Maintaining a therapeutic focus and sharing responsibility for student success: Keys to in-classroom speech-language services. *Language, Speech, and Hearing Services in Schools, 31*, 219–229.

Eisenman, L. T., Chamberlin, M., & McGahee-Kovac, M. (2005). A teacher inquiry group on student-led IEPs: Starting small to make a difference. *Teacher Education and Special Education, 28*(3), 195–206.

Etscheidt, S. (2006). Progress monitoring: Legal issues and recommendations for IEP teams. *Teaching Exceptional Children, 38*(3), 56–60.

Ferguson, D. L. (1995). The real challenge of inclusion: Confessions of a "rabid inclusionist." *Phi Delta Kappan, 77*, 281–287.

Fisher, D., & Frey, N. (2001). Access to the core curriculum: Critical ingredients for student success. *Remedial and Special Education, 22*(3), 148–157.

Fisher, D., Frey, N., & Thousand, J. (2003). What do special educators need to know and be prepared to do for inclusive schooling to work? *Teacher Education and Special Education, 26*(1), 42–50.

Fisher, M., & Meyer, L. H. (2002). Development and social competence after two years for students enrolled in inclusive and self-contained educational programs. *Research & Practice for Persons With Severe Disabilities, 27*(3), 165–174.

Foreman, P., Arthur-Kelly, M., Pascoe, S., & King, B.. (2004). Evaluating the educational experiences of students with profound and multiple disabilities in inclusive and segregated classroom settings: An Australian perspective. *Research & Practice for Persons With Severe Disabilities, 29*(3), 183–193.

French, N. (1999a). Paraeducators and teachers: Shifting roles. *Teaching Exceptional Children, 32*(2), 69–73.

French, N. (1999b). Paraeducators: Who are they and what do they do? *Teaching Exceptional Children, 32*(2), 65–69.

French, N. (2001). Supervising paraprofessionals: A survey of teacher practices. *Journal of Special Education, 35*(1), 41–53.

French, N., & Chopra, R. (1999). Parent perspectives on the roles of paraprofessionals. *Journal of the Association for Persons with Severe Handicaps, 24*, 259–272.

French, N., & Chopra, R. (2006). Teachers as executives. *Theory Into Practice, 45*, 230–238.

Friend, M., Cook, L., Hurley-Chamberlain, D., & Shamberger, C. (2010). Co-teaching: An illustration of the complexity of collaboration in special education. *Journal of Educational and Psychological Consultation, 20*(1), 9–27.

Gaylord, V., Vandercook, T., & York-Barr, J. (Eds.). (2003). *Impact: Feature Issue on Revisiting Inclusive K-12 Education, 16*(1). Minneapolis: University of Minnesota, Institute on Community Integration.

Giangreco, M. F. (1986a). Delivery of therapeutic services in special education programs for learners with severe handicaps. *Physical & Occupational Therapy in Pediatrics, 6*(2), 5–15.

Giangreco, M. F. (1986b). Effects of integrated therapy: a pilot study. *Journal of the Association for Persons with Severe Handicaps 11*(3), 205–208.

Giangreco, M. F. (2000). Related services research for students with low-incidence disabilities: Implications for speech-language pathologists in inclusive classrooms. *Language, Speech, and Hearing Services in Schools, 31*, 230–239.

Giangreco, M. (2004). The stairs don't go anywhere! A self-advocate's reflections on specialized services and their impact on people with disabilities. In M. Nind, J. Rix, K. Sheehy, & K. Simmons (Eds.), *Inclusive education: Diverse perspectives* (pp. 34–42). London, England: David Fulton.

Giangreco, M. F. (1997). Key lessons learned about inclusive education: Summary of the 1996 Schonell Memorial Lecture. *International Journal of Disability, Development & Education, 44*(3), 193–206.

Giangreco, M. F., & Broer, S. M. (2005). Questionable utilization of paraprofessionals in inclusive schools: Are we addressing symptoms or causes? *Focus on Autism & Other Developmental Disabilities, 20*(1), 10–26.

Giangreco, M. (1995). The stairs don't go anywhere! A self-advocate's reflections on specialized services and their impact on people with disabilities. In M. Nind, J. Rix, K. Sheehy & K. Simmons (Eds.), *Inclusive Education: Diverse Perspectives*. London: David Fulton Publishers in association with The Open University.

Giangreco, M., Broer, S. M., & Edelman, S. W. (2001). Teacher engagement with students with disabilities: Differences between paraprofessional service delivery models. *Journal of the Association for Persons With Severe Handicaps, 26*(2), 75–86.

Giangreco, M., Edelman, S., Broer, S., & Doyle, M. (2001). Paraprofessional support of students with disabilities: Literature from the past decade. *Exceptional Children, 68*(1), 45–63.

Giangreco, M., Edelman, S., Luiselli, T., & MacFarland, S. (1997). Helping or hovering? Effects of instructional assistant proximity on students with disabilities. *Exceptional Children, 64*, 7–18.

Giangreco, M. F., Prelock, P. A., Reid, R. R., Dennis, R. E., & Edelman, S. W. (2000). Roles of related services personnel in inclusive schools. In. R. Villa & J. Thousand (Eds.), *Restructuring for caring and effective education: Piecing the puzzle together* (2nd ed., pp. 360–388). Baltimore, MD: Paul H. Brookes.

Giangreco, M. F, Suter, J. C., & Graf, V. (2011). Appendix F: Roles of team members supporting students with disabilities in inclusive classrooms. In M. F. Giangreco, C. Cloninger, and V. Iverson, *Choosing outcomes and accommodations for children (COACH): A guide to educational planning for students with disabilities* (3rd ed., pp. 197–204). Baltimore, MD: Paul H. Brookes.

Giangreco, M. F., York, J., & Rainforth, B. (1989). Providing related services to learners with severe handicaps in educational settings: Pursuing the least restrictive option. *Pediatric Physical Therapy, 1*(2), 55–63.

Hapner, A., & Imel, B. (2002). The students' voices: "Teachers started to listen and show respect." *Remedial and Special Education, 23*, 122–126.

Hedeen, D. L., & Ayres, B. J. (2002). "You Want Me to Teach Him to Read?" Fulfilling the Intent of IDEA. *Journal of Disability Policy Studies, 13*(3), 180–189.

Heineman, M., Dunlap, G., & Kincaid, D. (2005). Positive support strategies for students with behavioral disorders in general education settings. *Psychology in the Schools, 42*, 779–794.

Hilton, A., & Gerlach, K. (1997, June). Employment, preparation and management of paraeducators: challenges to appropriate service for students with developmental disabilities. *Education and Training in Mental Retardation and Developmental Disabilities*, pp. 71–76.

Holt, G. L. (1971). Systematic probability reversal and control of behavior through reinforcement menus. *The Psychological Record, 21*, 465–469.

Hudson, M. E., Browder, D. M., & Wood, L. A. (2013). Review of experimental research on academic learning by students with moderate and severe intellectual disability in general education. *Research & Practice for Persons With Severe Disabilities, 38*(1), 17–29.

Hughes, C., Agran, M., Cosgriff, J. C., & Washington, B. H. (2013). Student self-determination: A preliminary investigation of the role of participation in inclusive settings. *Education and Training in Autism and Developmental Disabilities, 48*(1), 3–17.

Hughes, C., Guth, C., Hall, S., Presley, J., Dye, M., & Byers, C. (1999). They are my best friends: Peer buddies promote inclusion in high school. *Teaching Exceptional Children, 31*(5), 32–37.

Idol, L. (2006). Toward inclusion of special education students in general education. *Remedial and Special Education, 27*(2), 77–94.

Individuals with Disabilities Education Improvement Act, H.R. 1350, PL 108-446 (2004).

Ingram, K., Lewis-Palmer, T., & Sugai, G. (2005). Function-based intervention planning: Comparing the effectiveness of FBA function-based and non-function-based intervention plans. *Journal of Positive Behavior Interventions, 7*, 224–236.

Jameson, J. M., McDonnell, J., Johnson, J. W., Riesen, T., & Polychronis, S. C. (2007). A comparison of one-to-one embedded instruction in the general education classroom and one-to-one massed practice instruction in the special education classroom. *Education and Treatment of Children, 30*(1), 23–44.

Jameson, J. M., Walker, R., Utley, K., & Maughan, R. (2012). A comparison of embedded total task instruction in teaching behavioral chains to massed one-on-one instruction for students with intellectual disabilities accessing general education settings and core academic content. *Behavior Modification, 36*, 320–340.

Janney, R. E., & Snell, M. E. (2006). Modifying schoolwork in inclusive classrooms. *Theory Into Practice, 45*, 215–223.

Janney, R. E., Snell, M. E., Beers, M. K., & Raynes, M. (1995). Integrating students with moderate and severe disabilities in elementary general education classes. *Journal of the Association for Persons With Severe Handicaps, 21*(2), 72–80.

Johnson, J. W., McDonnell, J., Holzwarth, V. N., & Hunter, K. (2004). The efficacy of embedded instruction for students with developmental disabilities enrolled in general education classes. *Journal of Positive Behavior Interventions, 6,* 214–227.

Johnson, M. (Ed.). (2006). *Disability awareness—Do it right! Your all-in-one how-to guide: Tips, techniques, and handouts for a successful Awareness Day.* Louisville, KY: Advocado Press.

Jones, B. A., & Gansle, K. A. (2010). The effects of a mini-conference, socioeconomic satus, and parent education on perceived and actual parent participation in individual education program meetings. *Research in the Schools, 17*(2), 23–28.

Katsiyannis, A., Hodge, J., & Lanford, A. (2000). Paraeducators: Legal and practice considerations. *Remedial and Special Education, 21,* 297–304.

Kellegrew, D. H., & Allen, D. (1996). Occupational therapy in full-inclusion classrooms: A case study from the Moorpark model. *American Journal of Occupational Therapy, 50,* 718–724.

Kern, L., Delaney, B., Clarke, S., Dunlap, G., & Childs, K. (2001). Improving the classroom behavior of students with emotional behavioral disorders using individualized curricular modifications. *Journal of Emotional and Behavioral Disorders, 9,* 239–247.

Kleinert, H. L., Miracle, S. A., & Sheppard-Jones, K. (2007). Including students with moderate and severe disabilities in extracurricular and community recreation activites: Steps to success. *Teaching Exceptional Children, 39*(6), 33–38.

Kurth, J. A., Gross, M., Lovinger, S., & Catalano, T. (2012). Grading students with significant disabilities in inclusive settings: Teacher perspectives. *Journal of the International Association of Special Education, 13*(1), 39–55.

Kurth, J. A., & Keegan, L. (2012). Development and use of curricular adaptations for students receiving special education services. *Journal of Special Education.* Advance online publication. doi:10.1177/0022466912464782

Lee, S. H., Palmer, S., & Wehmeyer, M. L. (2009). Goal setting and self-monitoring for students with disabilities: Practical tips and ideas for teachers. *Intervention in School & Clinic, 44*(3), 139–145.

Lee, S. H., Wehmeyer, M. L., Soukup, J. H., & Palmer, S. B. (2010). Impact of curriculum modifications on access to the general education curriculum for students with disabilities. *Exceptional Children, 76*(2), 213–233.

Lieberman, A., & Miller, L. (2004). *Teacher leadership.* San Francisco, CA: Jossey-Bass.

Lingo, A. S., Barton-Arwood, S. M., & Jolivette, K. (2011). Teachers working together: Improving learning outcomes in the inclusive classroom-practical strategies and examples. *Teaching Exceptional Children, 43*(3), 6–13.

Liston, A. G., Nevin, A., & Malian, I. (2009). What do paraeducators in inclusive classrooms say about their work? Analysis of national survey data and follow-up interviews in California. *Teaching Exceptional Children Plus, 5*(5), 2–17.

Macfarlane, C. A. (1998). Assessment: The key to appropriate curriculum and instruction. In A. Hilton & R. Ringlaben (Eds.), *Best and promising practices in developmental disabilities* (pp. 35–60). Austin, TX: Pro-Ed.

Marks, S., Schrader, C., & Levine, M. (1999). Paraeducator experiences in inclusive settings: helping, hovering, or holding their own? *Exceptional Children, 65,* 315–328.

Martin, J. E., Van Dycke, J. L., Christensen, W. R., Greene, B. A., Gardner, J. E., & Lovett, D. L. (2006). Increasing student participation in IEP meetings: Establishing the self-directed IEP as an evidence-based practice. *Exceptional Children, 72,* 299–316.

Mason, C. Y., Field, S. L., & Sawilowsky, S. (2004). Implementation of self-determination activities and student participation in IEPs. *Exceptional Children, 70,* 441–451.

Mason, C. Y., McGahee-Kovac, M., Johnson, E., & Stillerman, S. (2002). Implementing student-led IEPs: Student participation and student and teacher reactions. *Career Development for Exceptional Individuals, 25*(2), 171–192.

Mastropieri, M. A. (2001). Is the glass half full or half empty? Challenges encountered by first-year special education teachers. *Journal of Special Education, 35*(2), 66–74.

Mastropieri, M. A., & Scruggs, T. E. (2001). Promotion inclusion in secondary classrooms. *Learning Disabilities Quarterly, 24,* 265–274.

Matson, J. L., & Boisjoli, J. A. (2009). The token economy for children with intellectual disability and/or autism: A review. *Research in Developmental Disabilities, 30,* 240–248.

McDonnell, J., Johnson, J. W., & McQuivey, C. (2008). *Embedded instruction for students with developmental disabilities in general education classrooms.* Arlington, VA: Council for Exceptional Children, Division on Developmental Disabiltiies.

McGahee-Kovac, M., Mason, C. Y., Wallace, Y, & Jones, B. A. (2001). *Student-led IEPs: A guide for student involvement.* Arlington, VA: Council for Exceptional Children.

McGregor, G., & Vogelsberg, R. T. (1998). *Inclusive schooling practices: Pedagogical and research foundations:* Baltimore, MD: Paul H. Brookes.

McIntyre, L. L., Eckert, T. L., Fiese, B. H., DiGennaro Reed, F. D., & Wildenger, L. K. (2010). Family concerns surrounding kindergarten transition: A comparison of students in special and general education. *Early Childhood Education Journal, 38,* 259–263.

McLeskey, J., Henry, D., & Hodges, D. (1998). Inclusion: Where is it happening? *Teaching Exceptional Children, 30,* 4–10.

McLeskey, J., & Waldron, N. L. (2007). Making differences ordinary in inclusive classrooms. *Intervention in School and Clinic, 42*(3), 162–168.

Menlove, R. R., Hudson, P. J., & Suter, D. (2001). A field of IEP dreams: Increasing general education teacher participation in the IEP development process. *Teaching Exceptional Children, 33*(5), 28–33.

Meyer, L. H. (2001). The impact on inclusion on children's lives: Multiple outcomes, and friendship in particular. *International Journal of Disability, Development & Education, 48,* 9–31.

Miner, C. A., & Bates, P. E. (1997). The effect of person centered planning activities on the IEP/transition planning process. *Education & Training in Mental Retardation & Developmental Disabilities, 32*(2), 105–112.

Modell, S., & Valdez, L. (2002). Beyong bowling: Transition planning for students with disabilities. *Teaching Exceptional Children, 34*(6), 46–53.

Mulvibill, B. A., Cotton, J. N., & Gyaben, S. L. (2004). Best practices for inclusive child and adolescent out-of-school care: A review of the literature. *Family & Community Health, 27*(1), 52–64.

Munk, D. D., & Bursuck, W. D. (2001). Preliminary findings on personalized grading plans for middle school students with learning disabilities. *Exceptional Children, 67*(2), 211–234.

Murawski, W. W. (2012). 10 tips for using co-planning time more efficiently. *Teaching Exceptional Children, 44*(4), 8–15.

Murawski, W. W., & Dieker, L. A. (2004). Tips and Strategies for co-teaching at the secondary level. *Teaching Exceptional Children, 36*(5), 52–58.

Murawski, W. W., & Dieker, L. (2008). 50 ways to keep your co-teacher: Strategies for before, during, and after co-teaching. *Teaching Exceptional Children, 40*(4), 40–48.

Oberti v. Board of Education of the Borough of Clementon School District, No. 995 F.2d 12014 (3rd Circuit 1993).

O'Brien, J., & Lovett, H. (2000). Finding a way toward everyday lives: The contribution of person-centered planning. In J. O'Brien & C. L. O'Brien (Eds.), *A little book about person centered planning* (pp. 113–132). Toronto, Ontario, Canada: Inclusion Press.

Palmer, S., Wehmeyer, M., Gipson, K., & Agran, M. (2004). Promoting access to the general curriculum by teaching self-determination skills. *Exceptional Children, 70,* 427–439.

Pickett, A, & Gerlach, K. (2003). *Supervising paraeducators in educational settings: A team approach* (2nd ed.). Austin, TX: Pro-Ed.

Pisha, B., & Coyne, P. (2001). Smart from the start: The promise of universal design for learning. *Remedial and Special Education, 22*(4), 197–203.

Pivik, J., McComas, J., & LaFlamme, M. (2002). Barriers and facilitators to inclusive education. *Exceptional Children, 69*(1), 97–107.

Powers, K., & Mandal, A. (2011). Tier III assessments, data-based decision-making, and interventions. *Contemporary School Psychology, 15*(1), 21–33.

Rainforth, B., & York-Barr, J. (1997). *Collaborative teams for students with severe disabilities: Integrating therapy and educational services* (2nd ed.). Baltimore, MD: Paul H. Brookes.

Reeve, C. E., & Carr, E. G. (2000). Prevention of severe behavior problems in children with developmental disorders. *Journal of Positive Behavior Interventions, 2*(3), 144–160.

Riggs, C., & Mueller, P. (2001). Employment and utilization of paraeducators in inclusive settings. *Journal of Special Education, 35*(1), 54–62.

Rusch, F. R., Hughes, C., Agran, M., Martin, J. E., & Johnson, J. R. (2009). Toward self-directed learning, post-high school placement, and coordinated support: Constructing new transition bridges to adult life. *Career Development for Exceptional Individuals, 32*(1), 53–59.

Ryndak, D., Ward, T., Alper, S., Storch, J. F., & Wilson Montgomery, J. (2010). Long-term outcomes of services in inclusive and self-contained settings for siblings with comparable significant disabilities. *Education and Training in Autism and Developmental Disabilities, 45*(1), 38–53.

Salend, S., & Duhaney, L. (2002). Grading students in inclusive settings. *Teaching Exceptional Children, 34*(3), 8–15.

Scott, T. M., Bucalos, A., Liaupsin, C., Nelson, C. M., Jolivette, K., & DeShea, L. (2004). Using functional behavior assessment in general education settings: Making a case for effectiveness and efficiency. *Behavioral Disorders, 29*(2), 189–201.

Shyman, E. (2010). Identifying predictors of emotional exhaustion among special education paraeducators: A preliminary investigation. *Psychology in the schools, 47,* 828–841.

Silva, M., Munk, D. D., & Bursuck, W. D. (2005). Grading adaptations for students with disabilities. *Intervention in School and Clinic, 41*(2), 87–98.

Sindelar, P. T., Shearer, D. K., Yendol-Hoppey, D., & Liebert, T. W. (2006). The sustainability of inclusive school reform. *Exceptional Children, 72,* 317–331.

Soukup, J. H., Wehmeyer, M. L., Bashinski, S. M., & Bovaird, J. A. (2007). Classroom variables and access to the general curriculum for students with disabilities. *Exceptional Children, 74*(1), 101–120.

Test, D. W., Mason, C. Y., Hughes, C., Konrad, M., Neale, M., & Wood, W. M. (2004). Student involvement in individualized education program meetings. *Exceptional Children, 70,* 391–412.

Thomson, C., Brown, D., Jones, L., Walker, J., Moore, D., Anderson, A., . . . Glynn, T. (2003). Resource teachers learning and behavior: Collaborative problem solving to support inclusion. *Journal of Positive Behavior Interventions, 5*(2), 101–111.

U.S. Department of Education, Office of Special Education and Rehabilitative Services, Office of Special Education Programs. (2011). *30th annual report to Congress on the implementation of the Individuals with Disabilities Education Act, 2008.* Washington, DC: Author.

U.S. Department of Labor, Office of Disability Employment Policy. (n.d.). *Disability employment statistics.* Retrieved from http://www.dol.gov/odep/topics/DisabilityEmploymentStatistics.htm

Villa, R. A., Thousand, J. S., & Nevin, A. I. (2013). *A guide to co-teaching: New lessons and strategies to facilitate student learning* (3rd ed.). Thousand Oaks, CA: Corwin.

Villa, R. A., Thousand, J. S., Nevin, A., & Liston, A. (2005). Successful inclusive practices in middle and secondary schools. *American Secondary Education, 33*(3), 33–50.

Wadsworth, D., & Knight, D. (1996). Paraprofessionals: The bridge to successful full inclusion. *Intervention in School and Clinic, 31,* 166–171.

Wagner, M., Cadwallader, T., Garza, N., & Cameto, R. (2004, March). Social activities of youth with disabilities. *NTLS2 Data Brief, 3*(1). Retrieved from http://www.ncset.org/publications/viewdesc.asp?id=1470

Wallace, T., Shin, J., Bartholomay, T., & Stahl, B. (2001). Knowledge and skills for teachers supervising the work of paraprofessionals. *Exceptional Children, 67,* 520–533.

Watson, S. M. R., Gable, R., & Greenwood, C. R. (2011). Combining ecobehavioral assessment, functional assessment, and response to intervention to promote more effective classroom instruction. *Remedial and Special Education, 32,* 334–344.

Wehmeyer, M. L., & Field, S. L. (2007). *Self-determination: Instructional and assessment strategies.* Thousand Oaks, CA: Corwin.

Wehmeyer, M. L., Lattin, D., Lapp-Rincker, G., & Agran, M. (2003). Access to the general curriculum of middle school students with mental retardation: An observational study. *Remedial and Special Education, 24,* 262–272.

Weiner, J., & Tardif, C. (2004). Social and emotional functioning of children with learning disabilities: Does special education placement make a difference? *Learning Disabilities Research & Practice, 19*(1), 20–32.

White, J., & Weiner, J. S. (2004). Influence of least restrictive environment and community based training on integrated employment outcomes for transitioning students with severe disabilities. *Journal of Vocational Rehabilitation, 21,* 149–156.

Williams-Diehm, K., Wehmeyer, M. L., Palmer, S., Soukup, J. H., & Garner, N. (2008). Self-determination and student involvement in transition planning: A multivariate analysis. *Journal of Developmental Disabilities, 14,* 25–36.

Worrell, J. L. (2008). How secondary schools can avoid the seven deadly school "sins" of inclusion. *American Secondary Education, 36*(2), 43–56.

York, J., Giangreco, M. F., Vandercook, T., & Macdonald, C. (1992). Integrating support personnel in the inclusive classroom. In S. Stainback & W. Stainback (Eds.), *Curriculum considerations in inclusive classrooms: Facilitating learning for all students* (pp. 101–116). Baltimore, MD: Paul H. Brookes.

York-Barr, J., & Duke, K. (2004). What do we know about teacher leadership? Findings from two decades of scholarship. *Review of Educational Research, 74,* 255–316.

York-Barr, J., Sommerness, J., Duke, K., & Ghere, G. (2005). Special educators in inclusive education programmes: Reframing their work as teacher leadership. *International Journal of Inclusive Education, 9*(2), 193–215.

Zhang, D., Hsu, H. Y., Kwok, O., Benz, M., & Bowman-Perrott, L. (2011). The impact of basic-level parent engagements on student achievement: Patterns associated with race/ethnicity and socioeconomic status (SES). *Journal of Disability Policy Studies, 22*(1), 28–39.

Index

A SAGE Company

Corwin is committed to improving education for all learners by publishing books and other professional development resources for those serving the field of PreK–12 education. By providing practical, hands-on materials, Corwin continues to carry out the promise of its motto: **"Helping Educators Do Their Work Better."**

CPSIA information can be obtained
at www.ICGtesting.com
Printed in the USA
LVHW062336061118
596264LV00007B/88/P